John Chippendall Montesquieu Bellew

Shakespere's Home at New Place, Stratford-upon-Avon

John Chippendall Montesquieu Bellew

Shakespere's Home at New Place, Stratford-upon-Avon

ISBN/EAN: 9783337309893

Printed in Europe, USA, Canada, Australia, Japan

Cover: Foto ©ninafisch / pixelio.de

More available books at **www.hansebooks.com**

SHAKESPERE'S HOME

AT

New Place.

STRATFORD-UPON-AVON.

Being a Hiſtory of the "Great Houſe" built in the Reign of King Henry VII., *by* Sir Hugh Clopton, Knight, *and ſubſequently the property of* William Shakespere, Gent., *wherein he lived and died.*

BY

J. C. M. BELLEW.

Imprynted in *London*,
FOR

1, Amen Corner, Paternoster Row.

MDCCCLXIII.

TO THE REVEREND

GRANVILLE JOHN GRANVILLE,

B.C.L.,

VICAR OF STRATFORD-UPON-AVON.

———o———

MY DEAR VICAR,

Allow me to Dedicate to you the following Account of NEW PLACE, which would never have been written but for your hoſpitality.

To you, and to our friend, Mr. Hunt, I, and a little circle of friends, have, on two occaſions, been under great obligations in making pilgrimages to Stratford. If you can ſpend half-an-hour pleaſantly with me, I hope you will receive my little Book as an aſſurance of my lively recollection of the happy hours which I have owed to you. That you may, in recruited health, long live to guard that Shrine which is committed to your keeping, and to enjoy the affectionate reſpect of your Pariſhioners, and troops of Friends, is,

My dear Vicar,

The ſincere wiſh of

Your much obliged,

J. C. M. BELLEW.

Thames Cottage, Hampton,
New Year's Day, 1863.

PREFACE.

****

ON entering a Continental Cathedral the traveller's attention is arreſted by an iron Corona ſtudded with burning tapers. They are the humble offerings of devotees.

The following pages are my humble offering at the ſhrine of that intellectual edifice, ſo vaſt in proportion and ſo lovely in detail, which our Shakeſpere erected by his works. Let me ſtand where the iron Corona does, cloſe to the portal, holding my feet in reverence, and not venturing to tread, with any pretence of critical ſurvey, the long drawn aiſles of that ſtupendous ſtructure which aſtoniſhes and delights the maſter minds of our race.

race. I ſhall not need to be told that the "farthing-candle ray" is a very appropriate ſimile to characteriſe the following pages. It is ſo. But let me pray that it be not blown out, or ſnuffed out, with cruel heedleſſneſs (puffed, of courſe, it is not likely to be), becauſe, though its quantity of illuminating power be but a "little "inch of light," ſo far as it does extend, I believe it diſperſes ſome darkneſs, and may prove uſeful in giving other pilgrims to the ſhrine, a momentary glimpſe of dim diſtances, which may excite curioſity, and the deſire to explore their hidden receſſes.

In ſimple language, I believe a great many facts regarding Shakeſpere remain to be brought to light; and that, while the critic or ſcholar has little left to ſay that is freſh or new regarding his works, the antiquary may have a great deal to diſcover and to ſay regarding the man.

It is remarkable what a labour of love has been expended by many eminent men of my own profeſſion upon the works of the Poet. In their wake I have not dared to follow; but I ſhall have done ſome good, I truſt, if I detect a need and point it out, ſo that others, wiſer, and better than I, may provide for its ſatisfaction. The title of my book ſuggeſts a ſubject upon which there reſts the darkneſs of an almoſt profound ignorance. What do we know of the man Shakeſpere in his home—in his domeſtic, ſocial, moral character, in his home aſſociations and his home aſſociates;—nay! what have we *cared* to know of him in them?

Let not the reader be deceived, and tempted into reading my book by ſuppoſing that I pretend to lift the veil, and with my tiny taper to illuminate the darkneſs. I do not. But *I do try to*

make

make the darkneſs viſible; and to the beſt of my opportunities, I have ſtriven to caſt a little light upon ſcattered points, and ſome few facts, which I think have not previouſly been publiſhed.

The ableſt and moſt learned man would ſpeak with modeſty and heſitation regarding any work he might publiſh referring to Shakeſpere. It is with the moſt ſincere diffidence that I venture to let the following pages paſs through the Preſs; but I take courage to do ſo from the belief, that every one who will honour me by reading what I have written, will ſee that I have honeſtly laboured at the facts of my ſubject, and that the opinions I venture to expreſs, are alſo honeſtly put forth.

If I extend this Preface to an inordinate length, it is from my anxiety to have my object underſtood—or, at leaſt, not miſunderſtood.

The

The Pedigrees introduced in this work have coſt an infinity of labour, which, the unintereſted or uninitiated, would never ſuppoſe, in glancing over their ſtatiſtical deſcents. It would be unfair to criticiſe them as if they bore the *imprimatur* of a King-at-Arms. Herald's College will only ſmile on them as the productions of a tyro. So they are. But, whatever amount of light they give, the flint and ſteel have been my own.

> *Ut varias uſus meditando extunderet artes*
> *Paulatim,* * * * *
> *Et ſilicis venis abſtruſum excuderet ignem.*

I believe I am turning inquiry in a uſeful, and much neglected direction, by preſſing ſuch pedigrees upon the conſideration of thoſe who are curious in Shakeſperian inveſtigations. My reaſons for ſo doing will be found in the body of my work. Whether I have laboured to a purpoſe and

and done good, or laboured in vain, I leave others to judge.

To the Clopton Pedigree I muſt draw particular attention, and eſpecially to that branch of it referring to the Combes family. In the Appendix (Article, "Combes") the reader will learn the difficulties and perplexities encountered: and will, I am certain, give me credit for a painſtaking purſuit of my object, and hold me pardonable if I ſhould be found hereafter to have made any miſtakes. In the Appendix, likewiſe, will be found many curious facts reflecting upon the perſons to whom reference is made, which I conſidered could not be legitimately introduced into the body of my work. The ſingular diſcovery made, with regard to the man Bott (Appendix A, p. 341), will explain how it came to paſs that New Place was originally ſold.

"*Qui ſ'excuſe, ſ'accuſe!*" If ſo, my excuſes

excuſes muſt amount to ſelf-accuſation; but of one thing I do not accuſe myſelf, and that is, of thankleſſneſs to the various friends who have given me their help. To Mr. T. Duffus Hardy, Deputy Keeper of Public Records; Mr. Burtt, and Mr. Cole of the Record Office; to Mr. Planché and his *confrères* at Herald's College; to the Vicar of Stratford, his Curates, and William Butcher, the Pariſh Clerk; to Mr. Clarence Hopper, in making a variety of reſearches for me; to Mr. Hunt, Town Clerk of Stratford, in patiently enduring my endleſs letters and inquiries;—to theſe gentlemen, and to a number of others, whoſe kindneſs has had my private thanks, (becauſe they object to being mentioned here,) I am greatly and ſincerely indebted. Let me offer my thanks likewiſe to another perſon. To John Middleton, Attendant in the Reading-Room of the Britiſh Muſeum,

not

not only of late, but for years, I have been indebted for conſtant attention. I thank him moſt heartily; and think I do myſelf honour when I go a ſtep out of my way to mark the obligations, which thoſe who frequent the Britiſh Muſeum, the Record Office, the Will Office, and all other ſuch public inſtitutions, owe to the courteſy always extended to readers and ſearchers, not only by the ſuperior officers of thoſe places, but alſo by their humbler aſſiſtants.

I ſhall be pleaſed, if, on cloſing my book, any of my readers feel a freſhened intereſt in the *Man*—William Shakeſpere; and above all, I ſhall be beſt ſatisfied if they are led to think with me, that this Prince of Poets was a worthier and better man than we vulgarly account him; that Shakeſpere's Home is a ſubject deſerving our ſtudy and reſpect; and that he was no hypocritical mouther of fine ſenti-

ments

ments, inditing with his pen the nobleſt and loftieſt teaching, and belying it in the conduct of his life.

I conceive that no one can teach effectively, that which he has not himſelf felt earneſtly; nor until good can be put for evil, and evil for good, can I bring myſelf to think that the pureſt intellectual refreſhment of a race thirſting after knowledge, pours from a polluted ſource. I picture Shakeſpere to myſelf as an embodiment of the manly, honeſt, and lofty virtues, which his Muſe delights to crown with honour; and half my reverence for him would be gone if I did not feel morally convinced that the greateſt of all human teachers, was not only a Great Man, but alſo a Good Man!

*** As Shakeſpere's name has been ſpelt by ſo many different people in ſo many different ways, I may remark that the orthography I have adopted is that of the Grant of Arms in Herald's College, 1596; believing, as I do, that the ſpelling in that document was dictated by Shakeſpere to Dethick.

CORRIGENDA.

Page 205.—" no one could," read " no one would."

Page 205.—" Gilrow," read " Gildon."

Page 218.—" thoſe years enjoying," read " thoſe years *as* enjoying."

Page 230.—" Revels," read " Revel."

NEW PLACE,

STRATFORD-UPON-AVON.

"ON the north ſide of this Chapell "was a Fair Houſe, built of brick "and timber, by the ſaid Hugh, wherein "he lived in his later dayes and dyed. "On the ſouth ſide of which Chapell "ſtands the Grammar School." Theſe words, quoted from Dugdale's "War-"wickſhire," and referring to Sir Hugh Clopton, Knt., were, until the other day, the chief record poſſeſſed by Engliſhmen of of the houſe in which William Shakeſpere alſo "lived in his later days, and "died." At length the ſtones prate of his whereabout, and it ſeems deſirable to lay their information before the public.

Every one, even remotely intereſted in the ſubject, is aware, that a ſhort time back, the land on which Shakeſpere's houſe was known to have ſtood (uſually denominated "Shakeſpere's Garden," and, as ſuch, pointed out to perſons viſiting Stratford-upon-Avon,) was for ſale. It is equally well known that an appeal was made to the public by Mr. Halliwell [*vide The Times*, October 15, 1861], and that the plot of land in queſtion, was reſcued from the graſp of private ſpeculators, or ſhowmen, to be veſted in the charge of truſtees, and by them to be preſerved for ever—ſet apart, and, in effect, conſecrated to the memory of the man who lived there, happily accordant with

with the prayer expreſſed in Garrick's words:—

> "*And may no sacrilegious hand*
> *Near Avon's banks be found,*
> *To dare to parcel out the land,*
> *And limit Shakespere's hallowed ground.*
> *For ages free, still be it unconfined,*
> *As broad and general as thy boundless mind.*"

As ſoon as the ſympathy of the public for the object in queſtion was exhibited, the ambition of its promoters expanded as the ſubſcriptions increaſed; and nothing leſs than the full and entire recovery of the eſtate once poſſeſſed by Shakeſpere at New Place, would ſatisfy theſe ardent and enthuſiaſtic individuals.

Goldſmith complained (to Dodſley after dinner) that his was an "unpoetic "age." There are many chatterers of the preſent day who repeat the complaint, which ſeems to have become ſtereotyped for all time. It was a fooliſh thought

thought to ſay "an unpoetic age," for every age muſt ſeem to the men of the day matter of fact and unpoetic. To-day always appears proſaic; yeſterday and to-morrow—ſubjects of retroſpection and anticipation, not objects in poſſeſſion—are the fit themes for poetry. Goldſmith's age, however proſaic it may have ſeemed, gave *him* good proof of its poetic appreciation; and ſo our age (iron age though it may be) gives equally good proof of its admiration for the real poet and for genuine poetry, wherever it finds the one, or reads the other.

If the true poet lives in the hearts and memories of his countrymen, how much more the Prince of all the Bards?

There are thoſe who will boldly aſſert that Shakeſpere's works do not attract, and that people generally, care little or nothing about Shakeſpere himſelf. It is not to the purpoſe in this place to enter into

into any difcuffion upon fuch topics. It might, however, be argued that the ftudents of his works have found themfelves compelled (unlefs contented with being guilty of ignorance) to make the Poet's plays the companions of the clofet; and that from the ftudent's clofet the moft valuable interpretations of his text have iffued of late years. Such an argument would infer that the marvellous creations of the Poet's mind command peculiar refpect at the prefent time; and it may be unhefitatingly afferted, that abundant evidence is forthcoming to prove that this is a fact. There has not been an era in Englifh literature more fruitful in labours of critical comment upon the text of Shakefpere, and more inquiring into every fort of evidence likely to throw light upon his life and hiftory. It might alfo be argued, that the people of England are

juft

juſt as proud of, and juſt as intereſted in, the fame of their countryman—are juſt as anxious to preſerve with ſacred care every relique and memento of the brighteſt genius the world has ever produced, as any of their forefathers have been. Circumſtances, perhaps, would warrant the aſſertion that the preſent generation exhibits more intereſt in him, and more reverence for everything connected with him, than any other ſince his death. The ſentiment of George II., that Shakeſpere's plays are bombaſt, no longer commands courtly acquieſcence; and the Carlton Houſe faſhion of depreciating his works (particularly by thoſe who had never ſtudied them) is a faſhion that has had its day. Doubtleſs, the conſervative feeling of this period with reference to the Poet's birthplace, his laſt reſidence, and the few reliques connected with him that ſurvive, has been operated upon by that

that revival of taſte for architecture, and that reverence for mediæval art, which does honour to the reign of Victoria, and will hereafter ſignaliſe it. The hiſtorian will tell how, from the ſixteenth to the nineteenth century, the eccleſiaſtical architecture of England univerſally, and the domeſtic generally, became baſer and ſtill more baſe; until, towards the cloſe of the Georgian era, it reached a depth of degradation (land-marked by the introduction of Roman Cement and Cockney Villas) than which nothing could be more infamous. The ſame hiſtorian will tell of the great work that Pugin did, of the conſequent reſuſcitation of taſte, and of love for architectural beauty becoming a neceſſary part of polite education. He will tell how (as the legitimate accompaniments of ſuch regenerated refinement) the Engliſh people awoke to the conviction that the fabrics of their churches

had

had been at the mercy of Goths and Vandals, and that the moſt intereſting hiſtorical remains of domeſtic architecture had been ſhameleſſly deſtroyed or barbarouſly mutilated. Then came the Reſtoration: a reſtoration in its particular province more beneficial and remedial than ſome chronological events deſignated by that phraſe have proved.

To the therapeutic ſpirit, ſo happily prevalent in England at the preſent period regarding mediæval art, may fairly be attributed ſome meaſure of the intereſt, and a great amount of the funds, which have been ſubſcribed to reſtore the birthplace of Shakeſpere, in Henley Street, at Stratford; and alſo to ſave his laſt place of reſidence from being utiliſed for "building lots," or vulgariſed by any ſpeculative Barnum.

For ſome months the ſubject has dropped out of public notice. The terrific calamity

calamity at Hartley Colliery, and the incumbent ſubſcriptions of all generous and charitable people, for the widows and orphans of the deceaſed; the heavy viſitation upon the Queen and country, followed by the Memorial Fund; and laſt of all, the increaſing want of our long-ſuffering and brave fellow-countrymen in Lancaſhire, calling for the admiration and ſympathetic contributions of thoſe who can aid them in their dire neceſſity, have, for a period, checked any appeals to public ſympathy, except thoſe of an urgent character.

In the face of ſuch griefs and ſuch wants, it was impoſſible for the Shakeſpere Fund ſubſcription liſt to keep its place before the public. It has, probably for this reaſon, been temporarily withdrawn. If ſo, the act has been judicious. While the ſubject is in abeyance, it may be well to conſider what has been done with

with the money ſubſcribed, becauſe a judicious expenditure already made, would be the beſt baſis of appeal to the public for further moneys to meet future outlays.

It is familiar to every one, that Shakeſpere's reſidence at Stratford was called "New Place." There are popular errors in exiſtence, both about the place, and the name of the place. It may be acceptable to the reader if a few facts are thrown together to tell its hiſtory, which will be no information to thoſe who have been intereſted in New Place, but may be inſtructive to many not "read up" in the ſubject.

New Place came from, and returned to, the family of Clopton. The Cloptons poſſeſſed it long prior to Shakeſpere's time, and repoſſeſſed it by intermarriage (ſubſequent to Shakeſpere's time) with a daughter of Sir Edward Walker.

Dugdale (as quoted) ſtates that the

houſe

Ockwells, Berkshire.

Face p. 11.

houſe was built by Sir Hugh Clopton, of brick and timber. Sir Hugh lived in the reign of Henry VII. The general appearance of the building can be eaſily imagined, though *there is no drawing of it in exiſtence.*

The plate on the oppoſite page gives a repreſentation of a houſe built about the ſame time that Sir Hugh Clopton erected "New Place." It preſents to us the front elevation of "Ockwells," in the pariſh of Bray, Berkſhire, at preſent poſſeſſed by Mr. Grenfell, of Taplow. This houſe is stated to have been built during the reign of Richard III., and is one of the very few ſpecimens of *domeſtic architecture* now remaining of that date. The Great Hall, until lately, was adorned by a beautiful ſtained-glaſs window, emblazoned with the armorial bearings of Henry VII., and the Duke of Somerſet; but, in a ſpirit akin to Vandaliſm, this moſt intereſting remnant

nant of antique heraldry has been removed from its proper place, and fixed up in Mr. Grenfell's new houſe, on Taplow Hill. It will not ſurpriſe the public, knowing this fact, to learn that Ockwells is turned into an ordinary farm-houſe; that its architectural intereſt and artiſtic beauty, as well as antiquity, are apparently unappreciated; and that its noble hall, with open-worked Gothic roof and oak wainſcoting, is made a ploughboy's lumber-room, filled with agricultural implements, ploughs, ſpades, ſacks, barrows, and rakes.* The accompanying drawing of Ockwells has been given in order to preſent a faithful repreſentation of a "great houſe, built of wood and timber," of the time of Henry VII. It is only to be

* An unſatisfactory hiſtory of the houſe, accompanied with two admirable drawings of the window referred to, will be found in Lyſon's "Magna Britannica," Berkſhire, Bray, pariſh of.

be regarded as a ſpecimen of a period, from which Sir Hugh Clopton's houſe would no doubt differ greatly in detail, but with which it would agree in character and effect.

The lovers of "illuſtrated works" have been indulged with a plate repreſenting Shakeſpere's houſe at New Place; but a drawing of a caſtle in the air would have been equally authoritative and correct. This is one error concerning New Place that needs to be exploded. No authentic repreſentation of it exiſts. When Dugdale uſes the words "brick "and timber," and tells us that the houſe was built in the reign of Henry VII., any one who has viſited Coventry, Cheſter, Shrewſbury, or the "Mint" at Briſtol, will be able, in his mind's eye, to picture the general appearance of Shakeſpere's houſe, with its multiplied gables, its overhanging eaves, its barge-boards, enriched

with

with the Tudor flower-ornament (as at the Coventry Almſhouſe), its projecting windows, its ſtrong framework of croſs-beamed, black, old Engliſh oak forming the ribs or ſkeleton of the houſe, the intervening ſquares built in with brick (probably plaſtered over and whitewaſhed), its wooden porchway, open-arcaded, with a room above, whoſe oriel windows diſplayed the falcon and tilting ſpear.

Of that houſe, which Sir Hugh Clopton built, and in which Shakeſpere ſubſequently lived and died, not a veſtige remained but yeſterday. Like the inſubſtantial pageant (of the Poet's play), not a rack was left behind, as far as any living man could tell.

Shakeſpere's Barn may, in a certain ſenſe, be ſaid to have exiſted up to 1861. In that year a couple of cottages occupying that portion of New Place garden which adjoins the theatre on the weſt,

were

were taken down, having, in the firſt inſtance, been photographed, and then ſtripped to the framework of which they were conſtructed. Theſe cottages had been contrived by ſubdividing the ancient barn belonging to Shakeſpere. On removing the thatch, the lath and plaſter work from between the beams, and reducing the building to its ſkeleton ſtructure, it was found that, in the lapſe of two centuries and a half, all the timbers of the barn had, from time to time, been replaced, with the exception of ſome three or four ſmall beams. Theſe were the ſole remains of the Poet's Barn.

The recent purchaſe of New Place led to a ſeries of excavations, and the diſcoveries which have reſulted, (though not very extenſive,) are extremely intereſting, and definitely ſettle ſeveral points which, heretofore, have been ſubjects of ſurmiſe and ſpeculation.

The

The leading facts regarding New Place are these:

1st. New Place was built by Sir Hugh Clopton, *temp.* Henry VII., *circ.* 1490. He died in London, 1496, and being a bachelor, devised it to his great-nephew, William Clopton, who died in 1521.

2nd. From the Clopton family it passed by purchase to the family of Bott, in the reign of Queen Elizabeth, 1563.*

3rd. By Willian Bott it was resold to Wm. Underhill, within a short space of time, between 1563 and 1570.†

4th. William Shakespere purchased from the Underhill family, for £60, New Place, consisting of "one messuage, "two barns, and two gardens, with "their appurtenances," during the Easter Term of 1597, in the 39th year of the reign of Queen Elizabeth,

* Appendix A. † Appendix B.

beth, and the year after his only ſon, Hamnet, had died. By him it was repaired, renovated, and fitted up for his permanent reſidence.

5th. March, 1616. Shakeſpere made his will, leaving it to his daughter, Mrs. Hall, for life; after her, to her daughter. The month following, April 23, 1616, his reputed birth-day, he died in this houſe, and was buried two days later, on the 25th, in the 53rd year of his age.

It was a happy accident that the reign of Queen Elizabeth had begun before the birth of the Poet, otherwiſe this country would have loſt the moſt valuable records regarding him. As ſoon as the Queen aſcended the throne, the regiſtries of the pariſh churches were carefully kept. The Regiſter-book of Stratford Church contains entries both of the baptiſm and the funeral of Shakeſpere.

"1564,

"1564, April 26. Gulielmus, Filius "Johannes Shakſpere." But this merely records his baptiſm, and not the date of birth, which baptiſmal regiſters have never done, and even now do not, although the value of ſuch entries is apparent.

The entry of the funeral runs thus:— 1616, "April 25, Will. Shakſpeare, Gent."

6th. Mrs. Hall ſucceeded to the property, and from her it paſſed to her daughter Elizabeth, Lady Barnard.

7th. Lady Barnard (Shakeſpere's granddaughter) according to an indenture dated 20th October, 1652, covenanted that New Place ſhould be had to the uſe of herſelf and her huſband, John Barnard, during their natural lives, and in default of iſſue, ſhould be left to the uſe of ſuch perſon or perſons as ſhe ſhould limit or appoint. Lady Barnard executed a will, 29th January, 1669, whereby New

New Place was left to Sir John Barnard for his life, and to the uſe of his executors for ſix months after his death. Lady Barnard died a few days afterwards, and was buried at Abington, February 17th, 1669. Her will was proved 4th March, 1669. The property continued in the poſſeſſion of Sir John until his death in 1673; ſubſequent to which, according to the proviſions of the aforeſaid will, New Place was ſold. An indenture, dated 18th May, 1675, conveyed it "to bee and "enure to the only uſe and behoofe "of Sir Edward Walker, Knt., "Garter Principall King at Armes," who completed the purchaſe for the ſum of £1,060.* He died, as the monument in Stratford Church ſtates, the following year—February, 1676.

8th.

* Appendix C.

8th. The only child of Sir Edward Walker, Barbara,* married Sir John Clopton,

---

* A native poet of Stratford, by name John Jordan, and by trade a wheelwright, publiſhed in 1777 a poem entitled "Welcombe Hills" (which are in the neighbourhood of Stratford). In alluſion to one of the Clopton marriages—that of Edward (the iſſue of the above Sir John and Barbara his wife) with Martha Combe, the laſt perſon of note of the family of John a Combe (Shakeſpere's friend)—the poet exclaims:—

> "*Till a late failure in the iſſue male,*
> *Turn'd, though unprejudiced, the lineal ſcale,*
> *An heireſs Combe, right well to be ally'd,*
> *Became the heir of neighb'ring Clopton's bride.*"

As Mrs. Partheriche, the deſcendant of this alliance, will be alluded to, the marriages are here ſubjoined, though the Pedigree of Clopton, *in extenſo*, will be found elſewhere.

Sir Edward Walker.
|
Barbara Walker = Sir John Clopton.
|
Edward Clopton = Martha Combe, last of the line of John a Combe.
|
Edward Clopton = Martha, *d.* of Thomas Middleton, Esq., of Mundham, Surrey.
|
1 2 3 4 5 6 — Children deceased while young.
7 — Frances Clopton, the last of her family. She survived her husband. *D.* 1793. = John Partheriche, Esq.

Clopton, of Clopton, in the pariſh of Stratford, and thus New Place returned again into the Clopton family. Sir John deceaſed, April 18, 1719. By him New Place was bequeathed

9th. To his younger ſon, Sir Hugh Clopton, of the Middle Temple, one of the Heralds of the College of Arms, and Recorder of Stratford.

10th. Sir Hugh Clopton *pulled down* New Place, *entirely rebuilt* it, and died in the *new New Place*, 1751, aged 80.—*Temp.* George II.

11th. Sir Hugh's ſon-in-law and executor Henry Talbot (brother of the Chancellor Talbot), ſold it to the Rev. Francis Gaſtrell, 1753.

12th. Gaſtrell deſtroyed the modern houſe, and razed it to the ground, in 1759.

13th.

13th. The ſubſequent hiſtory of New Place—1775 to 1862—may be told in a few words. Mrs. Gaſtrell ſold the property to W. Hunt,* Eſq., of Stratford, in 1775.

14th. The truſtees under the will of W. Hunt, on the 29th Sept., 1790, ſold to Charles Henry Hunt,† Eſq., who ſubſequently purchaſed of Fanny Mortiboys, ſpinſter, the adjoining houſe, now known as "Naſhe's "Houſe."‡

15th. The aſſignees of C. H. Hunt, on the 15th May, 1807, conveyed the whole of the property deſcribed upon

---

* Grandfather of W. O. Hunt, Eſq., the preſent Town-clerk of Stratford. He was a promoter of the Jubilee of 1769. Garrick correſponded with him.

† The ſecond ſon of the aforeſaid W. Hunt.

‡ It is only during the preſent year that it has been aſcertained that this houſe belonged to Thomas Naſhe, who married Shakeſpere's grand-daughter, Elizabeth Hall.

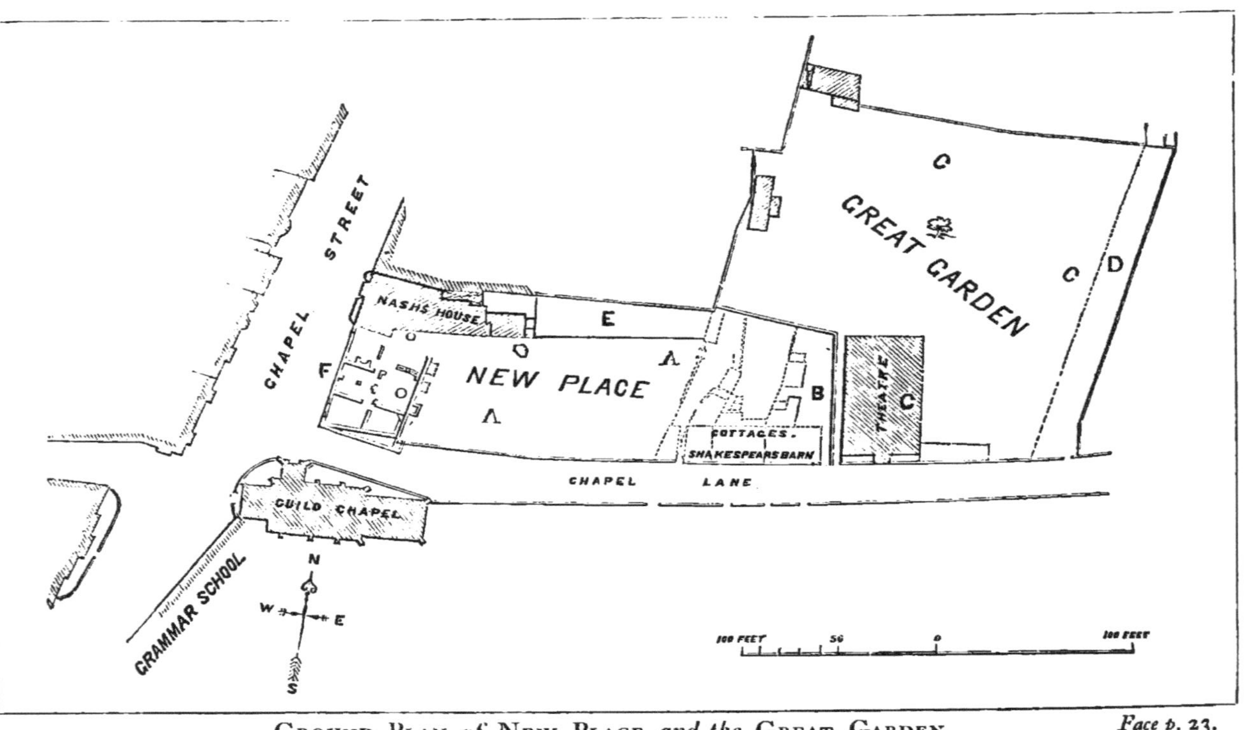

Ground Plan *of* New Place *and the* Great Garden.

Face p. 23.

upon the Ground Plan as "New "Place," including that now occupied by the "Theatre," to Edmund Batterſbee and William George Morris, Eſqs., Bankers.

16th. In January, 1829, the heir-at-law of E. Batterſbee, and the aſſignees of W. G. Morris, *ſold off the property in lots.*

A—including Naſhe's houſe, was purchaſed by Miſs Lucy Smith.

B—the Cottages formed out of Shakeſpere's Barn, were purchaſed, the one by Michael Prentice, the other by Thomas Webb.

C—the Great Garden (now a Bowling Green), including the ground now occupied by the Theatre, was purchaſed by Edward Leyton.

D—is a ſtrip of land which formerly belonged to the Clifford Charity, and was

was acquired by an exchange effected by Mr. Gaſtrell. It never belonged to the Great Garden in Shakeſpere's time, though it has continued a part of it ſince Mr. Gaſtrell acquired it.

E—is a ſtrip of Garden at the back of Naſhe's houſe, which always belonged to Naſhe's houſe until 1790, when it was purchaſed by C. H. Hunt, and became an integral part of lot A, of which it has ever ſince continued a part.

F—is the ruins of foundations lately uncovered, in which is identified a ſmall portion of Sir Hugh Clopton's "Great Houſe" of New Place, and a much larger portion of the ſecond houſe, built about 1720 (paragraph 10).

17th. In 1834, the ſaid Edward Leyton purchaſed Webb's cottage, and in 1838 he alſo purchaſed Prentice's; ſo ſo that he became poſſeſſor of the whole of the two lots B and C.

18th. On the 23rd of January, 1836, the truſtees of the above-mentioned Lucy Smith, under her will, ſold the lot A to Mr. David Rice, Surgeon. Some time about this period, between 1836 and 1844, Edward Leyton ſold that portion of the Great Garden whereon the Theatre now ſtands, for the erection of that moſt hideous ſtructure. By the knowledge of this fact, the reader will ſee what amount of "veneration" a ſtaring brick building, raiſed leſs than thirty years ago, can claim from the public.

19th. In July, 1844, the only daughter and child of Edward Leyton, contracted marriage with Chas. Frederic Loggin. Mr. Leyton then ſettled the whole of the remainder of lots

B and C

B and C to himſelf for life, to his wife after him for her life, and after her, to his daughter, under truſtees, for her life, *giving them power to ſell.*

20th. We are thus brought down to the preſent period, and to the laſt ſales that will ever occur upon the New Place eſtate.

A was purchaſed by Mr. Halliwell, by private contract, of the truſtees under the will of the above-named ſurgeon, Mr. Rice, for the ſum of £1,200. It was conveyed 21ſt March, 1862.

B and C were purchaſed by Mr. Halliwell, by private contract, of the truſtees under the ſettlement of Mr. Loggin, for £2,000. They were conveyed February 8, 1862.

Accordingly, there ſtill remains to be purchaſed that piece of ground whereon the theatre ſtands, ſold off from the

Great

Great Garden a few years ago. This "theatre" (ſo called) belongs, at the preſent moment, to a body of ſhareholders, who are prepared to ſell their rights—the ground, buildings, &c.—for £1,100. No doubt this purchaſe will, at no diſtant period, be made; and then the whole New Place property will belong to the public, veſted in the corporation of Stratford, to be preſerved by them for ever, for the contemplation and enjoyment of the Engliſh people.

The above detailed facts have been arranged in paragraphs, ſo that the reader may, with greater eaſe, carry in memory the changes and chances to which New Place has been ſubjected.

The familiar entries in the church books of Stratford regarding Shakeſpere's baptiſm and burial having been given, it will render the ſubject more complete if the

the principal facts regarding his marriage, and the iſſue of that marriage, are added in this place; for it can ſcarcely be doubted that Shakeſpere purchaſed New Place in order to provide a home for his wife and children during his long abſences in London—a home which he laboured hard to ſuſtain—a home to which he always retired when the ſeaſons of temporary repoſe arrived; when, being ſet free from the mental and phyſical exertions neceſſary to carry on the buſineſs of Blackfriars and the Globe Theatre, he could enjoy (as he ever loved to do) the ſweet aſſociations of that home, and the delights of the Garden of England—the luxuriant valley of the Avon.

Numberleſs efforts have been made to diſcover the regiſtry of Shakeſpere's wedding. Up to the preſent time, all ſuch efforts have proved vain. The probability—almoſt the certainty—is, that it has

has long ſince periſhed. His marriage bond and licenſe (bearing date 1582) are preſerved at Worceſter among the archives of the dioceſe. They run thus:—

“Noverint univerſi per preſentes nos
“ffulconem Sandells de Stratford in comi-
“tatu Warwici agricolam, et Johannem
“Rychardſon ibidem agricolam, teneri
“et firmiter obligari Ricardo Coſin gene-
“roſo et Roberto Warmſtry notario pub-
“lico in quadraginta libris bonœ et
“legalis monetœ Angliœ ſolvend, eiſdem
“Ricardo et Roberto hœred. execut. vel.
“aſſignat ſuis, ad quam quidem ſolu-
“cionem bene et fideliter faciend, obli-
“gamus nos, et utrumque noſtrum per
“ſe pro toto et in ſolice hœred, executor
“et adminiſtrator, noſtros firmiter, per
“prœſentes ſigillis noſtris ſigillit. Dat.
“28 die Novem. anno regni Dominœ
“noſtræ, Eliz. Dei gratia Angliæ, Ffrancæ,

“et

"et Hiberniæ Reginæ, Fidei Defenſor, "&c., 25°."

"The condicion of this obligacion ys "ſuche, that if hereafter there ſhall not "appere any lawfull lett or impediment "by reaſon of any precontract, conſan- "guitie, affinitie, or by any other lawfull "meanes whatſoever, but that William "Shagſpere one thone partie, and Ann "Hathwey, of Stratford, in the dioces of "Worceſter, maiden, may lawfully ſolem- "nize matrimony together, and in the "ſame afterwardes remaine and continew "like man and wiffe, according unto the "lawes in that behalf provided; and, "moreover, if there be not at this "preſent time any action, ſute, quarrell, "or demaund, moved or depending before "any judge, eccleſiaſticall or temporall, "for and concerning any ſuche lawfull "lett or impediment; and, moreover, if "the

"the ſaid William Shagſpere do not pro-
"ceed to ſolemnizacion of mariadg with
"the ſaid Ann Hathwey without the
"conſent of his frindes; and alſo if the
"ſaid William do, upon his own proper
"coſtes and expenſes, defend and ſave
"harmles, the Right Reverend Father in
"God, Lord John, Buſhop of Worceſter,
"and his offycers, for licencing them the
"ſaid William and Ann to be maried
"together with once aſking of the bannes
"of matrimony betwene them, and for
"all other cauſes which may enſue by
"reaſon or occaſion thereof, that then
"the ſaid obligacion to be voyd and of
"none effect, or els to ſtand and abide in
"full force and vertue."

Here follow the ſignatures, or *marks*, of the witneſſes; the firſt reſembling the attempt that an aged perſon would make to draw a triangle; the ſecond being a clumſy letter C. Two ſeals are added: the

the one is defaced, the other bears the impreſſion "R. H." Who was "R. H.?" Could this be the ſeal of the bride's father, Richard Hathaway? and inſtead of the licenſe being procured in ſecreſy, as Mr. Collier has ſuggeſted, may it not have been granted with the full knowledge and conſent of Richard Hathaway? Even ſuppoſing that there might be truth in the view which De Quincey and Mr. Collier have taken of this marriage—that it was accompliſhed hurriedly and ſecretly —ſuch an argument would ſtrengthen the ſuppoſition that "R. H." was the bride's father, and that he had accompanied Shakeſpere to Worceſter, in order to ſee that the licenſe was duly ſecured. Such a ſuppoſition would be moſt natural if there was any ground for ſcandal, which many perſons have ſhown a ſingular fancy for inſinuating. The "mature young "woman, five years paſt her maturity," being

being "led aſtray by the boy with two "and a half years to run of his minority," is objectionable to De Quincey's contemplation. Perhaps the idea is more abſurd than objectionable.

The evidence of "legal documents"—"a ſtory ſo ſignificant and ſo eloquent to "the intelligent,"—certainly ſhows that Shakeſpere procured his licenſe, 28th November, 1582, and that his firſt child, Suſannah, was baptiſed the following 26th May, 1583. But what then? Did the mature young woman lead the boy aſtray; and did the indignant R. H., on diſcovering the truth, inſiſt upon an immediate marriage, to hide his child's diſgrace?

This would be one way of explaining the procuring of the licenſe; and there might then be great ſignificance in the ſeal of "R. H." appended to the bond!

It has been concluſively ſhown, from the

the very regiſters of Stratford, that marriages, with the ſame "ſignificance of "dates" between the church ceremony and the baptiſm of the eldeſt child, were cuſtomary at Stratford.

It has alſo been ſhown, that they were cuſtomary in England, and on the continent; and before any ſcandal was hinted at, as to the purity of the "mature young "woman," it would have been well for the marriage cuſtoms of the age, and of people in Shakeſpere's rank of life, to have been carefully ſtudied. Even in this nineteenth century, there are ruſtic parts of northern England, in which the ſnort of the iron-horſe has never been heard, where ſuch primitive cuſtoms ſtill ſurvive, and contracts of marriage are made preciſely as they were in Shakeſpere's day.

In ſuch bucolic, or, as they might be called, "uncivilifed" parts, marriage

is

is "honourable among all men," and as duly celebrated as the contract is made.

> "*Is it a custom?*
> *Ay, marry, is 't.*"

It is difficult to understand how a youth of Shakespere's age, and of his disposition, could be suspected of secretly and suddenly binding, "in the prayers of holy "church," a connection that he had formed shamefully. Reverence for the memory of so great a moralist, and so warm a champion of female purity and innocence, should prompt every examiner of his life and acts, to compare those acts with the habits and customs of the days in which he lived. Knowing what were the marriage customs common among the folk with whom the poet was early associated, and seeing that his marriage was in accordance with their habits, it is most natural, and certainly most charitable,

able, to ſuppoſe that friends like John Shakeſpere and Richard Hathaway ſhould be well pleaſed for their families to be connected in marriage. That Ann Hathaway was older than William Shakeſpere might be her misfortune, but was not her fault. The "mature young "woman" could not help herſelf; and poſſibly ſhe may have been kept under her father's roof, denied to the ſwains of Shottery, waiting until ſuch time as young William Shakeſpere could, with any propriety, marry. At length the heads of houſes agreed that they might be contracted; there was a pleaſant trip to Worceſter for the licenſe; "R. H." went to ſee that everything was done duly and in order; William and Ann were married,—and, it is to be hoped, "they lived "happily ever after."

We are indebted to the antiquarian, Sir Robert Philipps, for diſcovering the bond

bond and licenſe in 1836, in the Conſiſtorial Court of Worceſter. In the original it is full of legal abbreviations, as given in Mr. Knight's Biography. For the ſake of ſimplicity, the full text, as rendered by Mr. Halliwell, has been adopted above.

The probability is, that the ceremony of marriage was performed in the Chapel of Luddington, a hamlet of the pariſh of Stratford, at a ſhort diſtance from Shottery, the reſidence of Ann Hathaway, and a place with which the Hathaways were connected. The Marquis of Hertford, to whom Luddington belonged, informed Malone that he remembered there were tenants of the name of Hathaway on the eſtate. One, John Hathaway, farmed part of the eſtate as late as 1775. It is alſo worthy of note that the curate of Luddington was the Rev. Thomas Hunt, who was ſchoolmaſter of

Stratford School when Shakeſpere would almoſt certainly be a pupil there.* If the maſter and pupil were good friends, the fact might be a ſtrong inducement to Shakeſpere to be married at Mr. Hunt's church. Licenſes granted for the pariſh of Stratford, would, of courſe, be available for all churches and chapels within the pariſh, at which marriages were allowed. Luddington Chapel was taken down many years ago, and its regiſters have either been deſtroyed or loſt.

The annexed Pedigree will give all neceſſary particulars regarding Shakeſpere's family, his marriage, and his iſſue. Writers upon this ſubject have commonly ſtated the marriages and deſcents in the ordinary letterpreſs of their works, which, in ſuch matters, is confuſing.

* Maſters of the School:—1570, Walter Roche; 1572 to 1577, Thomas Hunt (buried at Stratford, April 12, 1612); 1580, Thomas Jenkins.

THE PEDIGREE OF WILLIAM SHAKESPERE.

(COMPILED BY J. C. M. BELLEW.)

ARDERNE, or ARDEN.

SHAKESPERE.

HATHAWAY.

WILLIAM SHAKESPERE.

fusing. Where a Pedigree is set out, the eye instructs the memory much more easily and directly, and for this reason the present method has been adopted.

Allusion has been made to a popular error regarding Shakespere's residence. Paragraph 10 (p. 21) states that the house in which he lived was pulled down at the commencement of the last century. Any representation of that house, to be authentic, must therefore bear date previous to 1719. No such plate or picture exists, and there is no evidence of any such having existed. In order to satisfy public curiosity, two were invented; the one published by Malone, the other by Samuel Ireland, father of the notorious forger of Vortigern and other Shakesperian MSS. Malone's picture was a draft upon imagination, drawn by John Jordan, of Stratford, to whom reference has been made. Jordan was perfectly prepared,

prepared, for a confideration, to invent or compofe, or make himfelf generally ufeful. In firft publifhing Jordan's reprefentation of New Place, Malone accompanied the drawing with this title, giving it a place in his book, but preferving a complete filence himfelf as to the value or authenticity of the drawing:—

"New Place, from a drawing in the "margin of an ancient furvey, made by "order of Sir George Carew, (afterwards "Baron Carew of Clopton, and Earl of "Totnefs,) and found at Clopton, near "Stratford-upon-Avon, in 1786."

Jordan fubfequently confeffed that he had invented the porch of the houfe; and Malone himfelf approved of his adding Shakefpere's arms, becaufe "*they were* "*very likely to have been there*;" fuggefting, at the fame time, "neat wooden "pales, which might be placed with pro- "priety before the houfe." Ireland, in his

his work upon the Avon, produced an engraving of the houſe, which he boldly aſſerted was authentic, and taken from a drawing in the poſſeſſion of Mrs. Partheriche, of Clopton Houſe, the laſt of the Clopton family, *which drawing, however, had unfortunately been deſtroyed!* His words are as follows :—

" I have taken the liberty of giving a " view of the houſe as it ſtood at the " time he reſided there, which he did " from the period of his quitting London " till his death. The view is copied " from an old drawing of one Robert " Treſwells, made in 1599, by order of " Sir George Carew, afterwards Baron " Carew of Clopton, and Earl of Totneſs. " It was found in Clopton Houſe in " 1786, and was in the poſſeſſion of the " late Mrs. Patriche, who was the laſt of " the antient family of the Clopton's. " The drawing, I am informed, is ſince " loſt

" loſt or deſtroyed." Whether deſtroyed before Ireland made his copy, he omits to mention; but it is of no particular conſequence, as the impudent attempt at impoſition betrays itſelf.

In the ſtatements ſet forth by Malone and by Ireland, it is impoſſible to overlook theſe facts: they both aſſert that the drawing was found in the year 1786, and they both uſe the identical words, "made by order of Sir George Carew, " afterwards Baron Carew of Clopton, " and Earl of Totneſs."

Three improvements of the ſtory are introduced by Ireland, who favours us with the extra information that the drawing was made by one Robert Treſwells; that it was made in 1599, and that it was in the poſſeſſion of Mrs. Partheriche, the laſt of the Cloptons. Deſpite theſe additional baits to beguile the public, and give the ſtory an increaſed air of truth, it is impoſſible

poſſible to avoid the impreſſion that Ireland was pirating Jordan's invention; and that while he was pointing a moral for future writers, he was adorning a tale at the moment to anſwer his own purpoſes.

On comparing the drawings given by Malone and by Ireland, it is palpable that the one is a very slightly altered copy of the other, or that they are both copies of ſome third drawing. If a third—poſſibly genuine—drawing had exiſted, ſuch as Malone aſſerted, and Ireland reaſſerted, did exiſt, executed at the inſtance of Baron Carew, it is evident that ſuch drawing would not have exhibited a porch of Wren's era (*temp.* Charles II.) ſtuck in front of a drawing made in 1599 (*temp.* Elizabeth). But we have Jordan's confeſſion that "he added the "porch." A genuine drawing, therefore, in the poſſeſſion of Mrs. Partheriche, would have been minus the porch which Jordan

Jordan added, and minus the arms upon that porch, which Malone approved, because " they were very likely to have been " there." What ſhall be thought, then, of Ireland's picture, which preſents to us the confeſſed impoſition practiſed by Jordan, and improved upon by Malone?

There can be very little doubt that Ireland took Malone's drawing, added barge-boards to it, and reproduced it as copied from an original at Clopton Houſe.

Two queſtions of intereſt ſtill remain to be aſked. Did any ſuch drawing ever exiſt on the margin of a ſurvey? If ſuch did not exiſt, how came it that Malone lent himſelf to the impudent invention of Jordan, and publiſhed it as genuine, knowing that in ſome reſpects Jordan had " improved " it?

It is hard to believe that any ſuch drawing exiſted—certainly not as deſcribed by Malone, on the authority of Jordan—becauſe becaufe a furvey of his property, made by Lord Carew in 1599, would not be a furvey of other people's eftates. Lord Carew was contemporary with Shake-fpere, and might have known that New Place belonged to him two years prior to the making of the furvey—if fuch were ever made. But whether his lordfhip knew this or not, it is moft certain that his furveyors, in making plans and draw-ings of his eftate and the tenements upon it, would not introduce in the "margin "of their furvey" a houfe which, at leaft thirty-fix years previoufly, had been fold out of the Clopton family. When it is remembered who and what the "Poet "Jordan" was, and how ready he was to perpetrate any impofition upon the public, it feems moft probable that he invented the "margin of the furvey made by order "of Baron Carew," in order to impofe upon Malone, particularly as the exiftence of fuch ſuch a ſurvey or plan of a nobleman's eſtate was moſt likely to exiſt.

But was Malone impoſed upon? Did he believe Jordan's ſtatement, and regard the drawing as a genuine copy of an original repreſentation of Shakeſpere's houſe?

Malone may have been prediſpoſed to be deceived; he may have received the drawing with credence at firſt, as Walpole did Chatterton's records of ancient painters; but when Jordan got to improving the houſe, and adorning it with very probable coats-of-arms, it is hard to believe that Malone's faith was blind and unſuſpecting; while it ſeems ſtill harder to condemn him as *particeps criminis* in an attempt to paſs off upon the public, as a "great" Gothic houſe of the time of Henry VII., renovated in the time of Queen Elizabeth (when houſes were ſtill built in exactly the ſame ſtyle and manner—the only difference being in the

NEW PLACE: *as it was represented by* IRELAND.

(AN EXACT COPY OF THE ORIGINAL DRAWING.)

Face p. 47.

the "debaſed" *details* of ornamentation, pinnacles, tracery, &c.), a drawing which only needs to be glanced at, and it is inſtantly ſelf-condemned.

A fac-ſimile of this drawing will be found in Knight's "Biography of Shakeſpere" (note on New Place, p. 501). It has been repeatedly copied and preſented to the public, ſo that it ſeems unneceſſary to give it one more "laſt appearance" in this place. It and the drawing given by Ireland may be called *arcades ambo.* The plate on the oppoſite page, which accurately reproduces Ireland's, may ſafely be regarded as twin-brother to the Jordan-Malone picture, the details being the ſame in both, with the ſingle variation already noticed. The barge-boards, as ſeen in the accompanying plate, which Ireland furbiſhed up and added to the ſoiled impoſition of Jordan, may well be compared to the ſwaggering attempt of a gentleman,

out

out at elbows and deſtitute of a change of linen, who ſeeks to impoſe upon the public by mounting a clean collar on a manifeſtly dirty ſhirt.

The reader has only to examine and compare this picture with the picture of Ockwells to perceive, that though it might paſs muſter for the "oyſter-ſhell" Gothic of Horace Walpole's fancy, it is as unlike the genuine domeſtic architecture either of Henry VII.'s reign, or the "debaſed" of Queen Elizabeth's, as Walpole's lath and plaſter toy-ſhop at Strawberry Hill was a baſtard imitation of the ſtyle he pretended to affect.* It will be obſerved that the "timber and brick" deſcribed by

* The following letter, written by Horace Walpole, and now among the family papers of the Lord's Dacre, at Belhus, Eſſex, has never been made public. It has been kindly placed at the diſpoſal of the author by Sir Thomas Barrett Lennard, Bart., and will be read with intereſt, both as diſplaying the ſycophantiſh ſtyle in which Walpole addreſſed his ſuperiors, and alſo his architectural taſte:—

["STRAWBERRY

by Dugdale have altogether vanished in Ireland's repreſentation, and that a flat, paſteboard-like uniformity of frontage is preſented, in every reſpect oppoſite to the character of true Gothic architecture, in which the lines are invariably broken up by

"STRAWBERRY HILL, *July* 11*th*, 1777.

"I cannot receive joy from Bellhouſe, my dear Lord, "without giving it, and without telling your Lordſhip "how particularly kind I took it from Mr. Hardinge, "in acquainting me with his intended marriage,—I had "no right to expect ſuch attention, but by my zealous "wiſhes for his happineſs. When anybody that is "perfectly content, as he ſeems to be, thinks of making "others happy, it is the beſt proof of a good heart. "When miſery is communicative, it may flow from "want of pity, comfort, advice, or aſſiſtance; but when "happineſs is neither inſolent nor ſelfiſh, the monitor "muſt be benevolence. Without including myſelf in "this deſcription, I enjoy the ſatisfaction your Lordſhip, "Lady Dacre, Mrs. Harding, and Lord Camden muſt "have, in the felicity of ſo deſerving a young man. "It is talking, too, like an old one, but ſurely all the "riſing young men of the age have not Mr. Harding's "good qualities. Your Lordſhip did me the honour "of inviting me to Bellhouſe; it ſeemed ungrateful "not to thank you, and yet gratitude was the true "motive of my ſilence. I waited till I could tell you "that I could accept the honour of your offer. I "have had company, and various engagements that "prevented me, and am not yet at liberty from the "precarious

by gables, dormer windows, porches, and deep barge-boards, producing ſhadows, relief, and infinite variety. Ireland produced this wretched drawing in 1814. Mrs. Partheriche (concerning whom he was ſo ignorant that he could not ſpell her name correctly)* died in 1792. As the

"precarious ſtate of H.R.H. the Duke of Glouceſter's "health, and from expecting him and the Ducheſs in "England.[1]

"I was ſtill more flattered, though very unworthy, "by your Lordſhip's thinking of conſulting me on your "improvements at Bellhouſe; nobody is more attached "to the beauty of your ſeat, nor ſhall ſee your additions "with more pleaſure, but I have not the vanity to "preſume to direct them. You have not only done "everything there with taſte, my Lord, but to my taſte "of 'ancienne nobleſſe;' and ſince cheeſemongers can "be peers, I would have the manſions of old barons "powdered with quarterings for diſtinction; and ſince "Mr. Adams builds for ſo many of theſe, I wiſh he "would deviate from his ſtyle of Filigraine, and load "them with the Tuſcan order, which admits very "ſpeaking columns. "When

[1] His Royal Highneſs had married the Counteſs Waldegrave, daughter of Sir Edward Walpole, and niece to Horace Walpole.

* See quotation, p. 41.

the ſuppoſed original picture was unfortunately deſtroyed when in that lady's poſſeſſion, it might ſeem difficult for any ordinary mortal to make a copy of it in 1814: but difficulties of this ſort are trifles eaſily ſurmounted when genius, like another Joſhua, repeats the marvel of Ajalon, and puts back the courſes of time.*

Diſmiſſing both Jordan's invention and Ireland's impoſition, there is another matter of error which deſerves remark. Theobald aſſerts, that when Shakeſpere "repaired

"When I have a day at command, will Lady Dacre "and your Lordſhip allow me to make uſe of your "permiſſion, and wait upon you. I will not take that "liberty, however, without aſking if my viſit will be "ſeaſonable. I am, my dear Lord, with the trueſt "regards,

"Your Lordſhip's moſt obt.
"humble ſervant,
"Horace Walpole."

* Appendix D.

"repaired and modelled" New Place, he gave it that name. This is not the fact. In the survey of 1590 we find the following entry:—"Villielmus Underhill, "gen. tenet. libere quandam domum vo- "catam *the Newe Place* cum pertinentiis "per reddit. per annum, xij*d*. sect. cur."

Conclusive evidence is thus afforded us, that years before the Poet had any interest in the property, it was known by the name which has ever continued its "household "words." Sir Hugh Clopton, who built the house of New Place, happens to have styled it in his will "the Great House;" and such it has been supposed was its ordinary appellation. It is a supposition in search of a reason. The phrase seems rather an expression on the part of Sir Hugh, applied to his mansion as compared with the general size and importance of the tenements that surrounded it, than the title of the place itself. It well de-

served

ſerved the honourable deſignation; for when Queen Henrietta Maria, at the head of 3,000 foot, 1,500 horſe, beſide artillery and waggons, marched from Newark, in June, 1643 (on her progreſs to meet the king at Edge Hill, then proceeding to Oxford), and was met at Stratford by Prince Rupert, ſhe was conducted to New Place as the moſt commodious reſidence fitted to receive her Majeſty; and here ſhe ſojourned (as we are informed) "about three weeks."

Leſs direct, but important evidence of the "greatneſs" of New Place is afforded us by a conſideration of the wealth and ſocial poſition of Sir Hugh Clopton.

This Sir Hugh was a member of the ancient family of Clopton, of Clopton, in the pariſh of Stratford (Clopton Houſe being about a mile out of Stratford). The family name was derived from the manor, which had been granted to the Cloptons in in the reign of Henry III., ſo that Sir Hugh's anceſtors had been men of rank and importance for at leaſt two hundred and fifty years previous to his time. Sir Hugh became alderman of London, and ſerved the office of Lord Mayor in the ſeventh year of the reign of Henry VII., 1492. His name ſtill lives freſh and green in Stratford; for out of the abundance which he amaſſed as a wool-ſtapler in London, he not only adorned his native-place with the "Great Houſe," but he endeavoured to beautify the town itſelf, and alſo to benefit it by his charity. In the Guild Chapel of the Holy Croſs, adjoining New Place, there is a monument which was erected to his memory at the requeſt of the Corporation of Stratford, by that Sir John Clopton, his deſcendant, whoſe marriage with Barbara Walker brought back New Place into the Clopton family.

The

The monument tells us of his "pious "works, ſo many and ſo great, that they "ought to be had in everlaſting remem-"brance, eſpecially by this town and pariſh."

"He built ye ſtone bridge over Avon, "with ye cauſey at ye weſt end; further "manifeſting his piety to God and love to "this place of his nativity (as ye centurion "in ye Goſpel did to ye Jewiſh nation and "religion by building them a ſynagogue), "for at his ſole charge this beautiful "Chappel of ye Holy Trinity was rebuilt, "temp. H. VII., and ye croſs ile of ye "Pariſh Church."

The inſcription further relates his charities to the poor of Stratford and of London:—£100 to poor houſekeepers, 100 marks on their marriage to twenty poor maidens, both in Stratford and London; making of bridges and highways; founding exhibitions at Oxford and Cambridge; leaving money for poor priſoners,

money

money to hoſpitals, to the Mercers' Company, and "to ye parſon of ye pariſh "where he lived" (a wholeſome cuſtom that has ſingularly fallen into deſuetude). After all legacies and expenſes are paid, he leaves the reſidue of his goods and chattels to "repairing decayed churches," "mending bridges and highways," "maintaining poor children at ſchool," and in portioning "honeſt maidens."

"This charitable Gent. died a Batcheler, "15th Sept., 1496, and was buried in St. "Margaret's Church, Lothbury."

The ancient and beautiful altar-tomb among the Clopton monuments in Stratford Church, without any effigy, but with quatrefoil panels, originally fitted with armorial bearings in braſs, is moſt probably erected to his memory, becauſe it ſtands on the preciſe ſpot where, according to his will, he directed that he ſhould be buried, had he died at Stratford; and alſo

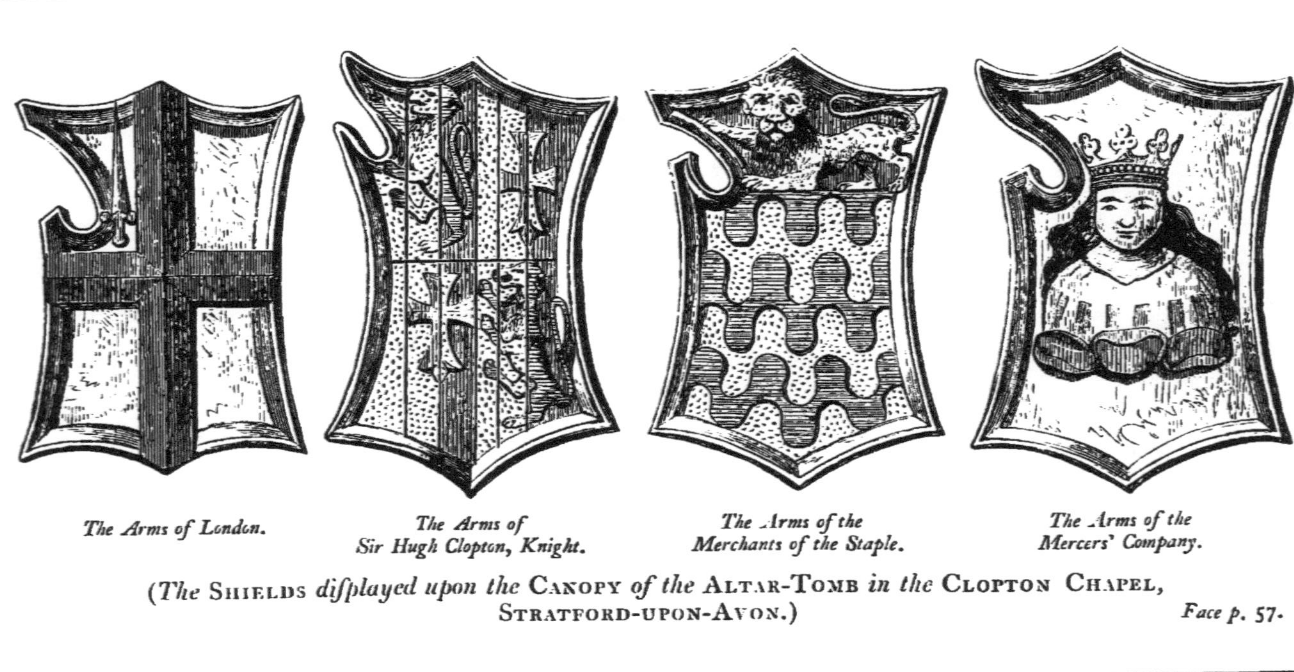

The Arms of London. *The Arms of Sir Hugh Clopton, Knight.* *The Arms of the Merchants of the Staple.* *The Arms of the Mercers' Company.*

(*The* SHIELDS *displayed upon the* CANOPY *of the* ALTAR-TOMB *in the* CLOPTON CHAPEL, STRATFORD-UPON-AVON.)

Face p. 57.

alſo becauſe the arms carved in the arch above it are thoſe of Sir Hugh, diſplayed with the arms of the Corporation of London, of which he was Lord Mayor, of the Mercers' Company, and of the Wool Staplers, to all which bodies he belonged.

In corroboration of this probability, which might be pretty ſafely aſſerted as fact, any viſitor to the Guild Chapel may obſerve on the face of the porch-way, over the arch, a ſeries of ſhields, in receſſes. It has been already ſhown that this portion of Holy Croſs—the nave and porch—were rebuilt by Sir Hugh Clopton. Accordingly, among the ſhields we find, ſimilar to the ſhields over the monument in the church, the arms of the City of London, the arms of the Wool Staplers, and the arms of Clopton, *quartered with Cockfield* (Clopton quartering, a Croſs patèe, fitchée in the foot; Cockfield, a lion rampant).*

The

* Appendix E.

The quarterings agreeing precifely with the difplay in the "Vifitation of Warwick-"fhire," and therefore fomewhat ftrengthening the affertion of the "Vifitation," that the Cloptons and the Cockfields were *temp.* Edward I. two diftinct families, and not that Walter de Cockfield was a Clopton, who affumed the furname of Cockfield, which name continued in ufe down to the time of Sir Hugh Clopton's grandfather, *temp.* Richard II., after which it difappeared, and Clopton only was ufed.

In his Survey of London and Weftminfter (under the title "Mercers"), Stowe alludes to Sir Hugh, as follows:—

"Sir Hugh Clopton, all his lifetime a "Bathchelaur, Maior, 1492, buried at St. "Margaret's in Lothbury, 1496. He "dwelt in Lothbury, where long after "was the fign of the *Wind-Mill;* and "where Sir Robert Large, fometime "Lord

"Lord Maior, had lived before.* This "man was born at Clopton, in Warwick-"ſhire, a mile from Stratford-upon-Avon, "where he builded a fair ſtone bridge of "eighteen arches, and glazed the chancel " windows

* This Sir Robert Large (Lord Mayor of London in 1439, died 1441), was the Mercer to whom Caxton was apprenticed when he came to London from the Weald of Kent. Stowe ſhows us that Caxton and Sir Hugh both lived in the ſame houſe in Lothbury, and we know they were both members of the Company of Mercers. When we remember that Caxton went over to Ghent and Bruges in the intereſt of the Mercers' Company, when the wool trade was ſuffering through the quarrel between England and Philip the Good of Burgundy, and that Sir Hugh Clopton was not only the ſucceſſor of Sir Robert Large in his houſe and place of buſineſs, but alſo a diſtinguiſhed member of the Company of Mercers, it ſeems almoſt a certainty that Caxton and Sir Hugh muſt have been well known to one another; and it is poſſible, perhaps probable, that by Sir Hugh the firſt books printed in England, "The Game "of Cheſs," publiſhed 1474, the "Poems of Chaucer," "Æſop's Fables," "Reynard the Fox," and others, would be taken down to his Great Houſe in Stratford, where the wonder and admiration of his neighbours would make the walls echo with the name of Caxton, the introducer of the invention which, in little more than a century later, was to carry forth from that ſame houſe the immortal thoughts of him, whoſe words, winged by Caxton's aid, have flown from pole to pole.

"windows of the ſame Pariſh Church "where his arms did ſtand. Which, "as William Smith, ſometime Rouge "Dragon, hath obſerved, differed much "from the coat ſet up for him, painted "in a target, in the Mercers' Hall, "which indeed was the arms of the "Cloptons of Suffolk."

Theſe facts preſent to the mind one of England's worthies, a true Chriſtian gentleman in the fulleſt and beſt ſenſe of the phraſe. It is a matter of ſurpriſe that a man of ſuch excellent parts and character, and ſo intimately connected with the houſe and place where Shakeſpere lived, ſhould be ſo much overlooked, as he is, by writers upon Stratford and its antiquities.

It is not, however, upon his genuine nobility of character that we have here to dwell; but upon his taſte, his love for art, and his delight in architecture. It is ſomething more than a fanciful idea

idea for us to believe that the taſte of Sir Hugh Clopton influenced the mind of Shakeſpere. Inſtead of a fancy, this ſeems to be a fact. The "New "Place," which he erected, was deſtroyed ſomewhere about 1720, and no repreſentation of it remains to portray it to us; but one piece of building, within a dozen yards of the ſpot where it ſtood, is indicative of Sir Hugh's taſte. The nave of the Guild Chapel was rebuilt by him, at preciſely the ſame period that Dean Balſhall (then Vicar of Stratford), was rebuilding the chancel of the Pariſh Church, to which it is clear that Sir Hugh generouſly contributed. Stowe informs us that the perpendicular tracery of the windows in this chancel was filled with ſtained glaſs, at the expenſe of Sir Hugh Clopton, whoſe arms Dugdale ſaw emblazoned upon the glaſs. There can be no difficulty

in

in conjecturing what ſort of reſidence "New Place" muſt have been—how architecturally correct—how excellent in proportion—how artiſtic in deſign—how pure in the ſtyle and detail of its ornamentation—how deſerving of its maſter's deſignating it the "Great Houſe" of Stratford, when we refer to his will, and compare its ſpecial proviſions for the repairing of churches, the building of bridges, the conſtruction of highways, with the work that he did himſelf accompliſh in erecting Stratford Bridge, building the nave of the Holy Croſs Chapel, and aiding in the erection of the chancel of the Pariſh Church. Thoſe portions of the Stratford churches, in which Sir Hugh was intereſted, are, even amidſt the laviſh richneſs of eccleſiaſtical architecture in Warwickſhire, juſtly reckoned ſuperb ſpecimens of the Perpendicular period.

Of "New Place" Shakeſpere became the

the lord and maſter in 1597. The houſe was then rather more than one hundred years old. It would need to be "repaired and modelled," particularly as it had belonged to three reſpective families within the half century before Shakeſpere purchaſed it, and had paſſed out of the Clopton family about a year prior to his birth. Of the repairs that he made, we know nothing; but it is eaſy to underſtand how much his mind may have been impreſſed with the ſtately beauty of New Place from his earlieſt childhood. No inhabitant of Stratford, ſeeing Sir Hugh's "Great Houſe" and the church that he alſo rebuilt alongſide it, could fail to know them and to admire them, much leſs a boy of Shakeſpere's obſervation and appreciative mind. New Place adjoins the Guild Chapel and the Grammar School. There the boy was taught; and day by day, as he went

bounding

bounding forth from school, the firſt objeƈt that met his view was Sir Hugh's houſe, next the church. While yet a child of between three and four years of age, a ſale took place. He may, on the very day of the ſale, have been holding to his nurſe's ſide, and making his earlieſt obſervations upon men and things, as he paſſed the chapel of Holy Croſs, and have ſeen the family of Underhill arrive to acquire poſſeſſion of "New Place." All this is perfeƈtly poſſible; and if this or anything ſimilar occurred, it might impreſs upon the boy's thoughts that New Place *had been ſold!* Might it not again? Who can tell, whether in his early days the boy Shakeſpere's mind had not been taught by old Sir Hugh's taſte to appreciate and admire the beautiful in art; had not been fired with ambition to go to London, as Sir Hugh (the pride of Stratford, and its benefaƈtor) had done, and

and by dint of labour and perſeverance to make an independence, and return like him to Stratford, and live honoured and beloved among the townsfolk of his native place? Who can tell whether this ſame boy may not often and often have ſtood ruminating under the ſhadows of the buttreſſes of Holy Croſs, admiringly examining the gables and caſements, the porch and antique barge-boards of the "great houſe," and reſolving, ſhould any ſale take place there again, if he were a man and had the means, it ſhould have but one maſter—one, himſelf poſſeſſed of taſtes like Sir Hugh's, who would "repair" and preſerve the anceſtral manſion?

In any biographies of Shakeſpere or hiſtories of Stratford which may have been written heretofore, New Place has been

been little more than mentioned. A houſe was built upon it at ſuch a date, ſold at another, purchaſed by Shakeſpere at another, and in it he died. No one has ever as yet opened the pages of ancient records to tell us much more about it than that it belonged to the Clopton family, and was built by Sir Hugh Clopton.

The time has perhaps come when it is deſirable that the public ſhould become poſſeſſed of more particulars concerning it; in fact, when every available information ſhould be produced to relate its hiſtory.

That it was Shakeſpere's dwelling-place is the cauſe of its intereſt in public eſteem; but that intereſt will be in no degree decreaſed if we know ſomething about the aſſociations of the place, and of the family to which it chiefly belonged, eſpecially as that family muſt have been well

been little more
houſe was built u
ſold at another, p
at another, and i
has ever as yet
ancient records tc
about it than th:
Clopton family, :
Hugh Clopton.

The time has
it is deſirable th:
become poſſeſſed
concerning it; in f:
able information ſh
relate its hiſtory.

That it was Sh
place is the cauſe of
eſteem; but that ir
degree decreaſed if
about the aſſociation:
the family to which
eſpecially as that fan

well known to Shakeſpere; and members of it, that were his contemporaries, play no obſcure part in the hiſtory of his times. Whoever he may be that undertakes to give the world a true and ſufficient account of New Place muſt inform his readers concerning the Cloptons of Clopton Houſe, ſince the hiſtory of New Place and its varied fortunes is as cloſely twined around the Clopton ſtem as the ivy around the oak.

On the oppoſite page will be found a pedigree ſet forth, which has appeared abſolutely eſſential to the accompliſhment of the author's purpoſe. By reference to it the reader will be able to follow him much more eaſily; and in order to ſecure perſpicuity—as the ſame names are repeated in ſeveral deſcents—thoſe have been alphabetically labelled to which it ſeems neceſſary to direct particular attention.

It

It has been ſhown (p. 16), that New Place was built in the reign of Henry VII., not later than 1490, by Sir Hugh Clopton, formerly Lord Mayor of London (pedigree Aa). Sir Hugh was a younger ſon of John Clopton, of Clopton — *temp.* Henry VI.,—and being a younger ſon, both he and his brother John ſought their fortunes as merchants of the Staple, in London. Dying a bachelor, Sir Hugh bequeathed his reſidence of New Place to his elder brother's grandſon and heir, William Clopton (Ab), in whom accordingly both Clopton Houſe and New Place became veſted.

The will of Sir Hugh Clopton, bearing date 14th Sept., 1496, was proved at Lambeth on the 4th day of October in the ſame year. He deſcribes himſelf therein as "citezein, mercer, and alderman of London," and deſires that if he die in London, or within twenty miles thereof,

thereof, he ſhould be buried in the church of St. Margaret's, Lothbury; but if at Stratford-upon-Avon, to be buried in the pariſh church there, within the chapel of our Lady, between the altar of the ſame and the chapel of the Trinity next adjoining, his body to be brought to ground with four torches and four tapers, and no more.

After detailing an agreement with one Dowland and divers other maſons about the building of the chapel of the Trinity, and the tower of a ſteeple to the ſame, and mentioning his father and mother by name (John and Agnes), there is a diſpoſition of ſundry legacies to charitable and religious uſes to conſiderable length; after which bequeſts to divers individuals; and, finally, entries relative to the deviſe of his property, in theſe words:—

Item.

Item.—I will as for my landes and rentes all such is of copy holde that Thomas Clopton the yonger and I be feoffed in remayne holy to hym and to his heires after my decesse for ever and for lak of issue to the right heires of the lordship of Clopton *And to William Clopton I bequeith my great house in Stratford upon Avon and all other my lands and tenements beinge in Wilmecote in the Brigge towne and Stratford with reversion and services and duetes thereunto belonginge remayne to my cousin Wm. Clopton* and for lak of issue of hym to remayne to the right heires of the lordship of Clopton for ever being heires males Also I will that CC marc that Doctor Balsale delyvered me be by the advise and discrecion of my executours employed to the use behoofe and moost profitte of the college of Stratford-upon-Avon by the consent and advice of the wardeyn with other sadde prestis and honest men of the towne And all such housing and tenementes as I have within the towne of Caleys I will remayn to my cousin Hugh Clopton the elder and also the reversion of the house that I dwell in att London and the termes of the same.

By the *inquiſition poſt mortem* upon *Sir Hugh Clopton,* it appears that he died ſeised of the following property in Stratford :—

De

De uno burgagio jacente in *Chapell strete* in Stretford predicta ex oposito capelle ex parte boriali et de uno dimidio burgagio jacente in *Ely strete* alias dicta *Swynne strete* et de uno burgagio in *High strete* et de uno orreo et gardino jacente in *Henley strete* et de uno dimidio burgagio jacente in *Church strete* in Stretford predicta et de duobus toftis quatuor virgatis terre quatuor acris prati et viginti acris pasture cum pertinentijs in *Brygge-towne* in parochia de Stretford Et quod idem Hugo ante obitum suum fuit seisitus in dominico suo ut de feodo de uno tenemento jacente in Stratford predicta in *Rother strete* vocato *Balsals place* et de uno gardino jacente in *Church strete* et de uno tenemento jacente in *High strete* super corneram de le Corne market in quo Johannes Balamy inhabitat et de aleo tenemento in *Chapel strete* buttante super le Corne market in quo Wolfridus Smyth inhabitat in Stretford predicta.*

Thefe documents will fhow that William Clopton (Ab), who had inherited the Clopton eftates in 1486, received a very

* According to this will, it appears that all this property here recited was demifed and let to Roger Paget and Elizabeth his wife, for term of life of the faid Roger.

very confiderable addition to his patrimony by the death—ten years later—of his great uncle, in 1496.

But, together with this acceffion, he found himfelf mafter of two confiderable manfions, removed little more than a mile from one another; viz., Clopton Houfe adjoining the town, and New Place within it.

Whether this gentleman kept up both the houfes there is no evidence to fhow; but as we have proof of New Place being let by his fon (B), it feems probable that William Clopton (AB) contented himfelf with the patrimonial refidence of Clopton, and fet the example which his fon followed. Having enjoyed his eftate for twenty-five years, he died in 1521, little more being known of him than that for fome offence to the Crown he received a pardon from Henry VIII.

By the *inquifition poft mortem*, it appears

pears that he was ſeiſed of the following property in Stratford, and retained poſſeſſion of New Place :—

In uno burgagio jacente in strata vocata *Chapel strete* in Stretford super Aven ex parte boriali capelle Sancte Trinitatis in Stratford predicta in comitatu predicto et de uno burgagio jacente in *Chapel strete* predicta uno capite inde abuttante versus Hugonem Raynold ex parte Australi et alio capite inde abuttante versus quandam stratam vocatam *Shepe strete* ex parte Boriali et de uno burgagio jacente in strata vocata *High strete* in Stratford predicta uno capite abuttante versus fundum Magistri Gilde Sancte Trinitatis de Stratford ex parte Boriali et alio capite inde abuttante versus stratam vocatam *Slystrete* ex parte Australi ac de uno burgagio jacente in strata vocata *High strete* in Stretford predicta uno capite inde abuttante versus tenementum Magistri Gilde Sancte Trinitatis predicte ex parte Australi et alio capite inde abuttante versus Willielmum Staffordshire ex parte Boriali Necnon de uno Burgagio jacente in strata vocata *Briggestrete* in Stratford predicta ac eciam de quodam orreo jacente in strata vocata *Henley strete* in Stratford predicta ac de quodam shopa jacente in strata vocata *Wode strete* quam Robertus Gonyatt modo tenet et occupat et de uno burgagio jacente

jacente in strata vocata *Rother market* in Stretford predicta in quo Deonisia Aylys vidua modo inhabitat ac de uno burgagio jacente in strata vocata *Grenhul strete* in Stretford predicta in quo Nicholaus Norres modo inhabitat necnon de uno burgagio jacente in strata vocata *Church strete* in Stretford predicta &c Necnon de alio burgagio jacente in *Church strete* in Stratford predicta in quo Johannes Ashurste modo inhabitat uno capite inde abuttante versus Episcopum Wigornensis ex parte Occidentali et alio capite inde abuttante versus vicum Regis vocatum *Church strete* ac de duobus gardinis in Stretford predicta abuttantibus versus Johem Hubandys ex parte Boriali et versus dictum Magistrum Gilde predicte ex parte Australi necnon de dimidio burgagio jacente in *Elystrete* in Stratford predicta nunc dimisso et locato pro quodam orreo.

The above William (AB) was ſucceeded by his ſon, bearing the ſame name (B), who lived in poſſeſſion of the combined eſtates from 1521 to 1560, at which latter date he died. His will is dated January 4th, and we learn from the inquiſition that he expired on the ſame day at Clopton. The death of this William Clopton

Clopton (B) brings to light the firſt fact explanatory of the cauſes which led to New Place ſubſequently becoming the property of Shakeſpere. The will bears the name of "William Bott," one of the atteſting witneſſes. There are traces of Botts in the regiſter of Stratford, though the author has vainly ſearched for ſome mention of this perſon, whoſe name is on record as one of the practiſing ſolicitors of Stratford at the period.

June 2, 1575.—William, sonne of Robt. Bott (buried).

September 2, 1576.—Sonne to Edward Botte.

July 18, 1588.—Margery, daughter of Ralph Bott, deceased.

January 19, 1591.—Anne Botte, deceased.

The probability is that the Botts were only profeſſionally connected with Stratford, and belonged to ſome outlying pariſh or hamlet. However this may be, it is certain that William Bott was a

lawyer

lawyer in practice at Stratford,* and that he was professionally engaged by William Clopton of Clopton (B).

After his death, the inquisition was taken on the 17th day of June, 2nd of Elizabeth (1560), at Warwyck, and the Jurors found that he died seised (inter alia) in his demesne as of fee—

De et in uno tenemento sive burgagio cum pertinentijs in Stratford super Aven in dicto comitatu Warr̃ in vico ibidem vocato la Chappell strete modo in tenura sive occupacione Willielmi Bott.

The same inquisition informs us, that the son and heir William Clopton (C) was at that date "twenty-two years of age."

In due course of years this William (C)

* Attorneys of Stratford about that date:—Mr. Thomas Trussell, Mr. William Court, Mr. Edward Davies, Mr. William Bott, Mr. Richard Spooner, Mr. Richard Symmons.

(C) came alſo to die, as the pedigree ſhows, in the year 1592.

The Book of Adminiſtrations, in an entry regarding the goods of this gentleman, reveals to us not only the buſineſs, but alſo the blood relationſhip between the Cloptons and the Botts; and thus we receive a complete inſight into a tranſaction that ſeems ſingular, regarding which no previous writer has given us any information.

The following extract is moſt important:—

Octobris, 1597.

WILLIELMUS CLOPTON.

Duodecimo die emanavit commissio *Johanni Bott*, PROXIMO CONSANGUINEO *Willielmi Clopton*, nuper dum vixit de Clopton, in comitatu Warwici, defuncti, habentis, &c., ad administrandum bona, jura, et credita ejusdem, per *Annam Clopton*, ejus relictam, jam defunctam, non administrata,

Blasij Johannis, 1603.

Administratio Comissa antea, mense Maij, 1592.

Johannis, 1605.

administrata, de bene, &c., in persona Thome White, notarij publici, procuratoris, legitime constituti, jurate. Blas'ij, 1605.

In what way John Bott happened to be "proximo consanguineo" to William Clopton the author must confess his profound ignorance; for Heralds' College can give him no relief. No doubt there has been an omission in the pedigree, wherever the link between the Botts and Cloptons occurred; but the above extract places it beyond all question that, in October, 1597, one John Bott, as the nearest of kin in the male line, after the death of Mistress Anne Clopton in 1596, the widow of William, administered the estate, it is to be presumed, as the friend and relative of the Countess of Totness, and Anne Clopton, of Sledwick, her sister, the co-heiresses of the late William Clopton (C).

What

What the connection between John Bott and William Bott was, the author has not discovered. They were probably father and son, or brothers—the latter being the more probable of the two conjectures. That they were close blood relatives is beyond a doubt.

Having dug up these facts, it will not surprise the most ordinary mind to find that William Bott, of Stratford-upon-Avon, solicitor, tenant of New Place, relative, and family lawyer to the Cloptons—witness to the will of a father, and adviser to his successor, aged twenty-two—took an early opportunity of improving upon the chances which fortune had cast in his way.

William Clopton (B) died 1560.

William Clopton, the administration of whose estate subsequently in 1597 is referred to above, (C) succeeded, and in 1563 he was induced to sell New Place to his

his late father's tenant, lawyer, and his own blood relative.

The transactions between Bott and William Clopton were considerable, for by the indenture which follows it will be seen that Bott had a knack of gaining possession of land belonging to the Clopton estate.

Indentur̃ int̃ Willm̃ Clopton et Willm̃ Bott.

This Indenture made the xth daye of Januarye in the syxte yere of the reigne of our so̾uaigne ladye Elizabeth by the grace of God quene of England Fraunce and Irelande defendor of the faith &c betwene Willm̃ Clopton of Clopton in the countye of Warr̃ Esquyer on the one partye and Willm̃ Bott of Stratforde uppon Avon in the said Countye gentleman on the other partye wytnesseth that the said Willm̃ Clopton for and in consederac̃on of and for dy̾use som̃es of money to hym in hande att and before the ensealinge hereof whereof and wherewyth the said Willm̃ Clopton doth acknowledge hym selfe thereof well and trulye satysfyed contented and paid and the said Willm̃ Bott his heires executors and administrators thereof clerely acquyted exon̾ated and dyschardged

chardged by these p̃ntes hath gyven and graunted bargayned and solde and by these p̃sentes doth clerelye and frelye gyve graunte bargayne and sell to the said Willm̃ Bott all those his three pastures of grounde called the nether Ingon alias Ington and all that his meadowe called Synder meadowe lyinge and beinge in nether Ingon alias Ington in the paryshe of Bisshopps Hampton in the said Countye of Warr̃ nowe or late in the tenure or occupac̃on of Rycharde Charnocke and Willm̃ Baylyes of Welon and the assignes of the said Rycharde Charnocke and all that his wyndemyll foure yardes of errable land and twentye and nyne leyes scituate lyinge and beynge in the Feildes of olde Stratforde and in the home nexte adioyninge to the said feildes and all that his meadowe lyinge in Shotterye meydowe nowe or late in the occupac̃on of John Combes and John Lewys alias Atkyns To have and to holde the said pastures meadowes wyndemylles lande and leys and all and singuler there app̃tenaunces to the said Willm̃ Bott his heires and assignes for eũmore to the onlye use and behoufe of the said Willm̃ Bott his heires and assignes for ever And also the said Willm̃ Clopton hath bargayned & solde by these p̃sentes all and all maner of evidences deedes wrytinges c̃hers and mynymentes that be touchynge and conc̃nynge onlye the p̃misses or any parte or parcell of them and the said evidences dedes wrytinges c̃hers and mynymentes the said Willm̃ Clopton couenaunteth and graunteth

graunteth by these p̃sentes to and wyth the said Willm̃ Bott his executors or assignes to delyuer or cause to be delyu̾ed to hym the said Willm̃ Bott his executors or assignes before the feaste of Easter next ensuinge the date hereof and fyrthermore the said Willm̃ Clopton for him his heires executors and administrators couenaunteth and graunteth by these p̃sentes to and wyth the said Willm̃ Bott that he the said Willm̃ Clopton shall before the feaste of Easter make or cause to be made to the said Willm̃ Bott his heires or assignes a good suer suffycyente laufull and indefycyble estate in the lawe in fee symple of and in the said pastures meadowes leyes of pasture wyndemyll and errable lande wyth all and singuler there app̾tenaunces be yt by fyne feoffament dede or dedes inrolled release confirmac̃on recou̾ye wyth voucher or vouchers wyth warrantye agaynste all men or wyth out warrantye as cane and shalbe deuysed or aduised by the learned councell of the said Willm̃ Bott his heires or assignes and furthermore the said Willm̃ Clopton for hym his heires executors and administrators couenaunteth and graunteth by these p̃sentes to and wyth the said Willm̃ Bott his executors and administrators that the said pastures meadowe wyndemyll and errable lande att the daye of the date hereof be clerelye dyscharged of all and from all former bargaynes sales dowres ioyntors leases statutes m̾chaunte and of the staple Recognisaunces iudgementes fynes am̾cyamentes condempnac̃ons and

and all other chardges and incomberaunces whatsoever they be the rentes and ꝯuices to the cheife lorde or lordes of the fee from hensforth dewe and accustomed to be paide onlye excepted and also the said Willm̃ Clopton for hym his heires executors and administrators couenaunteth and graunteth by these p̃sentes to and wyth the said Willm̃ Bott his heires executors and administrators that he the said Willm̃ Clopton and Anne his wyffe shall before the fourthe daye of Maye nexte ensuinge the date hereof knowledge a fyne before one of the quenes maiestyes iustyces of the Kinges benche or comon place to be levyed before the Quenes Justices at Westmꝰ of and for the said pastures meadowe wyndemyll leyes of pasture and errable lande wyth all and singuler there appᵱtenaunces and also the said Willm̃ Clopton for hym his heires executors and administrators couenaunteth and graunteth by these presentes to and wyth the said Willm̃ Bott his heires executors and assignes that he the said Willm̃ Clopton and his heires shall att all tymes hereafter and from tyme to tyme when and as often as he or they shalbe thereunto reasonablye required by the said Willm̃ Bott his heires or assignes doo suffer and cause to be done and suffered all and eụy suche further acte and actes thinge and thinges as shalbe reasonablye required by the learned councell of the said Willm̃ Bott his heires or assignes for the further assurance and suer makinge of the premisses to the said Willm̃ Bott his heires or assignes for

euermore

euermore In wytnesse whereof eyther party to these p̃sente Indentures int̃chaungeably have putto there seales the daye and yere firste above wrytten Et memorand q̄d t̃cio die Aprilis anno Sup̃script̃ p̃dcũs Wills̃ Clopton venit coram dc̃a dñа Regina in Cancellar̃ sua apud Westm̃ et recognouit Indentur̃ p̃dcãm et om̃ia et singula in eadem content̃ et sp̃ificat̃ in forma sup̃dict̃.

January, in the 6th of Eliz., would be 1563-4—three months before Shakeſpere was born. Upon the authority of Wheler, the author has aſſumed that the ſale of New Place occurred the year previous (1563). Wheler is commonly moſt accurate, and the above ſale gives weight to his aſſertion, becauſe it proves that Bott was at that time making purchaſes from William Clopton. The *Fines* of 1563 are ſilent, though it muſt be obſerved that there is a total abſence of all *Fines* in the Record Office for Michaelmas Term of that year ; which is to be accounted for by the fact that the plague was raging

raging. It is moſt probable that the ſale took place at that time; and that the late Mr. Wheler had met with ſome private trace of it for which the author has fruitleſſly ſearched among public papers.

That William Bott purchaſed New Place upon ſpeculation appears moſt probable, becauſe it only remained in his poſſeſſion for the period of four years. The *Fines*, Michaelmas Term, 9th Eliz., ſhow us that the ſale by Bott to Underhill took place at that date.

Warr̃ 1567.

Hec est finalis concordia fc̃a in Cur̃ Dñe Regine apud Westm̃ in crastino Sc̃i Martini anno regnor̃ Elizabeth dei grã Angł Franc̃ et Hibnie Regine fidei defensoris &c a conqũ nono coram Jacobo Dyer Ric̃o Weston Johe Walshe & Ric̃o Harpur Justic̃ et alijs dñe Regine fidelib3 tunc ibi p̃sentib3 int̃ Willm̃ Underehyll quer̃ et Willm̃ Botte et Elizabeth ux̃em eius et Albanũ Hetoñ deforc̃ de uno mesuagio et uno gardino cum ptiñ in Stretford sup Aven unde ptitum convenc̃ois sum̃ fuit

fuit int̃ eos in eadm̃ Cur scilt̃ qd̃ p̃dc̃i Willm̃s Botte et Elizabeth et Albanus recogñ p̃dc̃t teñ cum ptiñ esse jus ip̃ius Willm̃i Underehyll ut ill̃ que idem Willm̃s ħet de dono p̃dc̃or̃ Willm̃i Botte et Elizabeth et Albani Et ill̃ remiser̃ et quiet̃ clam̃ de ip̃is Willm̃o Botte et Elizabeth et Albano et hered̃ suis p̃dc̃o Willm̃o Underehyll et hered̃ suis impp̃m Et p̃terea idem Willm̃s Botte concessit p̃ se et hered̃ suis q̃d ip̃i warant̃ p̃dc̃o Willm̃o Underehyll et hered̃ suis p̃dict̃ teñ cum ptiñ cont^a^ p̃dc̃m Willm̃ Botte et hered̃ suos impp̃m Et ult̃ius idem Albanus concessit p̃ se et hered̃ suis q̃d ip̃i warant̃ p̃dc̃o Willm̃o Underehyll et hered̃ suis p̃dict teñ cum ptiñ cont^a^ p̃dc̃m Albanũ et hered̃ suos impp̃m Et insup ijdem Willm̃s Botte et Elizabeth concesser̃ p̃ se et hered̃ ip̃ius Elizabeth q̃d ip̃i warant̃ p̃dc̃o Willm̃o Underehyll et hered̃ suis p̃dc̃a teñ cum ptiñ cont^a^ p̃dc̃am Elizabeth et hered̃ suos impp̃m Et p̃ hac recogñ remissione quietaclam̃ warant̃ fine et concordia idem Willm̃s Underehyll dedit p̃dc̃is Willm̃o Botte et Elizabeth et Albano quadraginta libras sterlingor̃.

[Endorsed are the proclamations secundum formam statuti.]

By this sale New Place was rescued from the hands of a grasping lawyer, and passed into the possession of a family long connected

UNDERHILL PEDIGREE.

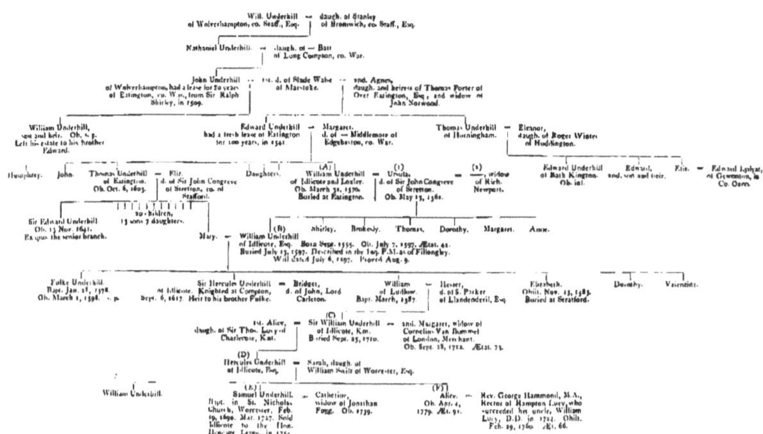

UNDERH

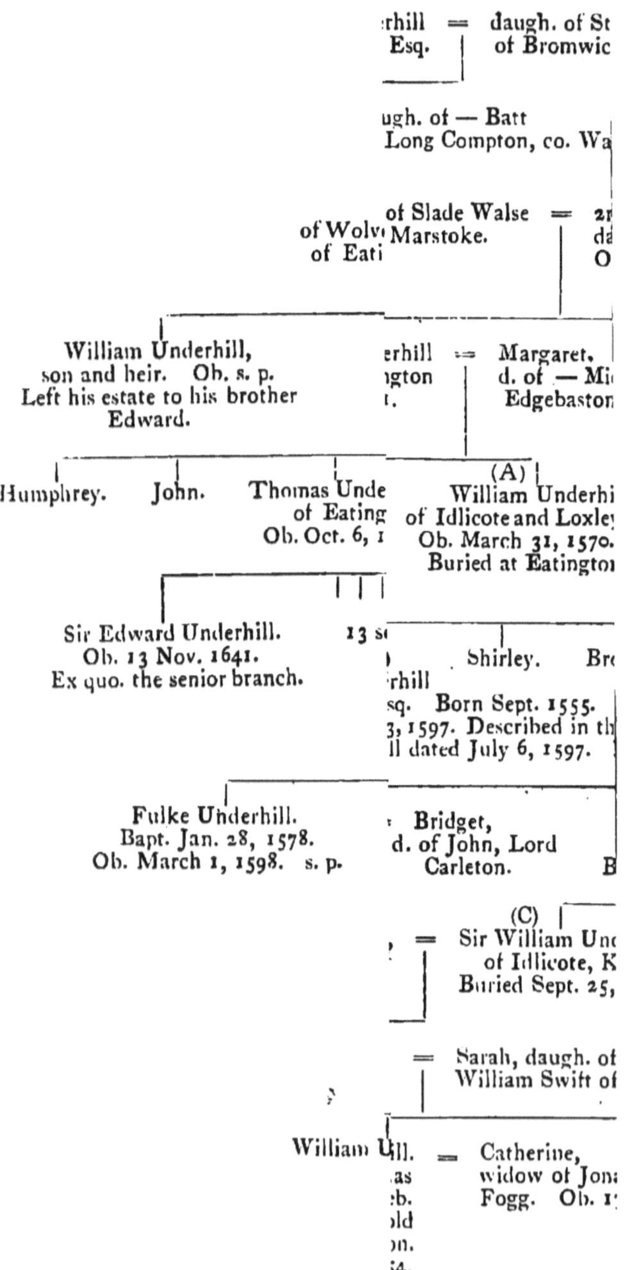

:rhill Esq. = daugh. of St of Bromwic
ugh. of — Batt Long Compton, co. Wa
of Wolv of Eati
of Slade Walse Marstoke. = 2r da O
William Underhill, son and heir. Ob. s. p. Left his estate to his brother Edward.
erhill ıgton ı.
Margaret, d. of — Mi Edgebaston
Humphrey.
John.
Thomas Unde of Eating Ob. Oct. 6, 1
(A)
William Underhi of Idlicote and Loxle Ob. March 31, 1570. Buried at Eatingto
Sir Edward Underhill. Ob. 13 Nov. 1641. Ex quo. the senior branch.
13 s
Shirley.
Br
rhill sq. Born Sept. 1555. 3, 1597. Described in th ll dated July 6, 1597.
Fulke Underhill. Bapt. Jan. 28, 1578. Ob. March 1, 1598. s. p.
Bridget, d. of John, Lord Carleton.
B
(C)
Sir William Un of Idlicote, K Buried Sept. 25,
Sarah, daugh. of William Swift of
William U ll. as b. old on. 54,
Catherine, widow of Jon Fogg. Ob. 1

connected with Eatington, and Idlicote, near Shipston-upon-Stour. The Underhills, as the abstract of pedigree herewith given shows, were originally a Staffordshire family, and settled at Eatington, a few miles from Stratford, on property belonging to the Shirleys.* The younger son of Edward Underhill purchased the estate of Idlicote, a short distance from Eatington, in the 10th year of the reign of Elizabeth (1568), from Ludovic Greville, and so established the junior branch of the Underhills as a family in Warwickshire. This William (marked A on the pedigree) had a son, also named William (marked B), who married his first cousin, Mary, of Eatington. His sons, Sir Hercules and William, were staunch and loyal supporters of the cause of Charles I., and were compelled to redeem

* Appendix F.

redeem their eſtate from the Republicans for £1,177 8*s*. 6*d*.

William Underhill (B) was the perſon by whom the purchaſe of New Place was made. By referring to the will of his father (in the Appendix G) it is evident that the Underhills poſſeſſed property in Stratford-upon-Avon; and therefore the purchaſe of New Place by William Underhill is readily underſtood. His name is repeatedly found among the fines levied about the years 1570 to 1590,* proving that he was anxious to accumulate as much landed property as he could in the neighbourhood of Stratford-upon-Avon; in fact, that he was ambitious to eſtabliſh the younger branch of the Underhills at Idlicote in as great affluence as the ſenior branch at Eatington. It was an ambition deſtined

* Appendix G.

deſtined to be diſappointed in the perſon of his grandſon (C), who having married Alice, the daughter of Sir Thomas Lucy, of Charlecote, had the misfortune to become a widower, and then to become enamoured of a widow, the relict of one Van Bommel, a rich Dutch merchant in London. This lady eſtranged Sir William from rural life, led him to London, and drew him into commercial ſpeculation. He embarked in the gunpowder trade; the mills were blown up, and the property blown to the winds at the ſame time. His ſon, Hercules (D), was involved, along with his father, and the reſult was, that in 1754 the eſtate was ſold to the Hon. Heneage Legge, by the grandſon Samuel (E), whoſe ſiſter Alice (F) was allied with the family of the Lucys of Charlecote, having married the Rev. George Hammond, Rector of Hampton Lucy, who ſucceeded his uncle, William

Lucy

Lucy, D.D., in the rectory, 1724. A monument to the memory of Mr. Hammond, and Alice Underhill, his wife, may be seen in the vestry of the modernly rebuilt church of Hampton Lucy; the apsidal east end of which, lately added by the present owner of Charlecote, aided by the genius of Mr. Gilbert Scott, has transformed this church into a sort of small cathedral; and, in the midst of the beauties and associations of Hampton Lucy and Charlecote, has furnished the lovers of architecture with a central object upon which the eye rests with gratitude to the liberality and taste of the present master of Charlecote.

From 1567 to 1597 William Underhill continued the proprietor of New Place.* It is vain at this remote date to speculate upon the causes which led to Shakespere's

* Appendix H.

Shakeſpere's purchaſe of New Place. Certainly there was no neceſſity for William Underhill to ſell any portion of his property. On the contrary, we have the beſt proof that he had the deſire and ability to increaſe his landed eſtate; and we can eſtimate its value when we recall the fact before ſtated, that his ſon, Sir Hercules, during the Civil War was glad to compound for it, by paying down £1,177. There is one fact concerning the ſale of New Place which is worth noting. It was ſold to Shakeſpere in the Eaſter Term of 1597; and Underhill was himſelf dead and buried July 13th of the ſame year.

This fact rather favours the idea that New Place was ſold from ſome private or perſonal motive to Shakeſpere; for it moſt certainly was not ſold as a buſineſs tranſaction. William Underhill is known to us as an accumulator of landed pro-

perty

perty, not as a man who had any neceſſity to part with a ſingle acre of his eſtate. It is probable that Shakeſpere was acquainted with the Underhills, and it may be that William Underhill was aware of the Poet's deſire to poſſeſs himſelf of the property at New Place. New Place would not be a reſidence at which Fulk, or Hercules—the future Sir Hercules, Royaliſt, and favourite of King Charles—would be ever likely to reſide, particularly as Idlicote itſelf was ſo contiguous to Stratford. It will be ſeen by the pedigree that Fulk died the year after his father, and the inheritance paſſed to his brother Hercules, a minor. Had Fulk Underhill died the year before his father's death, a reaſon for the ſale of New Place would have been ſupplied us. As it is, the probabilities are ſtrongly in favour of the belief that Shakeſpere was perſonally intimate with the Underhill family

family; and both Fulk and Hercules, youths of about ſeventeen and nineteen years of age, were poſſibly anxious that before their father died, the Poet and actor ſhould be gratified in his wiſh, and New Place ſecured to him. The facts, however, are theſe: in Eaſter Term, 1597, the ſale was effected, and on the 13th of July, William Underhill was buried. The preceding documents the author believes have never before been publiſhed; the following was diſcovered by Mr. Halliwell:—

Pasch. 39 Eliz.

Inter Willielmum Shakespeare quer̃ et Willielmum Underhill, generosum deforc̃, de uno mesuagio, duobus horreis, et duobus gardinis, cum pertinentijs, in Stratford super Avon, unde placitum convencionis sum̃, fuit inter eos, &c. scilicet quod predictus Willielimus Underhill recogñ, predicta tenementa cum pertinentijs esse jus ipsius Willielmi Shakespeare ut illa que idem Willielmus habet de dono predicti Willielmus Underhill, et ill̃ remisit et quietclam̃ de se et hered̃

hered suis predicto Willielmo Shakespeare et hered suis in perpetuum; et preterea idem Willielmus Underhill concessit pro se et hered suis quod ipsi warant predicto Willielmo Shakespeare et hered suis predicta tenementa cum pertinentijs in perpetuum. Et pro hac &c. idem Willielmus Shakespeare dedit predicto Willielmo Underhill sexaginta libras sterlingorum.

In glancing over theſe dry legal papers, unearthed from the charnel-houſe of hiſtory, we are brought into contact with the acts of men, whoſe lives would be unknown had they not been preſerved from oblivion by the embalming law. Shakeſpere's acquaintances, neighbours, perhaps friends, are brought before us in ſuch documents, and in the regiſters of pariſh churches. Theſe, and their tombſtones, are almoſt our only ſources of information concerning the men and women who were of note and conſequence in and about Stratford, who muſt have been familiar with the Poet, and who

who might, by the labour of a few hours, have left us records of him which would have made the world grateful through all its hours to come.

Let us be thankful, however, for possessing records that do survive the destruction of time; and accepting them, if we cannot re-people the past, at least we can catch a glimpse here and there of forms familiar to the Poet both before and during his New Place life.

Among the Special Commissions taken for the county of Warwick, now preserved in the Record Office, is an inquisition upon the estate of Ambrose, Earl of Warwick, dated 32 Eliz. (1591). The document is very lengthy, and one of very great interest. Some years back, attention was drawn to it by Mr. Cole, but as yet no antiquary has been found having a publisher of sufficient spirit to risk its publication.

The

The following epitome of ſuch portions as ſerve the object of the author will be read with intereſt. Among the commiſſioners will be obſerved the name of Charles Hales, to which the attention of the reader is eſpecially directed, for reaſons which will appear hereafter.

Special Commissions (Co. Warwick) *temp.* Eliz.

Inquisitio capta apud Warwic' et Stratford super Avon sexto die Octobris anno regni domine nostre Elizabethe Dei Gracia Anglie Francie et Hibernie Regine fidei defensoris &c tricesimo secundo coram Fulcone Grevile milite Thoma Leygh milite Johanne Puckeringe armigeris servientibus dicte domine Regine ad legem, Thome Dabridgcourt armigero, et Carolo Hales armigero, virtute Coñissionis dicte domine Regine extra Scaccarium nobis et alijs directe ad inquirendum et supervidendum de omnibus et singulis manerijs terris tenementis et hereditamentis in comitate predicto nuper Ambrosij comitis Warwicensis Et de quibusdam articulis eidem Comissioni annexis per sacramentum Johis Turner generosi Richardi Woodward generosi Radulphi Townesend generosi Johannis Fulwood generosi Humfridi Brace Radulphi Lorde Willielmi Wyatt Johannis Sadler Ricardi

Ricardi Walford Georgij Frauncis Thome Nosor Willielmi Harbage Georgij Gybbes Willielmi Taylor Thome Warde Johannis Collins THOME SHACKESPERE Johannis Barrett Thome Goddard Richardi Masters Willielmi Lapworth Thome Preyst Ricardi Williams et Roberti Farefax qui dicunt ut sequitur

* * * *

MANERIUM DE NOVO STRATFORD

Burgus sive villa de Stratford super Avon cum membris in comitatu Warr^{9}.

* * * *

Smythe strete

THOMAS SHACKESPERE tenet per copiam datam xxj die Julij anno xxvij regine Elizabethe unam croftam terre ad edificandum horreum ibidem continentem per estimacionem dimidiam acram terre vocatam Pookecrofte et unum gardinum cum pertinentijs pro termino quinquagenta annorum et reddit per annum . . . . iiij^{s} viij^{d}

* * * *

Vicus vocatus Henley strete

JOHANNES SHACKESPERE tenet libere unum tenementum cum pertinentijs per redditum per annum vj^{d} sectam curie . . . . vj^{d}

Idem JOHANNES tenet libere unum tenementum per redditum per annum xiij^{d} sectam curie . . . . xiij^{d}

Vicus

Vicus vocatus le Corne strete et Churche strete

WILLIELMUS UNDERHILL GENEROSUS TENET LIBERE QUANDAM DOMUM VOCATAM THE NEWE PLACE CUM PERTINENTIJS PER REDDITUM PER ANNUM xij^{d} SECTAM CURIE . . . . xij^{d}

[*Note*—Wm Underhill held also in "Walkers strete unum horreum &^{c}"]

Manerium de Shotterye reddit custumar^{9} tenen^{9} a Shotterie

JOHANNA HATHEWAY vid tenet per copiam unum messuagium et duas virgatas terre et dimidiam cum pertinentijs per redditum per annum xxxiij iiij^{d} finem et harriotam . xxxiij^{s} iiij^{d}

Manerium de Rowington cum membris customarij tenentes per copiam curie

THOMAS SHACKESPERE tenet per copiam sibi et heredibus suis unum croftum cum pertinentijs per redditum per annum ij^{s} ad festa predicta equaliter finem, heriotam, sectam curie . . ij^{s}

Liberi Tenentes

THOMAS SHACKESPERE tenet libere unum mesuagium et unam virgatam terre cum pertinentijs per redditum per annum &c . . . . . x^{s} x^{d}

Wood end

RICARDUS SHACKSPERE tenet per copiam ut supra

supra unum cottagium et dimidiam virgatam terre et unam acram prati cum pertinentijs per redditum per annum ad festa predicta equaliter vj^{s} x^{d} finem et sectam curie . . . . . vj^{s} x^{d}

Mulsowe ende

Thomas Shackespere tenet per copiam ut supra unum mesuagium et unam virgatam terre cum pertinentijs per redditum per annum ad festa predicta equaliter x^{s} iiij^{d} finem et harriotam, cum accederit, et sectam curie . . x^{s} iiij^{d}

Georgius Shackespere tenet per copiam ut supra unum cottagium et unum croftum terre cum pertinentijs per redditum per annum ad festa predicta equaliter ij^{s} finem et sectam curie ij^{s}

Ricardus Shackespere tenet per copiam ut supra unum mesuagium et dimidiam virgatam terre et duas parcellas prati cum pertinentijs per redditum per annum ad festa predicta equaliter xiiij^{s} finem et harriotam cum accederit xiiij^{s}

At the period of the above inquiſition being held, Shakeſpere was twenty-eight years of age. In a ſmall town like Stratford it ſeems that his family had induſtriouſly

"Scattered his Maker's image o'er the land."

There

There was a plentiful ſupply both of Shakeſperes and Hathaways in and about Stratford, not only at that date, but for many years previous. The regiſters and records of Rowington and neighbouring pariſhes have yielded their evidences to this procreative truth; but the author believes the following quotations from a Muſter Roll of the 28th Henry VIII. (1537), have not previouſly been publiſhed :—

Warwyke.

The certyficathe of George Throkmerton knyght John Grevyle Fulke Grevyle Edward Conwey Esquiers and Antony Skynner gent Comyssioners of our soueraync lorde the kings conserninge musters to be taken in the hundred of Barlychwey and libertye of Pathloc in the countye of Warwyke accordinge to the kinges highnes co(m)ission to them directed doe certyfie unto your lordships as well the names and surnames of all abell men withine the hundred and libertye aforesaid as horses harnes bowes arows billys and other thinges defensabell and mete for the warre with the diversitie therof whiche ar in every township of of the said hundred and libertye that ys to saye

* * * *

Rowington	Able men ther	
	* *	
(*Inter alios*)	Thomas Shakespere	Arch[er]
	* *	
	Ric: Shakespere	
	* * *	
Wraxsall	Able men ther	
	* *	
(*Inter alios*)	Willm Sakespere	Arch[er]
	* * *	
	Ric: Shakespere	
	* * *	
Shotery	Abell men there	
	John Hathewey	Arch[er]
Loxley	Abell men ther	
	Matthew Hathewey	Arch[er]

It will have been obſerved that William Underhill's father (A), the founder of the Idlicote family, was poſſeſſed of an eſtate at Loxley, a hamlet about three miles from Stratford. In this place alſo the

the Hathaways flouriſhed, for in the will office at Worceſter the author found the following entries:—

1541. Hathaway, Thomas . . Loxley.
1557. Hathway, Simon . . . Loxley.
1558. Hatheway, Joan . . . Loxley.
1617. Hathway, John . . . . Loxley.
1636. Hathway, Richard . . Stratford.
1637. Hathway, Richard . . Stratford.
1648. Hathaway, Andrew . . Bellbrougton.

Now, although William Underhill (B), the poſſeſſor of New Place, had his chief reſidence at Idlicote, it ſeems probable that New Place was a favourite town-houſe with him; and equally probable that it was purchaſed as a reſidence for him during his father's lifetime, as the ſale was effected by his father, three years prior to his death. That death may have occurred much more ſuddenly than was ever anticipated; and after his father was laid to reſt in Eatington church, William Underhill (B) may have been

unwilling

unwilling to retire entirely from a reſidence that had only been prepared for his reception three years previouſly. His ſocial rank and poſition are ſufficiently indicated by the preceding inquiſition, wherein he is ſtyled "generoſus;" and the author's reaſon for believing that this "William Underhill—generoſus" (though actually ſeated at Idlicote) always kept up his town houſe in Stratford, and occaſionally ſtayed there, although never making it a fixed reſidence, is drawn from the fact, that while the hiſtory of the family is to be read in the regiſters at Eatington, and the regiſters of Stratford are almoſt ſilent, it does ſo happen that the author has found one baptiſmal entry at Stratford, as follows:—

November 25, 1585.—Elizabeth, daughter of Mr. William Undrell.

The natural inference drawn from this entry being, that during the winter months

months of 1585, the Underhill family removed from Idlicote to their Stratford houſe, at which place it chanced that one of the children was born. We gather from theſe various documents that both at Loxley and in Stratford, William Underhill of New Place was ſurrounded by Shakeſperes and Hathaways. They muſt have been familiarly known to him, and he to them; for although there was a broad line of ſocial demarcation between the yeomen and able-bodied "archers," and the "generoſus" maſter of New Place, ſtill we muſt remember in the caſe of John Shakeſpere and his ſon there would not be ſuch a ſeparation, becauſe John Shakeſpere had attained a poſition in the town ſufficiently reſpectable to allow of a friendly intimacy exiſting between the Underhills and his branch of the Shakeſpere family.

From his childhood in 1567 until 1597

Shakeſpere

Shakeſpere would know William Underhill, Gent., as the owner of New Place.

That he muſt have known him ſocially, and that Underhill muſt have had ſome private and friendly motive in ſelling New Place to Shakeſpere, almoſt upon his death-bed, is a concluſion which the date and circumſtances of the ſale ſeem to force upon us. But Shakeſpere we know was intimately acquainted with John à Combe, of the "College," and in his will left his ſword to Thomas Combe. What of that?

The queſtion will be anſwered with the ſame explanation which the author would give to the companion queſtion, which we can well believe many time-worn lovers of Shakeſpere will be inclined to aſk: "Why do you burden your book "with a ſet of elaborate pedigrees which "no one has given before, and the uſe of "which is not obvious now?"

Let

Let ſuch queſtions receive this anſwer. Becauſe the writer believes, honeſtly and earneſtly, that much more fact, and infinitely more probability, concerning Shakeſpere's life, lies within our reach than is commonly ſuppoſed. Heraldry and pedigrees may ſeem to ſome perſons very dry ſtudy; but it may ſafely be aſſerted that, deſpite the flippant jokes of modern democratic writers at the expenſe of the Herald's Tabard, and the mediæval, quaint aſſociations of the College of Arms, that inſtitution, the Books of Viſitations, and the heraldic diſplays upon ancient church monuments, are becoming daily more and more valuable as contributors to the hiſtory of our country. However humorous it may ſeem to ſee the *novus homo* of Pie Corner or Pudding Lane aſſuming a creſt to which he has not the remoteſt pretenſion, and can ſhow no claim, nevertheleſs in the

the very aſſumption there is the indication of an Engliſhman's reverence and regard for the ancient landmarks of family and ſocial hiſtory.

What does it matter to any one if the inventor of the lateſt Delectable Soap or patentee of the Bifurcating-Baltic-Briſtle-Bruſh, drops in at one of thoſe terrific Holborn ſhops, which look like mediæval menageries for the exhibition of crimſon griffins and uproarious gamboge lions; and there, for the ſmall charge of 5*s.*, has his "arms found?" What though the brindle cat ſits and mews a-top his note-paper, curls its tail upon the flap of his envelopes, and ſpreads its whiſkers over the handles of his ſpoons? Do Garter or Clarenceux loſe their appetites becauſe the vaulting ambition of the ſhop has a ſneaking love for theſe things, and pays for it in the Queen's taxes, with hair-powder and ſuch like? Not

Not a jot. They know well enough that the honeſt citizen would have found his arms at Doctors' Commons if he could; and that, pleaſe God and his own induſtry, if he can found a family, ſome day or another the brindled cat may have its turn in that direction! Though the cynic may ſmile and ſneer at ſuch cockney pretenſion, and though it has a ludicrous aſpect, nevertheleſs it is not all ludicrous. There is ſomething genuinely Engliſh at the foundation. There is an evidence of the ſpirit of homage to antiquity; of reverence for even the humbleſt aſſociation with anything connected with the records of the country.

As all forms, eccleſiaſtical or civil, have their meaning and their moral, ſo the forms of heraldry—the quainteſt of all—are full of the deepeſt meaning and intereſt. Let the preſent writer make bold to ſay that a moſt intenſely intereſting book might be, may, perhaps, be yet written regarding Shakeſpere, by collecting together a record of the perſons and the incidents of thoſe perſons' lives with whom the Poet muſt of neceſſity have been aſſociated. Theſe pages cannot be devoted to ſuch an undertaking; and, therefore, there will be no further attempt made in them than to indicate the direction in which it ſeems well that ſome one ſhould travel.

It is by no means impoſſible to ſurround Shakeſpere with friends and acquaintances, concerning whom the world generally knows nothing up to the preſent time.

What is the common eſtimate of him and of his aſſociates? Vulgarity is ſtamped upon the traditional ſtories regarding his life and ſociety. We are told he was apprenticed to a butcher. He was a deer-ſtealer. He married a woman in a

hurry,

hurry, for a reaſon about which the leſs ſaid the better. He lived unhappily with his wife, and as an evidence of his indifference, left her his ſecond-beſt bed. Laſt of all, he died of a fever, caught from a bout of drunkenneſs. Poor Shakeſpere!

Can any one ſhow that there is a ſyllable of truth in any of theſe ſtories? Do ſuch low-bred vulgarity, immorality, and beaſtiality, ſuit with the mind of William Shakeſpere?

Has he not in his own words ſupplied for us the vixen-like revenge which littleneſs, and the worſt littleneſs of all, that of goſſips, takes upon any real greatneſs of mind and character:—" I'll give thee "this plague for thy dowry; be thou as "chaſte as ice, as pure as ſnow, thou "ſhalt not eſcape calumny."

Whence do all theſe ſtories about our Poet come? Plain, vulgar-tongued folk call

call them—goſſip. When ventilated in a ſuperior atmoſphere, and carried with the beefs and muttons from the ſcullery to the dinner-table, the word diſſolves into the politer phraſe—tradition. Be it ſo! But what is Tradition? Tradition is not to be believed; but always to be conſidered. Tradition is a perjured witneſs, who never yet came into court without a lie upon her tongue—for it is a lie to pervert, diſtort, exaggerate, or diminiſh aught of the truth; and where, either in the memory of man, or on the pages of hiſtory, was there ever a piece of "goſſip," "town's talk," "what everybody ſays," "tradition," that did not, on inveſtigation, turn out to be gorged with falſehood?

The ſtories current concerning Shakeſpere, which the lapſe of ages has conſecrated with the undeſerved title of tradition, might well aſtoniſh any ſtranger to Engliſh

Englifh habits; but they are not in the fmalleft degree aftonifhing, when we remember that it is one of the manners and cuftoms of the Englifh to try to knock a man over, the moment he lifts his head above the herd of his fellow-men. If by abufe and flander we can blight his fpirit, dull his brain, and break his heart, we give God thanks for having accomplifhed a worthy, Chriftian, and charitable end. But if he ftands the pelting, and wont be put down, there is a time coming when he can be cuffed and cudgelled to any extent. For your genuine lover of flander—the vampire of private life—the greateft treat on earth is the "poft-mortem" of a man's character, whom he has followed with envy, hatred, and malice through life. There are Cannibals, even in England, who want a gofpel preaching to them far more than their heathen brethren; for

while

while the latter whoop and dance around the dead, and then eat the periſhing fleſh, the former exultingly leap upon, and until they are ſick with ſurfeit, devour the more than body—the reputation, the life in death, of thoſe who lie defenceleſs in the grave.

There is no need to be ſurpriſed that even mighty Shakeſpere's memory has been handed down to us blackened and defamed by goſſip. In inverſe ratio, the higher a man attains, the lower and baſer he is likely to be repreſented. An unerring gauge whereby to meaſure the value of character and genius againſt goſſip, in the caſe of Shakeſpere, is here ſupplied.

The ſtory—which will hereafter be referred to—regarding the cauſes which led to Shakeſpere's death, is generally familiar, and has, as a matter of courſe, been commonly reported in Stratford. In order to

ſhow

ſhow how goſſip—otherwiſe tradition—improves as ſhe paſſes from mouth to mouth, the author lately encountered the ſtatement, gravely made to him by a clergyman at Luddington, who had been aſſured of its truth, that "Shake-"ſpere died drunk." That aſſertion will read to every one as wicked and pre-poſterous as it ſounded in the ears of the writer. But why wicked and pre-poſterous? It is the natural reſult, and inevitable development of the ſtory told in the Rev. Mr. Ward's Diary, which need not be further diſcuſſed in this place. This piece of goſſip of 1862, the author believes preciſely to the ſame extent that he does any and all of the before-mentioned ſtories. They all reſt upon one baſis, and that baſis is a rotten one.

A very clever, and, in its way, a very convincing pamphlet, was publiſhed a ſhort

ſhort time back, by Charles Holte Bracebridge, Eſq., entitled "Shakeſpeare no "Deerſtealer," the giſt of which is, that Shakeſpere did not kill the deer in Charlecote at all, but in Fulbroke Park; that in ſo doing he committed no offence againſt the law, or morals, but that he offended Sir Thomas Lucy thereby. Mr. Bracebridge quotes the ſtatement of the late Mr. Lucy to Sir Walter Scott, that "the park from which Shakeſpere ſtole "the buck was not that which ſurrounds "Charlecote."

Mr. Bracebridge's pamphlet is well worth reading, and he has done good ſervice by it to the memory of the Poet.

Now as to the value of tradition. Though tradition invariably ſpeaks falſely, as in one inſtance Mr. Bracebridge has ſhown, nevertheleſs, though a wretched bad witneſs in court to give evidence, ſhe ſerves as a very uſeful ſign-poſt upon the

the highways of time. She commonly (not always) points to ſomething that deſerves inquiring into, and indicates the direction in which we ſhall find it worth our while to travel. So with regard to the traditions about Shakeſpere: the author believes they are a mixture of abſurdity and of falſehood; but at the ſame time, while rejecting them as at all truſtworthy, they ſeem to him to ſerve a uſeful purpoſe in exciting inquiry, and making us ſeek for the truth that underlies them. As evil is commonly good perverted, ſo falſehood is often the wicked or idle miſrepreſentation of ſomething true at bottom; and as good as it is true.

Let any one of the ſo-called traditions concerning Shakeſpere be brought into court, and ſearchingly examined, and it will be committed for perjury.

But let us take the rambling old ter-

centenarian

centenarian crone at her real value; go and ſit with her in her timber and plaſter cottage at Stratford, and liſten to her as ſhe told her ſtory to Betterton, or to Ward, or in her later years to Malone or Stevens, and we ſhall thank her, not for what ſhe teaches us, but for ſending us off in the right direction in purſuit of ſomething we have yet to learn.

There is Mr. John Shakeſpere, in Henley Street—he is a glover, or a butcher, or a "yeoman," or wool-dealer! —what is he? Can no one ſum up all the ſuppoſed trades or buſineſſes, and ſay in a word, that they moſt probably mean he was a woolſtapler? Make him of any one of the above trades actually and ſolely, and we cannot reconcile the other ſtatements.

But like the variorum readings of the ſame names and the ſame employments in Shakeſpere's days, if we adopt

adopt the conclufion that he was a Merchant of the Staple, we fhall eafily be able to underftand his being called both butcher and glover. Confidering what a ftaple trade gloving was in John Shakefpere's time, in his own county, if he were connected with the mercers in London, he would of neceffity deal in gloves. The poffeffor of land, and the owner of cattle, it is the height of probability that he may have flaughtered his fheep in his own farm-yard, in order to have the fkins properly preferved. Butcher he might eafily be called, and fo might his fon William; and alfo be reprefented as apprenticed to a butcher, when he was in reality apprenticed to his father.

So, again, the ftory about Shakefpere killing an animal, or helping to kill one, may be true in origin, but tradition's reprefentation of it be as untrue, as if one of our princes or peers were nominated

nated a "butcher" becauſe he happened to be preſent when a ſtag's throat was cut.

And ſo, again, there is the deer ſtory. Mr. Bracebridge may be right as far as he goes; and yet, while tradition points to ſome fact that did occur, he might perhaps, though wanting evidence, and yet in truth, have gone much further. Might not Shakeſpere have been out, not merely for ſport, but as a matter of buſineſs? Might not his father have regularly killed, and paid for deer out of Fulbroke Park? Might not the quarrel with Sir Thomas Lucy have ariſen upon this ground; and an imperious, hot-headed country ſquire have attempted to interfere with Shakeſpere, thereby making himſelf ridiculous, and henceforward becoming famous in his folly?

Again, as regards Shakeſpere's removal to London. May not that have hap-

pened

pened for buſineſs motives? and may he not, during his whole London career, have benefited by a profitable trade, that gave him the poſition of a gentleman, and connected him with gentlemen? and alſo enabled him to realiſe that independence upon which he retired? It muſt never be forgotten that his father was in difficulties about the time when the Poet removed to the metropolis; and from that moment we never again hear of, or trace any domeſtic anxieties in the houſe of John Shakeſpere. The inference ſeems concluſive.

Look at Shakeſpere, in his home-life at Stratford: is he not continually engaged in commercial tranſactions—buying and ſelling corn, buying land, farms, tythes? Shakeſpere was a buſy man—an active, thrifty, accumulative man. He was evidently anxious to make money, and to found a family. His will, and the

records

records of Heralds' College, in his father's grant of arms, prove this.

When he became more permanently reſident at Stratford, we find him exhibiting the habits of life previouſly contracted. Men's habits are not changed in mid-life, and new ones aſſumed. What Shakeſpere was at Stratford we have every reaſon to ſuppoſe he was in London; but whatever the ſources of his accumulations, whether from one or various ſources—the ſtage, his plays, and commercial enterpriſes—we *know* that he did make money; and that at a very early time of life he was able to eſtabliſh himſelf and family in New Place. So far from the vulgar, baſeleſs conjecture, that Shakeſpere ran off to London to avoid Sir Thomas Lucy having anything to recommend it, it ſeems to the author as far-fetched and prepoſterous, as it is totally devoid of a ſcintilla of evidence in its favour.

Why

Why ſhould we delight in perpetuating ſuch miſerable fudge? Why ſhould one writer after another, and one generation after another, paſs on, from book to book, and from mouth to mouth, a ſet of ſtories that would be (diveſted of the grand-ſounding epithet "tradition," and branded with their proper deſignation, —pot-houſe goſſip) rejected as only ſuited to the ideas of tap-room topers? The term is uſed adviſedly. There is the faint, oppreſſive odour of that region—ſaturated with the ſtench of ſtale beer, and the deſpoiling of men's reputations—about almoſt all the "traditions" of Shakeſpere. Shakeſpere with merry companions, over the "cheerful bowl," is perpetually being preſented to our notice by tradition. Shakeſpere, and "the ſcience of drinking (at Bidford) the largeſt quantity of liquor without being intoxicated!" Shakeſpere dead-drunk, and ſleeping the night

night through "under the umbrageous "boughs of a crab-tree!" Shakeſpere making doggrel verſes at the expenſe of his particular and perſonal friend, at a tavern, ſaid to have been known by the ſign of "the Bear!" Shakeſpere drinking too hard at a merry-meeting, and dying thereby of a fever!

Oh! pundits of our literature! biographers of the greateſt man of all your craft! lovers of the Saxon tongue! is it by ſuch boozing tales as theſe that ye honour the High Prieſt of your profeſſion? Muſt the incenſe that you offer at his ſhrine reek with the coarſe odour of the village politician's and wiſeacre's foul tobacco, and ſtill fouler breath? Can no Neibuhr of Engliſh record be found ſtrong enough and manly enough to cleanſe the ſtream of hiſtory, by purifying and contemptuous ridicule of this corrupting garbage, polluting every-

thing

thing with its poiſonous "tradition?" We are taught to diſtruſt an autograph of Shakeſpere's, and cautioned not to believe a ſcrap of writing to be true, unleſs there is internal corroborative evidence to eſtabliſh its authority! Better, ſurely, to caution the world againſt believing a ſcrap of vulgar goſſip, unleſs there is ſome internal, and corroborative evidence to eſtabliſh its authenticity. No one is a jot the worſe or better whether a line of writing be genuine or forged; but a whole nation is made worſe,—every man who ſpeaks the Saxon tongue is worſe, becauſe his confidence and reſpect are ſhaken, if he diſcover that the teacher of the higheſt, nobleſt thoughts—the Poet who fills the heart with admiration for all that is noble and virtuous and honourable in human nature, began life as a thief, ſpent it as a vagabond, and ended it as a drunkard! Softer-ſpoken words might be culled from the

the dictionary; but these are the real and simple terms by which, in plain, unvarnished speech, Shakespere deserves to be described, if the self-condemning "traditions" in common currency regarding him are to be reproduced and re-believed.

It may be said, that the author has met tradition by nothing better than suggestion and that any one can draw pictures from imagination. But this would hardly be just. Which sort of evidence is more agreeable and acceptable,—that which is probably true because it rests upon conclusions derived from known facts; or that which is probably untrue, because it rests upon no other foundation than the loose and shifting stories of gossips?

Gossip represents Shakespere as a boozing and beer-drinking fellow. Facts do not prove that he was not; but facts provide us with evidences of his energy, labour,

labour, and thrift, leading us to conclusions from those facts which convince us he could not possibly have been so. *Ex uno disce omnes!* Gossip says he was a deer-stealer in Charlecote Park: facts now prove that statement to be positively false, and that if he killed a deer at Fulbroke, Sir Thomas Lucy had no power to prevent him. Gossip says he ran away to avoid the knight's displeasure; facts prove that his father was a man in considerable re-pute, connected with the Mercer's trade, but that he got into difficulties; and at that precise period we find young Shake-spere went to London. Facts truly do not prove, but they lead us to a reason-able conclusion based upon them, that Shakespere went to London for good and honest purposes; and that he went as a man of business, not as a homeless vagrant is the more probable, because facts show that his father retained posses-sion

ſion of his reſidence, and we hear no more of his troubles; while in a brief period of time his ſon returned to Stratford, able to eſtabliſh himſelf in the "Great Houſe" there.

Let us judge of Shakeſpere by what we really know of him, however ſmall and circumſcribed the amount of our information may be. Rejecting with ſcorn the old wives' fables, which other old wives ſeem to have delighted in perpetuating, it is a ſafer and more honourable path to purſue, if we ſet out upon a journey in ſearch of facts, and, like Pilgrim, eaſe our ſhoulders of that bundle of fictions which have burdened us. Let tradition be a finger-poſt, and nothing more! If the enthuſiaſtic lovers of the Poet would content themſelves with healthy exerciſe, they might perhaps find that there are ſtill many facts waiting to be dug out of ancient records that have been bruſhed

paſt

paſt by us ten thouſand times, and yet never detected. The ſilver mines of Potoſi were diſcovered by the tearing aſide of a bramble; and yet their treaſures had laid through the long centuries cloſe to the handling of men. So it may prove that there are treaſures of hiſtory that have been very cloſe to ſome among us, which an accident ſome day may diſcloſe. Even though it be not ſo, the ſubject is well worth diligent ſearch.

It ſeems extraordinary that many of the rapturous admirers of the genius of the Poet perpetuate, as if they were true, ſo many vulgar ſlanders and goſſips regarding the man. If they were true, we might begin to ſuſpect there is ſomething after all in that ſtrange theory that Shakeſpere's plays were never written by Shakeſpere, but by Francis Bacon; becauſe it would be impoſſible to reconcile the man that we ſhould picture from the writings

writings, with the man that we ſhould know in his aćts. In Mr. Charles Knight's moſt intereſting "Biography of "Shakeſpere" and running commentary upon contemporary hiſtory, manners, and habits of the country, a proper and contemptuous proteſt is entered againſt the ungracious doggrel attributed to Shakeſpere, as written at the expenſe of his friend and neighbour John à Combe, an eſtimable, worthy, and charitable gentleman, whom tradition has nick-named uſurer! Uſurer! Let any one read his Will, and it will be ſeen what a friend the poor of Stratford had in the kind old man who lived among them, and bountifully bequeathed his property for their benefit. The good that he did, has, indeed, been interred with his bones.

This ſtory, and others, Mr. Knight has diſmiſſed as they deſerve. It is heartily to be deſired that many more of the Poet's

Poet's biographers had done, and would ſtill do, the ſame.

Can no other picture of him be drawn? Let us make the attempt.

It will be admitted that Shakeſpere was a precocious and ambitious youth. Let the motive for his early marriage have been what it may, there was precocity in the ſtep. But if we diſcard the diſhonouring ſuggeſtions that have been made regarding it, and conſider it as the act of a young man who had a ſolemn and earneſt appreciation of the value and purpoſe of life, we ſhall find that ſuch a view of the tranſaction harmoniſes with the whole of Shakeſpere's conduct. Let it be ſaid—it matters not—that this is taking a very novel view of his conduct: is it not better, when we are attributing motives to a perſon, to try and find good rather than bad ones? Shakeſpere, it is true, needs no apologiſt, leaſt of all the advocacy

vocacy of ſo feeble a pen as that which traces theſe lines; but to furniſh motives for a man's acts is a paſtime at which all can play an even game; and therefore the fancy of one man is juſt as good as that of another. The Poet's character is read from a totally different point of view in theſe pages to that taken by De Quincey and by many others.* Let it be pardoned, if in love and admiration the author ſeems preſumptuous when he ſays, that he conſiders, in the glorification of the poet, Shakeſpere's character has wanted ſtaunch and faithful champions,—men

"To think no ſlander; no, nor liſten to it."

Let the ſuggeſtion above made be entertained for a moment, and in what a totally different light do the two momentous actions of the Poet's life preſent themſelves! —his early marriage, and his early ſetting out

* Appendix I.

out for London to fight circumſtance and conquer independence !

Precocity and ambition are herein combined. Who shall blame them ? This man commenced life as a good man ſhould begin it : there was no "ſowing of wild oats ;" no libertiniſm ; no exhauſtion of the ſtrength of youth amidſt the ſtews of a metropolis. Let Shakeſpere's acts—the facts of his life—be weighed againſt the words of goſſips who never knew him, and the author contends thoſe facts all go to turn the ſcale in his favour.

His firſt ſtep on the threſhold of manhood argues the ſenſe of reſponſibility, and the ambition for reſpectability. It was in the man ; and it came out and ſhowed itſelf at the earlieſt poſſible moment.*

There

* When it was ſtated, at p. 31, that there are two ſeals to Shakeſpere's marriage bond, one bearing the impreſſion "R.H.," it would have been more correct to ſay there "were," becauſe the ſeals have entirely vaniſhed, and there is ſcarcely a trace of them on the parchment.

There is another characteristic—the granting of arms to Shakespere's father. It

---

parchment. Nearly fourteen years have elapsed since the author last heard anything of that bond, and it was only by accident that, being in Worcester lately, he took the opportunity to give it a fresh examination. On doing so, he compared the text of Mr. Halliwell and Mr. Knight with the original, and found that the copy (given at pp. 29, 30) is perfectly correct, while that of Mr. Knight ("Biography," p. 275) contains these errors:—

"By reason of any p̄contract or affinitie, or by any other," &c., instead of "by reason of any p̄contract, consanquitie, affinitie," &c.

"May lawfully solemnize m̄riony," instead of "may lawfully solemnize m̄riony together."

"Laws in that case provided," instead of "lawes in that behalf provided."

With regard to Luddington, as the probable place of Shakespere's marriage, it may be well to put it on record that there is still living an old gentleman, named Pidering, at Colton, near Alcester, who, when a youth, resided at Luddington. This person distinctly remembers having heard it positively asserted by the inhabitants of the hamlet that Shakespere was married in their chapel; and he also remembers the books and registers of the chapel being burnt in a fire which occurred at his cousin's, the chapelwarden's house, *at the commencement of the present century.* (*Query.* Did Malone ever search those books?) Mr. Baldwin, who now occupies the farm on Luddington Green, preserves the remains of a Gothic font which belonged to the chapel, as also the Black-letter Bible which belonged to the reading-desk, and the key of the porch, which was dug up a few years since in the garden which now covers the ruins.

It is univerſally admitted that this was Shakeſpere's act; and that it was he who prompted John Shakeſpere's application to Herald's College.

It will be obſerved upon the Shakeſpere Pedigree, that the condition of his anceſtors and the grants of lands, as recorded in the draft of the pedigree in Herald's College, have been reproduced as correct, attributing them to the favour of Henry VII., to whom John Shakeſpere's great-grandfather did faithful and approved ſervice. William Dethick, Garter Principal King-at-Arms, has been charged with granting arms improperly; and Mr. Halliwell particularly dwells upon the ſcoring and interlining of the original grant of 1596. It ſeems to the author that this ſcoring and correction was moſt natural, and that in all probability it occurred from the fact of the evidence being taken down from the lips of William Shakeſpere.

Dethick

Dethick is not to be charged with the falſehood or miſrepreſentation, if any, appearing in the two drafts of arms, dated 1596 and 1599. In both theſe the faithful ſervices of the Shakeſperes to King Henry VII. is ſolemnly aſſerted; and it is hard to believe that the aſſertion is untrue, when it agrees ſo well with the probable ſettlement of the Shakeſperes in Warwickſhire, and was made, almoſt beyond doubt, by the Poet perſonally, to Dethick, ſince the draft bears date when Shakeſpere was buſy in London, and the *year before he purchaſed New Place*—a ſignificant fact!

Therefore, on the Pedigree in this book, that ſtatement is accepted and believed, becauſe the author believes the draft was drawn under information provided by William Shakeſpere himſelf; and he believes likewiſe that the man, with the chivalric feelings of a gentleman, would have ſcorned to tell a lie.

It has been ſuggeſted that becauſe, as it will be ſeen, the Ardens ſerved King Henry VII., Shakeſpere was confounding his maternal with his paternal anceſtors. So that we may take our choice as to whether, in the firſt caſe, he was a liar; or, in the ſecond, a fool. Pleaſing alternatives for thoſe who reliſh them! But it is to be hoped there are not wanting believers in the candour and truthfulneſs of the Poet; who, like Mr. C. Knight, in his "Biography," accept with credit the ſtatement found in both the drafts, for which we muſt hold Shakeſpere himſelf reſponſible, confidently believing that it was ſupplied as information by him in the drawing of the firſt draft of 1596, and repeated by Garter King in 1599.

But what was the motive for Shakeſpere inſtigating his father to obtain this grant? It can hardly fail to be obvious to any mind that is not tortuous. The author believes that the grant was ſought with the ſame motive that the early marriage was contracted,—that New Place was purchaſed,—and that Shakeſpere's will, finally, was made. It ſeems to him that in all theſe things, and in his wonderful mental activity and poſitive labour, there was the one noble, worthy, ambitious motive throughout: Shakeſpere wiſhed to found a family. He loved from his early days the honoured reſpectability of an Engliſh gentleman. He longed and deſired that his family ſhould achieve a place among the gentry of Warwickſhire. The ambition that we have ſeen in the preſent century, at Abbotsford, was preciſely what was ſeen at New Place in 1597. Perhaps there is a more extended parallel between Scott and Shakeſpere than this. Was there not the ſame hiſtoric feeling in both theſe men?

The

The love for antiquity, for defcent, for heraldry, for chivalric ftory and incident, is confpicuous in each of them! Shakefpere's plays are hiftoric chronicles; fo are Scott's novels. They prefent in a popular form, to the entrancement of the people, a moving fpectacle of events of which many would otherwife be profoundly ignorant. It requires a peculiar fympathy of mind to deal with fuch fubjects,—and that *thorough fympathy* was inbred in the characters of Shakefpere and Scott.

No carelefs reader of Shakefpere's works can poffibly mifs obferving the antiquary's tafte that pervades them. Let this be carried in memory, and the pride of anceftry, in the draft of the grant of arms, will be recognifed as his natural characteriftic, and not as Dethick's invention.

It will be obferved that the author treats with abfolute difbelief and dif-

guft

guſt the "traditions" current concerning the Poet; and he is impatient of them, becauſe he ſolemnly believes them to be injurious to the credit which the Man, as diſtinct from the Poet, deſerves to enjoy among his countrymen. He believes that the known and authenticated facts of Shakeſpere's life, taken by themſelves, preſent to us a Character to be reſpected and loved, juſt as much as his works do a Poet to be admired. Of thoſe leading events of Shakeſpere's life which have been ſummariſed above, he conceives that, when any mind diſengages itſelf from the mire of tradition, they can only be regarded in one light,—to his honour and fair fame.

This is a mighty contraſt and contradiction to the currently-received ſtories about ſtealing deer, marrying in ſhame, and running away to London! But thoſe are ſtories without confirmation or evidence,

dence, and the author holds they are positively irreconcilable with the proved and authentic facts of Shakespere's life, which uniformly exhibit him as an industrious, high-minded, aspiring citizen, and a man ambitious of taking rank with the families of English gentry.

We are informed by Rowe, who gives the story on the authority of Sir William Davenant, that Lord Southampton, out of his great friendship for Shakespere, presented him with £1000, to enable him to make a purchase for which he had a mind. This gift is supposed to have been made some time subsequent to the year 1593, when "Venus and Adonis" was published, and dedicated to his lordship!

We float aloft into a higher and purer atmosphere when we picture our Shakespere winning and holding such an "especial friend,"—being socially connected with such a man as Southampton; and befriended

befriended by William and Philip Herbert, Earls of Pembroke and Montgomery.

Something too much has been written about the inferior poſition of the Poet; and that poſition has been kept down by the everlaſting low-lived ſtories with which his name has been begrimed.

Shakeſpere's genius needs no eulogies. It were to paint the lily to laud that. But *Shakeſpere*—the man, the citizen, the high-minded poliſhed gentleman, ambitious of poſition and aſſerting his title to aſſociate with gentlemen—this is a perſon of whom we have heard too little. From all that his biographers have commonly put before us, we might naturally conclude that he was a ſort of dramatic penny-a-liner, ſcribbling by day from neceſſity—at the point of the literary bayonet—the pen—a certain amount of "copy," the value of which was unknown to himſelf, and delighting at night in the ſottiſh ſociety of taverns. It may be that on theſe pages this picture of him is expoſed in a broader and more glaring light than the public are accuſtomed to ſee it in. The author aſſerts that it is the true light; and believes that the ſocial and moral portraiture of the man, as painted by "tradition" (fiſh-wives' goſſip), is as groſs and prepoſterous as he alſo believes every one of thoſe daubs, (Chandos or otherwiſe), which are foiſted on the public as likeneſſes of the phyſical man, are like ſign-painters' portraits, having far leſs relation to the original than the "Saracen's Head" had to Sir Roger de Coverley. Is there not more ſatisfaction in contemplating Shakeſpere as the eſpecial friend of Southampton, than as regarding him as the "hale-fellow, well-met" companion of the ſwilling chaw-bacons of "Piping Pebworth, Dancing Marſton," &c. &c.?

Talk of reverence for this mighty man's

man's works!—it ſeems there is plenty of lack of reverence for the man himſelf.

Let us aſk ourſelves, when we prate about our love for the "Immortal Bard," where we find anything to juſtify our baſe-born traditional rubbiſh about that Immortal Man? Shakeſpere could not have acquired the independence he did, had he not been a ſober, cleanly-living, thrifty man.

Shakeſpere could not have inſtigated his father to acquire that coat-of-arms, had he not been an ambitious man: ambitious in the pureſt and beſt ſenſe of that word—ambitious to raiſe himſelf in ſocial poſition and reſpect.

Shakeſpere would not have completed the purchaſe of ſuch a property as New Place, and have made it his permanent reſidence, unleſs he had been what we now call commercially "a thoroughly reſpectable man," anxious to take his place

place amongſt gentlemen, and to be eſteemed as "generoſus" in his own county.

Every *known fact* of his life goes to ſupport theſe aſſertions. Let fact be weighed in the ſcale with fable, and the meaſure of the man will give us for reſult a character to reſpect, as well as a genius to admire.

Something has been ſaid in alluſion to Heraldry. There is one ſource of indirect information regarding Shakeſpere which has never as yet been thoroughly examined. Authors and biographers have riddled through the ſieve of criticiſm every grain of direct evidence regarding him, known of, and available. Cloſe Rolls, Records, Inquiſitions, Regiſters, have ſurrendered their ſilent teſtimonies. But Fines, Leaſes, Sales, Births, Deaths, and Marriages, while they give us direct and poſitive knowledge, do not give that indirect teſti-

mony

mony to be gathered from contemporary aſſociation. A Pedigree, quaint and formal as it may look, when well read and ſtudied, may yet be found to guide the antiquary's ſearch in ſome direction rich with indirect, and leading perchance to the most direct, evidence regarding the Poet.

As theſe lines are being penned, there lie before the writer twelve hundred cloſely-written foolſcap ſheets of Warwickſhire pedigrees and family hiſtories, compiled by the late Rev. Thomas Warde, Vicar of Weſton-under-Wetherley and of Barford, Warwickſhire. They are a part of the labour of a long life of an enthuſiaſtic antiquary's reſearch. They are interſperſed with pen-and-ink ſketches of ancient Warwickſhire timber-houſes, many of which are now deſtroyed; and their pages are crowded with the moſt intereſting family and local records, ſuch as have not

not been collected together by any one ſince Sir W. Dugdale publiſhed his famous book, deſpite its numerous errors. When the author firſt peruſed this MS., his intention was to quote from it largely; but he has relinquiſhed that idea, partly becauſe to do ſo properly would have involved the publication of a work of magnitude; and partly becauſe in doing ſo it would have been robbing the MS. itſelf of riches, which, in the author's opinion, would have been like rifling the tomb of the dead of its treaſure. Whole and undefiled the Rev. Mr. Warde's MS. ſhall remain, until ſuch time as its precious and ſingularly intereſting pages can be given entire to the public; though that portion of the public which takes intereſt in ſuch matters will grieve to hear that the documents now confided to the author's charge do not form more than a quarter of the number which once exiſted, and periſhed perifhed in a fire in London fome years ago. From the pages of the fragment of twelve hundred fheets ftill preferved, many items of information contained in this volume have been gathered; and a ftore of detail regarding the Lucys, Underhills, Combes, Boughtons, Shirleys, Cloptons, Carews, Grevilles, Throckmortons, and others who lived in Shakefpere's time, has proved to the author the value of the opinion he now expreffes, as to the wide field of indirect evidence ftill to be explored, calculated to convey moft interefting information, that may lead to a far more perfect knowledge of Shakefpere himfelf than the prefent age poffeffes.

The names juft given (and many others of the Warwickfhire gentry might be added), when we ftudy them by the help of the College of Arms, are found linked together by intermarriages, bringing before us curious and interefting facts elfe-where

where unattainable; and repeopling the paſt by ſuch aid, we are enabled to ſurround Shakeſpere with the forms and figures of men and women who, in the nature of things, muſt have known him well, and been known by him. The names of Sir Thomas Lucy, William Combe, Sir Thomas Throckmorton, and Fulke Greville paſs before us as Members for the county of Warwick. By turning to the Clopton Pedigree, we find John Combe married to Roſe Clopton, of Clopton.* On the tomb of Judith Combe, in Stratford, we find the arms of Combe quartered with Underhill, and the hiſtory of the two families puts before us the intermarriages. In the ſame way we learn of the alliance between the daughter of Sir Stephen Hales, the contemporary of Shakeſpere, and Edward Combe.

Again,

* Appendix J.

Again, the grandſon of Thomas Underhill married the daughter of Sir William Lucy. And again, Jocoſa, or Joyce Clopton (three years younger than Shakeſpere, born 1568), married George Carew, afterwards Earl of Totneſs. Theſe were people aſſociated with Stratford, with many of whom Shakeſpere muſt have been familiar. The Combes, the Underhills, the Cloptons, the Carews, it may be aſſerted without any heſitation, were his friends. What does the world know of theſe people? It has heard John Combe libelled as a uſurer; and been told that he was Shakeſpere's friend until the Poet lampooned him. It has learned that the Earl of Totneſs was a brave ſoldier. And this is all. The evidence of John Combe's regard for Shakeſpere has paled before a doggrel verſe. The evidence of Shakeſpere's attachment to the Combes has been made nothing of.

The

The fact that Lord Totnefs, living at Clopton Houfe, was a man of letters and an author, has efcaped notice beyond the record of the fact itfelf. And the ftory that Lord Southampton prefented Shakefpere with £1000 to complete a purchafe on which he had fet his heart, has never, it is believed, been pointed at the acquirement of New Place.

When people have been fufficiently naufeated with the fentimental rubbifh with which the prefs has teemed about the "Immortal Bard," and when the tap-room talk, yclept tradition, has been poured out into the gutter with its kindred dregs, the healthy and honeft refearches of the good and true fearchers of this age after fact, will lead to the gathering of new materials for writing the hiftory of Shakefpere. In fo doing it will be well to furround him with the focial facts of Stratford at the time when he lived, having

having ſtripped him of the fables of half a century after he died. It is ſurely more profitable to know the perſons among whom he dwelt, than to liſten to the looſe ſtatements of people that he never ſaw. Inquiries about his contemporaries may bring us to diſcover ſomething about *him*; but if they never teach us anything poſitive as to his hiſtory, there is ſome ſatisfaction in contemplating the men and women who had the privilege of his acquaintance.

Let us glance at one or two of the Stratford worthies of the Shakeſperian age.

There were three houſes which we of the preſent generation would give much to have reſcued from deſtruction: New Place, the Poet's home; the College of Stratford, the home of his friend John à Combe; Clopton Houſe, the home of the Cloptons and Carews. Of theſe three, two have utterly periſhed: the third, Clopton

Clopton Houſe, exiſts as it was reconſtructed by Sir Edward Walker (F) in the time of Charles II. Happily one morſel of the original houſe, built in the time of Henry VII., has been ſpared. It ſtands at the back of the preſent manſion, and was a porch-way entrance acroſs the ancient moat. One hundred and forty years have paſſed away ſince a Sir Hugh Clopton (H), and withal a Herald of the College of Arms, deſtroyed the houſe in which Shakeſpere died. The preſent generation, therefore, has been robbed of nothing which it has contemplated and poſſeſſed. Not ſo with the College. That venerable ſtructure, erected in the reign of Edward III. by Ralph de Stratford, Biſhop of London, and adjoining the yard of Stratford Church, was ſhamefully deſtroyed within the memory of living men. This monaſtic eſtabliſhment had been "embelliſhed" at the

front

front towards the church, with Georgian facing; but at the back it ſtill retained many of its mediæval architectural features. Unfortunately, in the year 1796, it was ſold to one Edmund Batterſbee, a man who had made money in Mancheſter, and curſed Stratford by ſettling there. The MS. records in the author's truſt, allude to the College as follows:—

"In 1797, the furniture of this "manſion, the College, was diſpoſed of "by auction, together with a collection "of paintings. Many of them were very "curious, ancient, and valuable; and "ſome very intereſting family portraits, "which were, unfortunately for the "antiquary, ſold and diſperſed. Whole "lengths of Queen Elizabeth, Charles II. "and his Queen, Louis XIII. and his "Queen. Charles II. and his Queen, "Louis and his, are now in the Town

"Hall

" Hall at Lichfield, having been purchaſed
" for a trifle each, for Mr. Green's
" muſeum in that town, and ſince its
" being diſcontinued, theſe pictures—*not*
" *finding a purchaſer!*—have been all
" hung up in the Town Hall. Full
" length paintings of George, Prince of
" Denmark, George I., and II. alſo de-
" corated this antique manſion. A large
" piece, bearing the date 1641. A half-
" length portrait of Juxon, Biſhop of
" London, who attended the unfortunate
" King Charles I. to the ſcaffold. This
" painting very likely was an original, as
" the pious Biſhop, at the time of the
" uſurpation of Cromwell, retired to his
" houſe at Little Compton, in Glouceſ-
" terſhire, which is not far from Strat-
" ford. A very beautiful half-length
" portrait of Lady Radnor, *and innume-*
" *rable family portraits!* and others too
" numerous to mention.

" This

“This venerable manſion,—which had “exiſted through a lapſe of 446 years, “and ſince the ſuppreſſion of the religious “houſes in the reign of Henry VIII. “had been the reſidence of ſeveral very “honourable families,—was now doomed “to fall, and its ancient walls to be “pulled down to the ground, though the “whole of the manſion was in perfect “repair, and ſome parts of it fitted up in “the modern ſtyle by its purchaſer, who “very unfortunately had purchaſed it. “Being an entire ſtranger to the town of “Stratford, having lately purchaſed the “houſe ſtanding near the large gates of “the entrance to the church, where he “reſided, and having more money than “any regard for venerable antiquity, or “any reſpect for antiquarian lore, or the “ancient poſſeſſors of this noble manſion, “he, tradeſman-like,—for he was a Man-“cheſter tradeſman,—not liking that the

“ground

" ground facing his own houſe ſhould be " encumbered with ſuch an old anti- " quated building, determined to have the " whole pulled down, like Mr. Gaſtrell, " who deſtroyed the famous mulberry- " tree. By the taking down of this an- " cient pile the town of Stratford had to " lament the deprivation of one of the " chief and greateſt ornaments. But Mr. " Batterſbee, regardleſs of public opinion, " and deſirous of the land on which it " ſtood, to make uſe of part for a kitchen- " garden and the reſt for paſture for his " cattle, deſtroyed the whole of the old " College in 1800. *Sic tranſit, &c.*"

The above quotation has been made in full, that the reader may have a ſpecimen of the ruthleſs manner in which, little more than half a century ago, the moſt intereſting family reliques were diſperſed, and the houſe in which Shakeſpere had ſpent many an hour with the Combes and the

the Cloptons was deſtroyed! Can it be that when old ſwords, and halberds, and ruſting antiquities were turned out with the pots and kettles, Shakeſpere's ſword went along with them? *It is quite poſſible.*

Paſs we on now to Clopton Houſe, which, happily, remains. As before ſtated, one remnant of the antique Shakeſperian edifice ſtill ſtands: the remainder of the manſion being Carolean. Neſtling under the weſtern ſweep of Welcombe Hills, the ſlopes rich with verdure, dotted with copſes, and ſhadowed with ancient trees, among which the deer feed, ſtands Clopton Houſe. As we look upon that ſolitary remnant of the Tudor Houſe, we feel a thrill of pleaſure in the conviction that under its portal Shakeſpere and his friends muſt have paſſed ſcores of times. The moat ran directly in front of it, and was a few years back diſturbed, in

order

order to lay ſome modern foundations. Various trifling reliques of by-gone days were recovered, and among others three ſack-bottles of ſtunted form, made of the coarſeſt glaſs. Two of them had the creſt of Combe upon them. There is a theme for a reverie! Sack from the College, taken up to the Houſe! Was it an offering from John à Combe to Lord Totneſs? Was it a ſpecial preſent at ſome Chriſtmas time, when the lips of the Lady Joyce or the Poet pledged the cup, and did honour to the "Boar's "Head?" Who can tell? The empty bottles ſunk in the mud of a moat for centuries come back to light, and tell us on what friendly terms the families of Combe and Clopton were, in the days when they pledged the toaſt in ſack.*

There

* One of theſe bottles is now in poſſeſſion of the author. From the length of time that it has been buried, it has acquired thoſe priſmatic colours which grow upon glaſs under the ſoil.

There is but one place left which, in its reliques and aſſociations, brings Shakeſpere vividly back to the imagination, and that is Clopton Houſe!

We enter its noble hall, with receſſed bay-window full of the Clopton coats of arms, and running our eyes round the walls we light upon the manly, maſſive head of George Carew, Lord Totneſs. There hangs his portrait as freſh, and in as fine preſervation as the day it was painted.* There, too, are numerous members of the Clopton family—Joyce, the Counteſs, venerable men, and noble ladies, coming down in ſucceſſion to Mr. and Mrs. Partheriche. There is a ſplendid original of the "Lady Elizabeth," Cromwell's

* There are two portraits of Lord Carew at Clopton Houſe. The one here referred to came from Aſton Hall, Birmingham; the other, which has always been in the houſe, hangs in one of the galleries. Both pictures ſeem to have been painted at one date, and the treatment is the ſame; but the Aſton is in far the beſt preſervation.

Cromwell's mother: and a moſt intereſting painting of the river front of Whitehall Palace in the days of the Stuarts. Among a multitude of others, is a beautiful portrait of Sir Edward Walker, wearing his badge of Garter King.

In turning over the papers and MSS. of Clopton Houſe the author met with an ancient written and *emendated* copy of the third part of "Jewel's Apology!"

What ſtory could this manuſcript tell! It is in the handwriting of the time of Mary and Elizabeth. Whoſe was the book? Could it ever have belonged to Jewel himſelf, or was it made for ſome member of this Clopton family? Who can gueſs?

Perhaps the moſt precious book of all at Clopton is a ſmall volume by Richard Pynſon—a collection of Statutes. It is as complete and perfect as the day it iſſued from the preſs of the King's Printer.

This book tranſports us back to Shakeſpere's own times. It was in his day exactly what we ſee it now. Whence it came, whoſe it was, none can tell. But it is among the old books and papers of ſuch a place as Clopton that we beſt like to meet with ſuch a book. Tumbling about in unknown nooks and corners there may yet be found other ſuch, and more direct evidences connected both with the Poet's period and the Poet himſelf. Here, at leaſt, is one book publiſhed before Shakeſpere's birth, which we find preſerved not only in Warwickſhire, but in the very houſe with which all his circle of friends is aſſociated. Let the fact ſpeak for itſelf.

From the houſes let us glance at their maſters and miſtreſſes!

Much ſtreſs has been laid upon heraldic reſearch, and the author,—it may be ſomewhat boldly, but, neverthelesſ, very ſincerely,—

cerely,—has expreſſed not merely his opinion about the value of heraldic records, upon which there needs no opinion to be expreſſed; but his conviction that there is yet much knowledge to be gained from reſearches, to which a compariſon of the Warwickſhire pedigrees of Shakeſpere's age, would lead the inquirer. In preparing theſe pages for the Preſs, the examination of the Viſitations has led the author again and again upon the track of information of which he was previouſly in utter ignorance. May not the ſame reſult await other inquirers? Moreover, we experience a freſhened intereſt when we gain a knowledge of the perſons who ſurround the Poet in familiar intercourſe. That marriage regiſter—

"1561. June 4.—Johannes Combes, *Generosus*, "et Rosa Cloptonne"—

brings Shakeſpere into connection with the great folk at Clopton from his earlieſt years.

years. Roſe was married the year after her father died, and her brother William had come into poſſeſſion. She was miſtreſs of the College during the firſt fifteen years of the Poet's life, and as ſhe watched him growing, and ſaw him attain his fourth year, ſhe would hear the news from the Houſe that her brother's wife had brought him a little girl—duly chriſtened Jocoſa or Joyce. This was the future Counteſs. The Poet would be juſt old enough to remember her being born, the year after William Underhill, Eſquire, had come to reſide at New Place. The boy and girl grew up to man's and woman's eſtate, familiar with the ſame people and having the ſame friends. In 1575, Queen Elizabeth arrived at Kenilworth, and Maſter Langham, in his letter to Maſter Martin deſcribing the Queen's viſit, diſcovered that "Olld Hags, prying into every place, "are az fond of nuelltiez az yoong girls "that

"that had never ſeen Coourt afore." Then did the men of Coventree make petition that they "moought renue now "their old Storical Sheaw,"—"of late "laid dooun they knoe no cawz why, "onleſs it wear by the zeal of certain "theyr preacherz. Men very commend-"able for their behaviour and learning, "and ſweet in their ſermons, but ſome-"what too ſour in preaching awey theyr "Paſtime."*

Among the young girls who had never ſeen Court afore we may probably reckon Joyce Clopton, for the author has diſcovered, among the pedigree MSS. in his cuſtody, that at an early age Joyce was appointed

* A curious MS. copy of the celebrated "Letter "wherein part of the Entertainment unto the Queen'z "Majeſty at Killingwoorth Caſtl: in Warwickſheer in "this Soomerz Progreſt, 1575, is ſignified," is in the author's poſſeſſion. The writer notes "this manuſcript "is valuable." The author's name is given, Langham. Mr. Knight calls him "the entertaining coxcomb, "Laneham."

appointed a Maid of Honour to Queen Elizabeth, being "a great favourite and "remarkable for her virtues." Moſt likely the Queen firſt ſaw the little girl, aged ſeven, on this memorable occaſion, when William Clopton (C), her father, came to Kenilworth to do honour to Leiceſter. However this may be, the lithe Joyce muſt have been brought about the Queen's perſon at a very youthful period, for young George Carew, a Captain in the army, met her, made love to her, and married her without her father's knowledge when ſhe was 19 years of age! "Mr. Clopton was greatly diſpleaſed "with his daughter's marriage with Cap-"tain Carew, which was without his "knowledge and conſent, and intended to "diſinherit her. But upon an accidental "meeting and converſing with Captain "Carew, he found him a man of ſuperior "genius and fine addreſs, which quali-

"fications

" fications ſo effectually recommended " him to his favour that he was recon- " ciled, and ſettled his eſtate at Clopton, " which was very conſiderable, upon him " and his daughter."

By reference to the Pedigree, it will be found that Clopton House was in the poſſeſſion of three perſons during the whole of Shakeſpere's life. William Clopton (C) inherited it three years before the Poet's birth, and enjoyed it until 1592, when Shakeſpere was 28 years of age. Joyce and her huſband ſucceeded, and long outlived the Poet.

In theſe three perſons we have individuals of rank, importance, and intellectual power. The traditions which aſſociate Shakeſpere with Clopton Houſe would be of little value, were it not that they are finger-poſts directing us to inquiries which give us every confidence that he was ſo aſſociated. The Combes,

Cloptons,

Cloptons, Underhills, Boughtons (of Lawford), we find linked together by family ties and ſocial bonds. In the midſt of them, in the "Great Houſe," that had belonged to the families of two of them, Shakeſpere reſided. It is a happy, pleaſant picture that the mind creates for itſelf, as in imagination it repeoples the College, and New Place, and Clopton Houſe, and the neighbouring reſidences of Idlicote and Boughton. We ſeem to ſee our Shakeſpere enjoying, and enjoyed in, ſuch ſociety. When we turn to the Pedigree, and learn what was the character and fame of George Carew, Earl of Totneſs, we can conceive in the brave ſoldier's periods of leave and repoſe how greatly he would appreciate ſuch converſation as he might find in New Place. Carew was himſelf an author, and eſteemed a literary character in his day. Being ſent by James I., in 1609, on an embaſſy

to

to France, he drew up on his return a relation of the ſtate of that country, and gave portraitures of Henri Quatre, and of the principal people about the Court. He alſo wrote the "*Pacata Hibernia,*" a hiſtory of the wars in Ireland, which Biſhop Nicholſon ſays contained the tranſactions of three years of much fighting, in Munſter, from the latter end of the year 1599 to the death of Queen Elizabeth. He alſo tranſlated into Engliſh a hiſtory of Iriſh affairs, written by Maurice Regan, a ſervant of the King of Leinſter, in the year 1171; the MS. of which work was formerly in the library of the Duke of Chandos.

Without purſuing the records of pedigrees further, it is to be hoped that enough has been brought forward to anſwer the queſtion at page 105, which the author ſuppoſed being put to him.

It is true there is no poſitive and direct evidence

evidence that Shakeſpere ever aſſociated with many of the perſons that have been named. Heaven forbid that there ever ſhould be found any direct evidence that he aſſociated with any of the perſons into whoſe ſociety he is degraded by tradition!

But which is the truſtier of the two—the fair and natural concluſions which the mind draws from the contemplation of contemporaneous facts; or the idle, looſe, and ſhifting ſtories of perſons who had never ſeen the Poet, or could ſpeak a word from their own knowledge?

Shakeſpere's character, read by the offenſive taper-light of village goſſip, is not the character which the ſtudent of his works would expect to meet, and be miſerably diſappointed if he did not meet.

The weights and meaſures of conſcience—the things ſhe approves, or diſapproves—have one eternal, unchanging ſtandard. In every age there is the ſame

ſenſe

ſenſe of right and wrong, clean and unclean, ſober and diſſolute. Shakeſpere either was or was not a man to love and reſpect, as well as a Poet to admire. If he ſank ſo low as to have his paſtime with tipplers and drunkards, then our diminiſhed regard tarniſhes the brilliancy of our admiration. But if there is abſolutely no evidence whatever to prove aught againſt the man; if deer ſtealing, and vagabondiſing, and hard drinking are unſupported by a ſingle eſtabliſhed, proved fact; and if, on the contrary, they are ſingularly at variance with what *are the known facts* of this great man's life, it is but juſt to his memory, and giving him the honour which is his due, if we ſcout with contempt the wrencings of tap-tubs and the vulgar goſſip of clowns.

The view of Shakeſpere's life and character which the writer takes, is not drawn from imagination, preſenting

ing an outline which will admit of no faults. It is eaſy to mount a Pegaſus, and ſoar aloft on the wings of grandiloquent words about his genius, and his poetry, and his dramatic ſkill. It is the proſaic, and not the ſentimental, view of the man Shakeſpere with which theſe pages are engaged. It is Shakeſpere's Home which is their concern. Planting our feet on a few acres of land, under the ſhadow of Holy Croſs, in Stratford, the object is to know as much as poſſible about that home hiſtorically and ſocially, and to know what the man was who inhabited it.

His ambition to acquire poſſeſſion of New Place was as honourable and laudable as it ſeems natural. Was not John Shakeſpere, the Poet's father, engaged in the ſame trade as the great Sir Hugh Clopton, however wide the difference in the extent of their dealings? That Great

Houſe

Houſe had been the London mercer's home. It had belonged to the man who made his money in Old Jewry and the Cheape. Before Shakeſpere ſet out for London, when his father was in difficulties, he very probably took a lingering look at the houſe,—took courage from the memory of the man who had lived in it,—and ſet out for London town with a ſtern determination to win independence himſelf, and return to live in Stratford, enjoying it. Let us review the circumſtances of his life, and we ſhall find all this is moſt natural, and harmoniſes with what we know *are facts.* His running away to London, like a thief, to eſcape Sir Thomas Lucy, is a wretched, crack-brained ſtory, baſed upon no fact whatever; but invented ſolely to try and make out a reaſon for Shakeſpere's going, when a natural and ſufficient reaſon laid cloſe at hand.

Lord

Lord Southampton gave him £1000 to complete ſome purchaſe he greatly deſired. There was a purchaſe completed, and probably completed in a hurry, for the vendor ſold in Eaſter term, and was dead in July! May not Lord Southampton's money have been given for this particular purpoſe? And when Shakeſpere was ſettled at New Place, what are the evidences, the *facts*, we know of him? They uniformly go to prove that he was a careful, induſtrious, money-making man, ſeeking to acquire property and to found a family. His proper ambition is diſcoverable in every movement of his life: in his acquirement of New Place; in his grant of arms by the College; in his will; in his various purchaſes of property; and, laſt of all, in the ſociety of the perſons with whom we conclude, both by poſitive and alſo by indirect evidence, that he aſſociated.

As

As we tread the garden of New Place, and recall the mighty dead that once trod that ſame plot of earth, and called it his, let thoſe who love to think of him as the Poet, think of him alſo as the Gentleman. The idle talk of men who never knew him has wafted down to us unproved and diſcreditable ſtories. At his threſhold, when we enter New Place, let us ſhake them, with the duſt, from off our feet. Shakeſpere's honeſt, anxious life deſerves better from us than a readineſs to hear him defamed. As we tread his garden let us think of him, and judge of him *by what we know of him.* It is not much, indeed, but it may ſome day be more. Such evidence as we have, all tells in his favour. It preſents to us a man with goodly ambition raiſing himſelf and his family to preſent independence, and to everlaſting fame. It preſents to us a cautious, careful labourer—

a painſtaking artiſt, a moſt ſkilful anatomiſt of human nature. It preſents to us no hurried ſcribbler of plays, careleſſly throwing off, without an idea of their beauty, the teeming imaginations of his brain, as it has been impudently aſſerted; but a man who chaſtened his muſe with ſevere caſtigation, and applied himſelf through life with unhalting ſelf-devotion, not only to ſeek out the treaſures of thought, but to poliſh, and ſet his gems in ſuch marvellous frameworks of plot, as in *Othello*, *Lear*, *Hamlet*, and *Macbeth*, that the world has gazed theſe three hundred years with admiration and delight upon his wondrous workmanſhip.

And when we tread his garden let us think of him as the greateſt, loftieſt teacher of mankind who has ever ſpoken with uninſpired lips. "There are," ſaid Watſon, Biſhop of Llandaff (to the late Duke of Rutland, when retiring from his

tutorſhip),

tutorſhip), "two books to adhere to in "your future life; one is the Book of the "Child of God; the other the Book of "the Child of Nature."

From Shakeſpere's House at New Place, many of the pages of that book went forth to the world; and in that garden, among its trees and flowers, their thoughts were meditated. Let us honour his memory where his very preſence ſeems to overſhadow us.

"A gleam of daylight ſet
Will gild the cloud of eve;
And the ſoul's light linger yet
O'er the place it ſighed to leave."

In writing about Shakeſpere, inches of fact have been fringed with acres of conjecture. When once an author has entered upon the field of conjecture he can wander along at his will, unchecked and

and unhindered! But if conjecture is ſuggeſtive of inquiry, where inquiry may not have been ſufficiently made, perhaps it is not altogether worthleſs.

Where did Shakeſpere obtain his knowledge? That queſtion has been aſked by every ſtudent of his works, and has never yet been ſatisfactorily anſwered. Ben Jonſon aſſerted that he had "ſmall Latine, and leſſe Greeke," by which, it is to be preſumed, he meant to ſtate that Shakeſpere had received the rudiments of a claſſical education, without being diſtinguiſhed as a ſcholar. Such a concluſion might be fairly arrived at from a ſtudy of his plays. But though he might not have been able to tranſlate the Medea or Antigone with eaſe, it does not admit of a doubt, that in ſome way or other, and at an early age, he muſt have read extenſively — perhaps indiſcriminately.

At

At eighteen he married. The youth, whether he was a lawyer's clerk, or apprenticed to busineſs, had finiſhed his curriculum at ſchool before that event. We are conſequently reduced to the neceſſity of conſidering his "education" (technically ſo called) as finiſhed when he was ſeventeen years of age. Had he acquired the maſs of information with which his mind was ſtored, previous to that date? or, during the labours of author and actor in London, did he find time to purſue the cultivation of his mind, as well as to inform himſelf of the data and hiſtorical facts regarding any particular play which he was going to write? A diſtinguiſhed magiſtrate of the preſent day once anſwered the writer of theſe lines (on his expreſſing ſurpriſe at the minutely accurate information diſplayed by a popular noveliſt regarding the local hiſtory and hiſtorical records of a place he had

had never visited), "Oh! give a man a "fortnight at the British Museum and he "will get up any period or place you "please." No doubt there is much truth in this remark; but, *imprimis*, Shakespere had no British Museum to which he could refer; and, in the next place, the knowledge he displays in *Romeo, Hamlet, Macbeth*, or any of the plays, the plots of which he borrowed from historical books, tracts, or stories he had read, is of a very much deeper and profounder character, than results from cursory reading. It is not the knowledge of a "common-place "book," or a "cram," but the result of keen observation and close study.

Not in the technical, but in the broadest sense of the term "education," insufficient inquiry has been made, as to how, or by what means, Shakespere became self-educated? for it does not admit of dispute that his profound knowledge of human

human nature, and his marvellous capacity for the acquiſition of facts, were the reſult of ſelf-cultivation. No grammar ſchool of King Edward VI. inſtructed a boy's mind as Shakeſpere's mind was inſtructed.

Conjecture ſpeculates as to how he gained his information?

Suggeſtion, with a ſurmiſe, may inquire whether the hiſtory of the "Guild" at Stratford has ever been narrowly ſcrutiniſed, with a view to arriving at a concluſion.

Shakeſpere's lines in the Third Act of the *Twelfth Night* have been repeatedly quoted:—

> MARIA. *He's in yellow ſtockings.*
> SIR TOBY. *And croſs-gartered.*
> MARIA. *Moſt villainouſly; like a pedant that keeps a ſchool i' the church.*

Whether Shakeſpere had his own preceptor before his mind's eye, may be doubted; but there can be no doubt that he he alludes to a cuſtom of his time, which had come under his own obſervation, which was the very common habit of holding public ſchools in the Lady chapels, or chancels of churches which had formerly been connected with monaſtic eſtabliſhments.

There are many perſons alive who have belonged to ſchools kept in the church—as, for inſtance, the Queen Elizabeth School, which was held in the Lady chapel of St. Mary Redcliffe at Briſtol, and in which they received their education. Schools in the church were not uncommon. The ſchool at St. Alban's continues to be held in the Lady chapel of that ſtupendous Norman abbey, to the preſent hour. A ſchool was kept (perhaps ſtill is) in the Triforium of Chriſt Church, Hants. The college ſchool at Worceſter alſo has been held in a noble hall within the Cathedral precincts. A long liſt of ſuch ſchools in the church might

might be given. But there is one remarkable fact connected with them; they have, as a general rule, been established or held in the Lady chapels, or chapels of suppressed monastic institutions, and not in buildings that were parochial churches before the Reformation. In connection with these suppressed monasteries, or cells, there were frequently valuable libraries, rich in ancient chronicles, tales of the wars, histories of royal heroes and valiant knights, as well as in the lives of the saints, missals, and breviaries.

Such an establishment was the Guild of the Holy Cross. Henry VIII. suppressed its conventual character. His son Edward VI. erected it into a grammar school. The Corporation records of Stratford prove that the chancel of the Guild Chapel was used as a "school i' the church," and it is altogether uncertain whether such use was continuous or temporary. Mr. Halliwell

well and others imagine it was temporary, founding their opinions upon probabilities as they ſuggeſt themſelves to their minds from an examination of the Corporation books. The items of allowances there alluded to in 1568 are:—"for repayryng "the ſcole;" "for dreſſyng and ſweepyng "the ſcole houſe;" "for ground and "ſellynge in the olde ſcole;" "for takyng "doun the ſoller over the ſcole." Mr. Halliwell comments upon this—"This "laſt entry would alone ſeem to prove "that the ſchool was not then in the "chapel, but in another building."

The difference in the terms of deſignation ſeems to warrant the opinion that there may have been an intended diſtinction between the "ſcole" and "olde "ſcole." The uſe of the word "olde" appears to ſignify that there were two ſchool-rooms, or places of teaching, belonging to the one "Grammar School,"

anſwering

anſwering probably to what is called in the preſent day, the upper and lower ſchool. And if the chancel of the Guild Chapel had lately been appropriated for ſcholaſtic purpoſes, it was very natural in the Chamberlain's accounts, to deſcribe the ſchool-room in the monaſtic buildings of the ancient guild as "the "olde ſcole." It was the trueſt deſcription, for the ſame place had been "a "ſcole" for fifty-two years previous to the ſuppreſſion of the monaſteries, having been founded in the laſt year of the reign of Edward IV., 1482, by a Thomas Jolyffe, under charge and control of the Guild of the Holy Croſs.

There is another entry and date in the Corporation books, of great importance. In February, 1594, an order directs, that there ſhall be no ſchool kept in the chapel from that date. It will be fair to conclude, that up to that year, from the

new

new foundation of the ſchool in the 7th year of the reign of Edward VI., 1553, the Guild Chapel had been uſed for ſchool-teaching; and in all probability about that date, the "olde ſcole" had ſuch additional accommodation given to it, that it was no longer neceſſary to appropriate the Guild Chapel to ſuch a purpoſe. Whether it was habitually uſed as a ſchool from 1554 to 1594 (as the Lady chapel of St. Alban's ſtill is, and St. Mary Redcliffe was until lately), is of no great moment, becauſe diſtinct evidence proves, that, whether occaſionally or habitually, to ſuch uſe it was devoted during the years when Shakeſpere was at ſchool, and (ſuppoſing he continued at ſchool until he was ſixteen) for fourteen years ſubſequently.

It may yet be diſcovered that greater impreſſions were produced upon the mind of the boy Shakeſpere by the advan-

tages

tages he derived from the "ſchool i' the "church," than have ever been ſuggeſted by commentators upon his life! Many obſcurities have of late years been cleared up, by a careful peruſal of documents hitherto neglected.

There are poſſibly in exiſtence many documents, which, if diſcovered, would throw a flood of light upon the buſineſs of his manhood and his authorſhip, that remain for the preſent ſhrouded in obſcurity. Probably enough, on that night in June, 1613, when Burbage was performing *Henry VIII.* in the Globe Theatre, Blackfriars, and the thatched roof catching fire, the entire building was deſtroyed, many MSS., plays, and note-books of the Poet's, may have periſhed in the flames, which would have ſet at reſt the unſatisfactory queſtion—How did Shakeſpere acquire his varied, profound, and alſo deſultory knowledge?

The

The inquiry ſeems to force us to one or other of two concluſions: either he enjoyed peculiar advantages from the "ſchool i' the church" which could not be derived from the ordinary croſs-gartered pedants' routine of *Hic, Hæc, Hoc,* or he muſt have been enabled, by Lord Southampton, or ſome other influential perſon, to obtain acceſs to a library in London. At the preſent moment, in the utter abſence of all direct evidence upon the ſubject, we are thrown back upon probabilities, and the indirect internal evidence of Shakeſpere's writings. They appear to bear a twofold witneſs in favour both of Stratford and London; but ſuch knowledge as ſo buſy a man could acquire in London, was much more likely to be obtained for the occaſion, and ſtudied in hiſtories and chronicles hurriedly, in order to conſtruct the plots of his pieces, than to be of that profound and equally diſ-

curſive

cursive character, which remains to the present time the admiration and equally the puzzle of the world. In the plays which we know that Shakespere wrote, when one of the "owners" or "partners" of the Globe Theatre, and in the full strain of mental and physical exertion, we do find an immense amount of that "knowledge of a period" before alluded to, which is rather the business of a searcher of records, than of a student of literature. This, after all, is the mere skeleton of a play. The flesh and life that clothe those dry bones of history, could not be so read-up or crammed. The plays of *Henry IV.* and *Henry VI.* may serve for example. No Garter-King-at-Arms, no F.S.A. could supply us with more accurate knowledge of descent and pedigree, than do such speeches as those of Mortimer (First Part *Henry VI.*, Act ii.), and of the Duke of York (Second

Part

Part *Henry VI.*, Aƈt ii.). No hiſtorian could ſketch character more admirably, or render narrative more tranſparent, than do the princes and prelates who ſpeak in Aƈt iv. Second Part of *Henry IV.* But while ſuch knowledge might have been ſtudied for the purpoſe, let it be remembered that this ſame Aƈt is world-famous for a knowledge of a very different character—a knowledge of human nature, exhibited in the two phaſes of high and ordinary life,—King Henry and the Prince; and Juſtice Shallow, Falſtaff, and Bardolph,—in itſelf ſufficient to have eſtabliſhed the fame of a humoriſt or ſatiriſt of any age. It is not a queſtion of probability, but a known faƈt, that Shakeſpere did model the ſkeletons of many of his plays upon the chronicles which he read while aƈtively occupied at the Globe Theatre. Still, that does not account for the fleſh, and blood, and life, with which

which they are quickened; and in order to do ſo, it ſeems neceſſary to retrace our ſteps to Stratford, and to attribute them to a precocious acquiſitiveneſs, as well as natural quickneſs of obſervation. Quickneſs of obſervation ſeems neceſſarily allied with the keeneſt ſenſe of the ludicrous. The *traditions* of Stratford concerning the Poet's humour, *may well be truſted when we read his plays;* and when we regard him as a ſatiriſt of the follies of mankind, in compariſon with the ſatiriſts of modern times, their attacks are but as the prick of a bodkin or a pin, compared with the flaying of a ſcalping-knife!

Shakeſpere's knowledge was two-fold: it was the moſt wonderful that any human being has ever exhibited, regarded as knowledge reſulting from obſervation; but it was alſo knowledge acquired by reading and ſtudy. In him every one recog-

niſes

nises the student as well as the observer. When did he study? Where did he study? A great amount of his knowledge of life, as exhibited in his rustic characters and clowns, was, we know, the photographing of persons with whom he had come in contact in Warwickshire! There also most probably was his study! It has been asserted that, towards the close of his life, he regularly retired to Stratford for the purpose of writing his plays. The assertion carries with it every probability, and it is likely enough the truth, that at Stratford he was habitually a student to the very close of his career. If the *Tempest* or *Henry VIII.* were the last plays he wrote, he must have been such. We may well incline to the belief, when we remember the touching farewells of Prospero and Wolsey to that power which they had so long exercised. Shakespere himself might be speaking

to

to us in the "long farewell," or in the lines:—

> *"I'll break my ſtaff,*
> *Bury it certain fathoms in the earth,*
> *And deeper than did ever plummet ſound,*
> *I'll drown my book."*

It is not, however, with the cloſe but with the commencement of his career, that we have to do. Was not Stratford the ſchool-houſe of his life? Did not his mind,—with a precocity ſuch as has been exhibited in Milton and Chatterton, and for which Lord Byron was nervouſly anxious that the world ſhould give him credit,—eagerly and thirſtily drink at the ſources of ſuch knowledge as were capable of being reached in his youthful years? Though it may ſeemingly be a very unſatisfactory manner of anſwering a queſtion, to put another; nevertheleſs, when every lover of Shakeſpere has aſked, and will continue to aſk until the queſtion is anſwered, "Where did the Poet gain his

"diverſified

"diverſified learning?" it may not be altogether uſeleſs to reply to ſuch inquirers—Have you not paſſed over, without ſufficiently ſearching conſideration, the days that were ſpent at "the ſchool i' the "church?" Have you thoroughly inveſtigated the character of that ſchool, and of the Guild of the Holy Croſs, with which it was originally incorporated? Have you ſatisfied yourſelves, whether, in that very church, Shakeſpere might not have found thoſe ſources of knowledge which he evidently found ſomewhere and ſomehow?

Between the date when King Henry VIII. ſuppreſſed the monaſtic eſtabliſhment in 1536, to the date of his ſon, Edward VI., reviving the School of the Guild in 1553, only ſeventeen years intervened. Thoſe years were long enough to complete the work of diſperſion or deſtruction among the libraries of abbeys that

that were themſelves reduced to ruins, but no ſuch ruin overtook the Guild of the Holy Croſs. It was not an eſtabliſhment of ſufficient importance to be ruined, and accordingly it changed hands, and followed the deſtinies of the Reformation.

What became of its furniture—its chattels—above all, its books? Was there any library connected with the Free School of the Guild? If ſo, what object could there be for the officers of Henry VIII. to deſtroy it, or diſperſe it?

The problem as to where Shakeſpere gained his extenſive knowledge, can never be ſolved until inquiries in this direction ſhall be—if ever—ſatisfactorily anſwered. The ground, to the beſt belief of the author, is almoſt, if not altogether, unbroken ground. Whether the readers of theſe pages will feel the ſame conviction that he does, it is not for him

him to know; but, while the moſt interesting of all inquiries regarding the life of Shakeſpere ſtill waits for an anſwer, the author has convinced himſelf, that if that anſwer is ever rendered, it will come from Stratford, and not from London;—it will prove that William Shakeſpere, while a ſchool-boy, with little Latin and leſs Greek, had neverthele ſs a thirſt for knowledge in his own mother-tongue, a love for acquiring information of the moſt diverſified character, and a marvellous power, or natural gift, for *hiving* his ſtore in the cells of memory, and bringing forth that knowledge, "ſweeter than honey or "the honeycomb," whenever it was required. With a conviction, which nothing but abſolute evidence to the contrary would ever ſhake, the author feels morally certain that at the "ſchool i' the church" Shakeſpere had free acceſs to ſome valuable ſtore of books, whether belonging

to

to the Guild proper, or to the ſchool of the Guild, or to ſome other library that was contiguous and eaſily acceſſible; and that from the ſame ſources at which the thirſting ſchool-boy drank, the man, in his occaſional and eventually permanent retirement, drank alſo. Perhaps there may have been a peculiar charm and attraction for this teacher of mankind in ſettling at New Place, becauſe its gables and caſements were ſhadowed by the glorious architecture of that Holy Croſs Chapel, wherein he had diſcovered, and ever after fondly ſought, thoſe ſilent teachers—dear and precious books!—the unquarrelling friends, the unchanging companions, the charmers whoſe charms never fade;—alike welcome to the man in the zenith of literary fame, and to the ſchool-boy with ſatchel and ſhining morning face, eagerly ſeeking (as King Edward named the maſter of the Stratford

School)

School) the Pedagogue and "the ſchool "i' the church."

Though the remains are very ſcanty that ſerve to give us any information regarding Shakeſpere, it is ſomewhat remarkable that one of the moſt valuable relics connected with him ſhould have belonged to his library. One book of Shakeſpere's, with his autograph on the fly-leaf, exiſts. It is Montaigne's Eſſays. Amidſt the goſſip of literature with which the modern Preſs abounds, it is no ſmall teſtimony to the worth of ſuch books as Montaigne's Eſſays, and Burton's Anatomy of Melancholy, that they ſtand without rivals to the preſent hour; approached only by Hallam, by D'Iſraeli's "Curioſities of Literature," and one or two other works of like character, but unſurpaſſed by any, in their own quaint

quaint and captivating ſtyle of hiſtorical anecdote.

That Montaigne ſhould be a favourite author with Shakeſpere will be readily underſtood by any one who has ſtudied the minds of the two men. They were both ſatiriſts of the eccentricities of human nature. They had both a reliſh for conceits. They were both philoſophers of life. We can well imagine that Montaigne would be as valued on the ſhelves of New Place, as Charles Lamb deſcribes a new book to have been valued, when it was at laſt acquired after the careful ſtoring of every ſpare farthing, and carried home in triumph to his ſiſter!

Shakeſpere's one book! And ſuch a book! What more humorous, inſtructive, entertaining, and improving companion could a man need than Montaigne's Eſſays? Leaving to Mr. Emerſon

Emerſon and Mr. St. John the taſk of apologiſing for the occaſionally eccentric tendency of the Gaſcon's fancy—remembering the faſhion of the times in which he lived, and the vernacular even of courts and kings, which in modern days would make the hair of ſociety ſtand on end—we might be permitted to arrange in imagination the bookſhelves of New Place, and with the ſingle vertebra of a library —Montaigne's Eſſays — proceed to the formation of the body of Shakeſpere's fireſide literature, as Profeſſor Owen conſtructs an animal upon the authority of a bone. Aſtoniſhing as the number of works is which Caxton contrived to produce between the publication of the "Game of "Cheſs," in 1474, and his death in 1491—*the year before Sir Hugh Clopton was Lord Mayor of London*—equalling as much as five thouſand cloſely printed folio pages, this leaping of the giant in the womb of time

time (as Mr. Hallam called it) was nothing in comparifon with the production of books during the feventy years that intervened between the date of Caxton's death and Shakefpere's birth. The great printer's favourite apprentices, Pynfon and Wynkyn de Worde, had between them publifhed more than fix hundred volumes at the end of the firft quarter of the fixteenth century. When once the preffes had been eftablifhed at Oxford and other large provincial towns, the iffue averaged feventy-five volumes a year. So that, by the clofe of the century when Shakefpere modelled and furnifhed his houfe at New Place, he had the pick of ten thoufand volumes publifhed in the Englifh tongue, and could adorn his ftudy either with Cranmer's Bible, publifhed by Grafton, or with one of John Day's; or with that edition of 1551 for which Tindall was ftrangled, and his body burnt. In addition

addition to this, the retirement of Stratford would be enlivened for him by the arrival of "Mercuries" or "Flying "Couriers," in which the lateſt intelligence from Town would be recorded, and he might ſee what Heminge and Burbage were about at the Globe.

When ſpeculations are hazarded as to the knowledge of Shakeſpere, and its ſources, it is deſirable to have facts of this deſcription recalled to mind. We ordinarily labour under the impreſſion that books were very ſcarce in Shakeſpere's days; and if we may take Lord Macaulay's celebrated picture of England's country houſes in the time of Charles II. as ſomething like the truth, we may make a pretty fair gueſs at what would be the amount of intellectual food enjoyed by the gentry and ſquires of Warwickſhire juſt one century earlier. If, between 1660 and 1665, "the difficulty and ex- "penſe

" penſe of carrying large packets from " place to place was ſo great that an ex- " tenſive work was longer in making its " way from Paternoſter Row to Devon- " ſhire or Lancaſhire than it now is in " reaching Kentucky," . . . . and " few " Knights of the Shire had libraries ſo " good as may now perpetually be found " in a ſervants' hall," the ſubject of rural intellectuality would be depreſſing indeed, on glancing backwards one hundred years prior to ſuch Bœotian darkneſs, were it not that the crab-like movement in this inſtance would be poſitive progreſs, ſince there can be no queſtion that learning degraded in England between the dates 1560 and 1660.

Upon Shakeſpere's claſſical knowledge, or maſtery of languages, there is little to be ſaid, or that needs to be ſaid ſince the publication of Dr. Farmer's (the Maſter of Emmanuel College, Cambridge,) " Eſſay

" Essay on the Learning of Shakespere." That exhaustive pamphlet, Malone candidly admitted, was overwhelming in its evidence, and conclusive, that the Poet's classical plays and poems were not constructed upon a knowledge of the classic authors, but upon translations of those authors. Whether Ben Jonson ever uttered the slighting words attributed to him or not, he would be a rampant enthusiast indeed who would dare to contravene the truth of the words themselves. Nothing can be more conclusive of Shakespere's mere schoolboy knowledge of Latin than his absurd misquotation from Lily's Grammar of a line which, for the purpose of example, is given one way in the grammar, but runs very differently in the " Eunu-" chus" of Terence, from which, had our Poet really been quoting, he would have quoted correctly. In the

the *Taming of the Shrew*, we read (Act i. Scene 1)—

> TRANIO. *Master, it is no time to chide you now;*
> *Affection is not rated from the heart:*
> *If love have touch'd you, naught remains but so,—*
> *"Redime te captum quam queas minimo."*

In the original ("Eunuchus," I. i. 29) the passage stands thus:—

> PHŒDRIA. *Nec quid agam, scio.*
> PARMENO. *Quid agas? Nisi ut te redimas captum quam queas*
> *Minimo: si nequeas paululo, at quanti queas*
> *Et ne te afflictes.*
> PHŒDRIA. *Itane suades, &c., &c.*

The truth was that Shakespere had learnt Lily's Grammar at school (with its "Epistle" and directions by Cardinal Wolsey).

We have no possible reason for supposing that he ever pretended to scholarship. He put into the mouth of Tranio a line with which, in his day, every schoolboy was familiar; but from whence

derived,

derived, it is very probable, Shakeſpere neither knew nor cared. Probably, with his keen humour, no one could have enjoyed a laugh more than he, could he have liſtened to the rubbiſh which Shakeſperian "ſcholars" have talked about the claſſical knowledge of a man who was too honeſt even to pretend to any familiarity with the Greek and Latin poets.

The well-worn ſtory of Mr. Hales, of Eton, filtering through the works of Rowe, Dryden, and Gilrow, is equally honourable to Mr. Hales, and probably cloſe to the truth.

Rowe writes: "In a converſation be-
"tween Sir John Suckling, Sir William
"D'Avenant, Endymion Porter, Mr.
"Hales, of Eton, and Ben Jonſon, Sir
"John Suckling, who was a profeſſed
"admirer of Shakeſpere, had undertaken
"his defence againſt Ben Jonſon with
"ſome warmth; Mr. Hales, who had

"ſat

"sat still for some time told them, "'*That if Mr. Shakspeare had not read* "'*the ancients, he had likewise not stolen* "'*anything from them; and that if he* "'*would produce any one topick finely* "'*treated by any one of them, he would* "'*undertake to show something upon the* "'*same subject at least as well written by* "'*Shakspeare.*'"

Fifteen years before Rowe's Life of Shakespere had been published, Gildon's Letters and Essays (in 1694) told the story. "The enemies of Shakespere "would by no means yield him so much "excellence: so that it came to a reso-"lution of a trial of skill upon that sub-"ject. The place agreed on for the dis-"pute was Mr. Hale's chamber at Eton. "A great many books were sent down by "the enemies of this Poet; and on the "appointed day, my Lord Falkland, Sir "John Suckling, and all the persons of

"quality

" quality that had wit and learning, and " interefted themfelves in the quarrel, " met there; and, upon a thorough dif- " quifition of the point, the judges, " chofen by agreement out of this learned " and ingenious affembly, unanimoufly " gave the preference to Shakfpeare, " and the Greek and Roman poets were " adjudged to vail at leaft their glory in " that to the Englifh hero."

Dryden's allufion to the ftory (" Effay " on Dramatic Poefy," 1667,) is as follows: " The confideration of this made " Mr. Hales, of Eton, fay, ' that there " ' was no fubject of which any poet ever " ' writ, but he would produce it much " ' better done by Shakfpeare.' "

The " ever-memorable " John Hales was a fcholar of diftinguifhed European reputation, and, therefore, he muft have been as familiar with the Greek and Latin poets as with Shakefpere. He was one of of thoſe ripe and broadly read ſcholars—not thick as blackberries even in the nineteenth century—who are as familiar with the poetry of their own country as with that of the ancients. Hiſtory has aſſured us of this: and how very few there are like him! How very few thoſe who can "cap verſes" in that higheſt range of literary knowledge, where Terence, Horace, Sophocles, and Euripides, can be inſtantly anſwered by the quotation of a kindred line from Spenſer, Shakeſpere, or Milton. Hales was one of theſe few athletes of ſcholarſhip, and therefore his opinion is worthy of all conſideration, while his celebrated victory deſerves to make him, as Malone prayed he might remain, "ever-memorable."

The mental gymnaſtics thus performed in Mr. Hale's room at Eton, ſeem to point out very diſtinctly the ſtrength and the weakneſs of Shakeſpere! "If he

"had

"had not read the ancients!" What then? Mr. Hales knew he had not. Deeply read himſelf in the claſſics, he knew that his favourite was not ſo. But, what then? Point out any moral, any philoſophic reflection, any noble and elevating ſentiment, produced by the ancient poets, and "I will produce it "much better done by Shakſpeare," ſaid Mr. Hales.

From the crucible to which Dr. Farmer ſubjected the writings of Shakeſpere, they came forth purged from that alloy of ſilly eulogy which was a droſs, giving to the Poet what never belonged to him, and depreciating the pure coinage uttered by his brilliant brain. The marvel of Shakeſpere's works is in the beauties that are all his own. The prodigality of his genius may in ſome degree be eſtimated when one of England's greateſt ſcholars challenges the ancient poets, and declares

himſelf

himſelf ready to "cap" any ſentiment of their verſe by a ſimilar ſentiment, equally well or better expreſſed in Shakeſpere. And who, in the trial, wins the victory? Let it be granted frankly that Shakeſpere, in writing his *Troilus and Creſſida,* followed Caxton's Hiſtory of Troy; that he borrowed from Plutarch; that he read Hollinſhed in order to conſtruct *Richard III.;* that he ſtudied a tranſlation of Belleforeſt before he wrote *Hamlet!*—Let the ſame ſort of facts be quoted againſt *Henry IV., Richard II.,* and all the hiſtorical plays: and what does it amount to? Both the cloſet and the ſtage are witneſſes to the truth, that the more "hiſtorical" the Poet is—the more he depends upon and adheres to chronicles or legends—the leſs powerful he is. Thoſe plays are the leaſt popular which are the moſt hiſtorical, for the ſimple reaſon that

that where he has to trace the hiſtory of a reign in the cramped limits of a play, he is neceſſarily fettered, and the ſcope of the Poet's fancy is more or leſs ſubjected to the inevitable rehearſal of facts. How different is it in the unapproached perfection of treatment, progreſſive development of plot, and poetry of diction in *Othello* and *Macbeth.* In thoſe, as in *Hamlet,* and *Romeo,* and *King Lear,* a ſcheme of the play has been derived from ancient writers, or tranſlations, but nothing more. The genius of the Poet has been left free to portray character, and to clothe ſentiment with words as no other poet ever did.

There is every difference between learning and language. Shakeſpere's knowledge was not a knowledge of language, but it was the knowledge of learning. It is highly probable that he never derived a ſingle claſſical incident, alluſion, or ſtory

ſtory, direct from a claſſical author. It is equally probable that he never in his life read a Greek play, and knew no more of Terence than he had learnt of him in Lily's Grammar!

The more we realiſe theſe facts (for they are facts), and the more ſurpriſing the learning of the Poet becomes, he does not thereby ſink, but rather riſes in our admiration. We ſtrip him of pretenſions—*poſt-mortem* honours to which he laid no claim—and regard him ſolely as what he is, the Poet of England, and uttering in Engliſh verſe the thoughts gathered from, or ſuggeſted by, Engliſh literature.

We have ſeen that there were ten thouſand volumes publiſhed in Engliſh during the century in which he flouriſhed, and that every year contributed largely to the information of ſtudious men. Whatever truth there may be in

Macaulay's

Macaulay's ſtrictures upon the ignorance prevailing in the reign of Charles II., the buſineſs of Shakeſpere's life involved reading and ſtudy. And although it is true that the circulation of books in the rural diſtricts of England may have been very ſlow, ſtill this objection would not be any impediment to Shakeſpere, who, living conſtantly in London, and travelling to and fro between Stratford and town, would have ample opportunity to take down with him into the country any books which he wiſhed to read. Chronological tables of the order in which his plays were written, founded upon internal evidence, dates of performance, or of publication, have frequently been publiſhed. Such tables are after all conjectural, and it is no proof of the date when a play was written, to learn when it was printed or played. In the abſence of demonſtration, the conjectures of

Malone

Malone and Chalmers attribute, the one ſeven, the other eleven plays to Shakeſpere prior to his purchaſe of New Place in 1597. The far more ſatisfactory, becauſe poſitive, facts which Mr. C. Knight gives us, ſhow that only three plays had been publiſhed prior to 1597. With a very trifling amount of exception it may, therefore, be ſtated that the maſs of his plays were written during his tenancy of New Place; and all the greateſt, without doubt, during the latter period of his life. Within ſixteen years thirty-four plays of Shakeſpere's were either printed or ſpoken of in print, giving us an average of two plays a year; their actual publication, or direct alluſion to them in particular years, being as follows:—

In 1597	. . . . .	3 Plays.
„ 1598	. . . . .	8 „
„ 1600	. . . . .	5 „
„ 1602	. . . . .	3 „

In

In 1603	 1	Play.
„ 1604	 1	„
„ 1607	 2	„
„ 1609	 2	„
„ 1611	 2	„
„ 1613	 1	„

It is very remarkable that, according to this liſt, the Poet worked the hardeſt during the year he became poſſeſſed of New Place, and for the four or five years ſubſequent. It ſeems natural to conclude that Shakeſpere purchaſed New Place with a view to making it his literary ſanctum; for it is impoſſible to reſiſt connecting with the purchaſe, the fecundity of his pen. Let us only conſider the character of work in which he was employed when in London, and let any man ſo engaged anſwer whether it would be poſſible for Shakeſpere, regularly employed at Blackfriars or the Globe, rehearſing and performing, to ſtudy the plots and produce the MSS. of eight or five tragedies and comedies per annum. If he could have

have done ſo, he would have been a far greater prodigy than the world has ever yet accounted him. Such an Herculean labour of mind and body is beyond the capacity of any human being. But if we attach the purchaſe of New Place to Shakeſpere's ſucceſs as a play-writer, and contemplate him withdrawing there from the excitement and buſtle of Blackfriars to produce the *Merchant of Venice,* and *Midſummer Night's Dream,* then that garden, and the ſlender remains of the foundations of his houſe ſeem to become doubly precious to Engliſhmen. As time wears on his labours ſlacken; but almoſt to the end he continues bringing forth from the treaſures of his mind the immortal works which gild his fame. The opinion of many writers has been that Shakeſpere was undomeſticated, and that he rarely viſited Stratford. Humbly, but confidently, the writer embraces a

directly

directly oppoſite opinion. To him it appears impoſſible that Shakeſpere could have accompliſhed the literary work he produced, immerſed in the buſineſs and diſtracting engagements of Blackfriars or the Globe. Circumſtances ſeem to give credit to the ſuppoſition that a larger amount of his time was ſpent at New Place than is commonly eſtimated; and as to his being undomeſticated, or unhappy in his home, ſuch an uncharitable and purely conjectural idea has not even as much reſpectability as the mare's-neſt which De Quincey diſcovered in the marriage licenſe. The minds that give welcome to the one notion will, moſt likely, cheriſh the other.

Inſtead of Shakeſpere reſiding in London and occaſionally viſiting Stratford, it may be much nearer the truth to ſay that he lived the latter years of his life chiefly at New Place, and only viſited London at

thoſe

thoſe periods of the year when his preſence was abſolutely neceſſary. The probabilities are ſtrongly in favour of this opinion, and there is no evidence to the contrary. For the laſt eighteen years of his life he is preſented to our imagination as the maſter of New Place. He is not to be regarded during thoſe years enjoying retirement and repoſe, like many of the great men who have followed him in his profeſſion, as Garrick at Hampton, John Kemble at Lauſanne, or Macready at Sherborne and Cheltenham.

The "ſilver livery of adviſed age," which it was permitted the two firſt—and long may it be allowed to the third—to wear, was never donned by Shakeſpere. He died in the freſhneſs and vigour of life; and, as we know of a certainty, continued actively employed until the cloſe of his exiſtence. It is ſaddening to think how little aſſociated with his private life remains

remains to us. A letter, a will, a deed, a book—and that is all! How different the fate of the maſter and his apprentices. There are happily preſerved to us the chief incidents in the life of Garrick; and many articles of perſonal property belonging to him, which are highly prized. When Shakeſpere was dead a hundred years, ſcarce a trace of him remained. A few ſtories gathered from goſſips hung about his track in Stratford; but anything actually aſſociated with him would have been as hard to diſcover there, as the Philoſopher's Stone. The hundred years was only juſt completed, when the houſe in which he had lived and died was razed to the ground. The deſcendants of his ſiſter, Joan Hart, as the pedigree ſhows, have reached down to our own days. Poſſibly ſome of them may ſtill exiſt in the neighbourhood of Tewkeſbury or Glouceſter. To Joan he bequeathed not only

only his houſe in Henley Street, and twenty pounds, but alſo "all my wearing "apparel."

What would the world now give to ſee a ſuit of wearing apparel that had been worn by Shakeſpere? If the coat of Napoleon in the Louvre, or of Nelſon in Greenwich Hoſpital, attracts the attention of tens of thouſands, what would be the value of and intereſt in the black gown, "garded with velvet and faced with "cony;" the ruddy coloured hoſe, the caſſock, the jerkin, the "fryze bryches," the rapier, and "the hat of a certain kind of "fine haire, fetched from beyond the ſeas, "which they call 'bever hatte.'"?*

Shakeſpere's wardrobe muſt have been ſtocked with articles of this deſcription. They were all left to his ſiſter; and his ſiſter's deſcendants certainly ſurvived to the

* Fairholt's "Coſtume in England," p. 216 (1860, Ed.)

the end of the laſt century. It would have ſeemed natural for them to have preſerved ſome of the coſtume of the Poet, but there is not a trace of anything of the ſort.

In the ſame way he bequeathed to Mr. Thomas Combe his ſword. The pedigree ſhows us how the Combe property paſſed into the Clopton family, by the marriage of Martha Combe with Edward Clopton. What would his countrymen not give to recover Shakeſpere's ſword? Its preſervation would have been moſt eaſy. If the ſword of the Conqueror could be preſerved in the family of the late Sir Godfrey Webſter, with the Roll of Battle, down to the middle of the laſt century, and only then periſhed through the misfortune of a fire, why could not the Combes and Cloptons have preſerved Shakeſpere's ſword? Why might it not have been depoſited ere this

in

in ſome national treaſury? If there is an article of uſe which has the quality of defying accident and time, it is a ſword. Very probably Shakeſpere's ſword ſtill exiſts, but has been loſt or ſold! Who knows whether it may not have been among the furniture and chattels ſold off by Mr. Batterſbee, previous to the demolition of Stratford College, the reſidence of the Combes?

What became of the broad ſilver-gilt bowl bequeathed to Judith Shakeſpere—Mrs. Quiney? What became of the "chattels, plate, jewels, and houſehold "ſtuff" bequeathed to Dr. Hall and Mrs. Hall? Theſe would naturally deſcend to Lady Barnard; and at her deceaſe would continue in the uſe of Sir John Barnard, until his death in 1673. Neither Lady Barnard's will, nor the indenture relating to her property, make any mention of Shakeſpere's heir-looms. The

broad

broad ſilver-gilt bowl, the plate, the jewels, all vaniſh from ſight. Articles of this deſcription do not periſh or conſume away. They may exiſt now in as excellent preſervation as in 1616! If ſo, what has become of them? Unleſs the ſilver bowl was ſold by the Quineys, and melted down, it would moſt probably be engraved with a creſt, or a monogram, or ſome device whereby it could be recogniſed. Is it yet too late to inſtitute a ſearch for ſuch an invaluable relic of the Poet? A man of Sir John Barnard's ſtation would naturally leave plate, jewels, and property, to his heirs or relatives. It is ſaid that this family has died out within a very ſhort time at *Abingdon, in Berkſhire.* If ſuch is the fact, family heir-looms do not deſcend to the grave: they paſs to ſome one. If the inquiry has not yet been diligently made, it is well worth while to know in what di-

rection

rection the Barnard property has gone; and to trace—failing direct male descent—the female issue, and the marriages which may have carried property into other families. It seems impossible but that Elizabeth Hall must have inherited the plate and jewels which belonged to her grandfather; and as she makes no direct mention of them in her will, it is natural to suppose they continued in possession of her husband.

We see Shakespere's personal property divided among his children and his sister: to one his wardrobe is bequeathed, to another his plate, to another his broad silver bowl, and to Thomas Combe his sword! It is hard to believe that a man valued during his lifetime as Shakespere was, and immortalised so quickly after his death, should be held in the least esteem by those of his own household. It is hard to think that no one belonging to to him ſhould deſire to preſerve the mementoes which he had particularly bequeathed to them in his will. And yet the fact ſtares us in the face that not a ſingle heir-loom of the Poet has been handed down, by any one branch of his family, to the preſent day! All, all are loſt and gone, ſave one book, the preſervation of which has been purely accidental!

Rowe, who acknowledges himſelf indebted to Betterton for a conſiderable part of the paſſages relating to the Poet's life introduced in his Biography (publiſhed 1709), informs us that Betterton's "vener-" ation for the memory of Shakeſpere . . . " engaged him to make a journey into " Warwickſhire, on purpoſe to gather " up what remains he could of a name " which he had in ſo great veneration." Conſidering that Betterton was born in 1635—the ſame year in which Dr. John

John Hall died—and that his daughter ſurvived until 1669, when Betterton was thirty-four years of age,—and conſidering alſo that ſhe was eight years of age when her grandfather died, and therefore perfectly able to ſpeak of him from her own recollection,—it does ſeem extraordinary that the remains which Betterton went to Stratford to gather up were ſo ſcanty. He would find Shakeſpere's children all dead, but his reſidence in the poſſeſſion of his grandchild, who, though living at Abington, was probably an occaſional viſitor to her property in Stratford. Had he even made her acquaintance, with what a fund of information might Rowe's Life have been enriched! and what treaſures connected with the Poet might have been chronicled, and poſſibly preſerved, through his intereſt! But the fates ſeem to have ordered it otherwiſe. The Poet had not been dead twenty years

years when Betterton was born; and within half a century of Shakeſpere's deceaſe, this venerator of his memory probably viſited Stratford. From that place he does not ſeem to have brought back with him a ſingle memento of the Poet; or to have ſeen his ſword, his ſilver bowl, his books, or any of his chattels, at a deſcription of which the ears of every antiquary in England would now tingle, while to recover one of them would make any preſent diſcoverer famous.

Fifty years, and the treaſures of the Poet were unnoticed or unknown! One hundred years, and the domeſtic aſſociations of his pupil and interpreter, David Garrick, are as freſhly and carefully preſerved as if he had been in their midſt yeſterday! Within a mile of one another, at Hampton and Hampton Court, are two reſidences, which, ſo ſo long as they exiſt, will be for ever aſſociated with Shakeſpere and Garrick. Thanks to Mr. Peter Cunningham's timely diſcovery in the Audit Office of the "Revel's Booke," we now know when "Shaxberd's" *Plaie of Errors*, his *Marchant of Venis*, his *Meſur for Meſur*, and his *Merry Wives of Winſor*, were performed before James I. We know with certainty of two noble chambers — and thoſe royal chambers—in which Shakeſpere was ſeen and heard, and of none other; for though it would be almoſt a profanity to diſturb the tradition which identifies the houſe in Henley Street, Stratford, as the birthplace of the Poet, there is no abſolute certainty of ſuch being the caſe. The Banqueting Houſe, at Whitehall, and the miſnamed "Wolſey's Hall," at Hampton Court, wherein Shakeſpere's company performed before the king in the winters of 1603 and 1604,

are

are chambers for ever aſſociated with the hiſtory of England; and not among their minor aſſociations is the recollection that in them the King of England liſtened to the Poet's plays—ſaw the Poet himſelf as one of the players—and "be-" ſtowed eſpecial honour upon Shake-" ſpere," in "an amicable letter." The letter was in the poſſeſſion of Sir William Davenant as reported, and there ſeems no reaſon to queſtion the truth of the report. But whether it be true or not, there is no queſtion regarding the enactment of the tragedies and comedies before the Court at Whitehall and Hampton. We are thus enabled to interweave the memory of our Poet with two ſtructures utterly diſſimilar in architectural detail, but each a princely pile, and each cloſely connected with the moſt ſtirring events of hiſtory.

Prince Charles, a child of four years of

of age, may have ſported at the King's knee, and witneſſed the deed of blood done by the Moor in the ſame hall through which he was to paſs to a darker deed of blood years afterwards. The hiſtory of that Palace of Whitehall is familiar to every ſchoolboy, but not ſo familiar that of the two halls which have adorned the Palace of Hampton Court. For contraſt, for light and ſhade in hiſtorical painting, what four pictures of ſunſhine and ſhower could be more dramatic than a vigorous repreſentation of Wolſey's Banqueting Hall, as it muſt have appeared when he entertained the French Ambaſſador,—when the Court Revels was held there after the acceſſion of James, and Shakeſpere performed in the hall which now occupies the ſame ſite as Wolſey's, which was moſt probably deſigned by him, but not erected until the 22nd Henry VIII., ſix years after the

Cardinal

Cardinal had left the Palace for ever;—and on the oppoſite or ſhadowed ſide of the picture, when Mary inhabited the Court, liſtening to the maſſes and prayers of her prieſts, praying for her ſafe deliverance of an heir to the throne of the realm, which was never deſtined to be born; or when Cromwell, in his domeſtic gloom, paced up and down that Hall, liſtening to the muſic of the "box of whiſtles," which Puritanic opinion thought too Popiſh for the chapel of Magdalen College, but was a fit inſtrument, erected in the Minſtrel's Gallery at Hampton, to ſoothe the throbbing breaſt of the Lord Protector.

George Cavendiſh deſcribes Wolſey's entertainment to the Ambaſſador of Francis I. Nearly three hundred bed-rooms were fitted up to receive his ſuite, each provided with a baſin and ewer of ſilver, wine and beer veſſels of ſilver, bowls, goblets, and ſilver ſconces.

At

At the banquet, bouffets ſtretched acroſs the end of the Hall, having ſix ſhelves one above the other, crowded with gold and ſilver plate. During the ſecond courſe the Lord Cardinal came in, booted and ſpurred, and giving all welcome, took a golden bowl filled with hypocras, and drank to the health of his Sovereign Lord and of the King of France. What a contraſt to the ſpectacle witneſſed on the ſame ſpot in the following century, when the King-killer, quivering with emotion as his child lay dead in an adjoining chamber, wandered in his ſolitude about that Palace! There Mary likewiſe had wandered in her ſolitude! and there, too, Charles had paſſed ſome of his bittereſt days! Strange aſſociations theſe, with the Hall in which Shakeſpere and his company had performed before Charles's father, and perchance in Charles's preſence!

The deſtruction of New Place, and the loſs and deſtruction of every article of perſonal property that the Poet bequeathed to his family, excepting one book,—Florio's tranſlated edition of Montaigne (1603), with his ſignature inſcribed,—muſt for ever remain a matter of the deepeſt regret. We only know of ſix ſignatures of Shakeſpere. All, ſave one, are appended to legal documents. The autograph in Montaigne is the only ſcrap of writing by the Poet which aſſociates us with him in his literary life. However valuable his ſignature may be, a far higher value attaches to his writing in a book that was one of his companions and friends, and poſſeſſed a place in his home, than the mere execution of a hard, dry, legal document. A very intereſting account of Shakeſpere's copy of Montaigne was written by Sir Frederick Madden, which ſtates that it was purchaſed

chaſed in 1838 for the Britiſh Muſeum, from the Rev. Edward Patteſon, of Eaſt Sheen, and had belonged to his father, the Rev. Edward Patteſon, of Smethwick, near Birmingham, by whom, previous to the year 1780, the volume uſed to be exhibited as a treaſure, on account of its containing the autograph of Shakeſpere. In other words, the book and its autograph were ſhown with pride, *and not for ſale*, prior to Ireland's forgeries, and the vulgar attempts to imitate Shakeſpere's ſignature by ſuch impoſtors as Jordan, "*the Poet of Stratford*," ſave the mark!

Sir Frederick Madden ſays, and ſays properly, "the preſent autograph chal-"lenges and defies ſuſpicion." The book of itſelf is intereſting, apart from its connection with Shakeſpere; and as it is a treaſure which can only be inſpected by ſpecial leave, it may be well to publiſh its title.

THE

THE

ESSAYES,

OR

MORALL, POLITIKE, AND MILLITARIE DISCOURSES,

OF

LO: MICHAELL DE MONTAIGNE,

KNIGHT,

Of the Noble Order of ST. MICHAELL, *and one of the* GENTLEMEN IN ORDINARY *of the French King,* HENRY THE THIRD, *his Chamber.*

The First Booke.

(***)

First written by him in *French,*
and
Now done into *English*

By

By him that hath inviolably vowed his labours to the Æternitie of their Honors,
Whofe names he hath feverally infcribed on thefe his confecrated Altares.

The First Booke.

To the Right Honorable
LUCIE, CO: OF BEDFORD,
and
LADIE ANNE HARRINGTON,
Her Ho. Mother.

The Second Booke.

To the Right Honorable
ELIZABETH, CO: OF RUTLAND,
and
LADY PENELOPE RICHE.

The Third Booke.

To the Right Honorable
LADIE ELIZABETH GREY,
and
LADIE MARIE NEVILL.

JOHN FLORIO.

¶ *Printed at London, by* VAL. SIMS *and* EDWARD BLOUNT, *dwelling in Paules Churchyard.* 1603.

That Shakespere was familiar with this translation is put beyond all doubt by the fact that, in Act ii., Scene 2, of the *Tempest*, he quotes from it almost word for word:—

> *"I' the commonwealth, I would by contraries*
> *Execute all things: for no kind of traffic*
> *Would I admit; no name of magistrate;*
> *Letters should not be known; riches, poverty,*
> *And use of service, none; contract, succession,*
> *Bourn, bound of land, tilth, vineyard, none;*
> *No use of metal, corn, or wine, or oil;*
> *No occupation; all men idle, all;*
> *And women too; but innocent and pure."*

The passage thus quoted, in Florio, Book i., Chap. 30, runs as follows:— Speaking of a newly discovered country, which he calls Antartick France, Montaigne observes:—"It is a nation—would "I answer Plato—that hath *no kind of* "*traffike; no knowledge of letters;* no in-"telligence of numbers; *no name of* "*magistrate*, nor of politike superioritie; "*no use of service, of riches, or of poverty;* "*no contracts; no successions;* no divi-"dences;

"dences; *no occupation, but idle;* no "respect of kindred, but common; no "apparell, but naturall; no manuring of "lands; *no use of wine, corne, or "mettle,"* &c.

That the volume in question belonged to a library in Shakespere's time, its binding shows, particularly in the Tudor-fashioned *fleur-de-lis* and crown ornamentation with which the leather is stamped.

That the volume belonged to Shakespere himself, the autograph which "challenges and defies suspicion" proves.

Having re-asserted Sir Frederick Madden's words, it would be unfair not to quote the following passage from Mr. Halliwell's "Life of William Shake-"speare," pp. 280-81:—

"It is unnecessary to say that many alleged autographs "of Shakespeare have been exhibited; but forgeries of "them are so numerous, and the continuity of design, "which a fabricator could not produce in a long docu-"ment, is so easy to obtain in a mere signature, that the "only safe course is, to adopt none as genuine on internal

"evidence

" evidence. A ſignature in a copy of Florio's tranſla-
" tion of Montaigne, 1609, is open to this objection.
" The verbal evidence as to its exiſtence only extends
" as far back as 1780, after the publication of Stevens'
" fac-ſimile of the laſt autograph in the will, of which
" it may be a copy with intentional variations."

Mr. Halliwell's general accuracy makes an error, in what he ſays of this book, remarkable; and excites the ſuſpicion that, in his ſcepticiſm, he may have diſdained to give the book that honourable conſideration which it really deſerves. He ſays, " tranſlation of Montaigne, 1609." The title above given will ſhow that the date is 1603. The error is hardly worth notice in itſelf, but well worth it when fallen into by a gentleman to whoſe painſtaking and ſearching accuracy we are ſo greatly indebted. It awakens an impreſſion that Florio's Montaigne may be worthy of a cloſer examination than it has yet received, and may perhaps contain more intereſting evidence in favour of its having belonged to Shakeſpere than has

has as yet been ſhown. For inſtance, Sir Frederick Madden, in his deſcription of the book, notices the manuſcript notes which are found in it, and the quotations and references on the fly-leaves at the beginning and ending of the volume. He ſtates that he had at firſt hoped theſe notes might have proved to be in the handwriting of Shakeſpere, but on examination he concluded they were written at ſome period later than Shakeſpere's time, though not much later, as the character of the writing proves. There Sir Frederick leaves the matter. But it is well worth while to take the book in hand, and reſume its examination at the point where Sir Frederick has dropped it. On the fly-leaf are Italian quotations, references to the claſſic poets, and references to ſubjects in the book. Theſe prove that the writer was a literary man and a claſſical ſcholar. Taking up the references, and

turning

turning to the body of the work, we find the margins annotated in ſeveral places, and Montaigne's Latin quotations verified or corrected. Sometimes a wrong author's name is given: if ſo, the annotations correct the preſs. Sometimes a quotation is given without the name of the author: if ſo, the annotation throws in "Livy," "Virgil," or ſome other claſſical name—ſuch a book, ſuch a line. We are thus put beyond all doubt that the writer was ſome ſcholar who had the claſſical poets, as we ſay, at his fingers' ends. But here comes the marvel of the matter. Upon the edges of the leaves is printed with pen and ink the name A. HALES.

Hales! Is it poſſible that the connection of that name with Shakeſpere entirely eſcaped the recollection of Sir Frederick Madden, and all other examiners of the book? Did no one remember the Poet's champion at Eton, who

Lord

Lord Clarendon declared "was one of the "leaſt men in the kingdom, and one of "the greateſt ſcholars in Europe." Sir Frederick is perfectly correct in ſtating that the orthography in the volume, though not Shakeſpere's, belongs to a date of the Shakeſperian age. When we link together theſe facts—that Mr. Hales, of Eton, was the Poet's enthuſiaſtic admirer; that he was a profound ſcholar, and therefore the very man who would ſupply the names of claſſic authors to quotations, and correct errors of reference to them, or inſcribe on a fly-leaf a parallel paſſage from ſome Italian poet; that if there was a ſale of Shakeſpere's goods and chattels at New Place, his books would be preciſely the memorials of the man which Mr. Hales would covet and purchaſe; that a volume containing his autograph would be a prize eagerly ſought and religiouſly preſerved; that

ſuch

ſuch a work would be read and annotated by Mr. Hales with the intenſeſt pleaſure; and that the name "Hales" is actually inſcribed upon the edges of the leaves,—it does ſeem that a ſtrong teſtimony to the value of the book has been overlooked, and that a moſt intereſting piece of internal evidence as to its hiſtoric value has been unappreciated. It is true that it falls ſhort of abſolute proof; but the links of the chain couple themſelves ſo naturally, and the probabilities are ſo ſtrongly in favour of this book having belonged to Mr. Hales, that if ſuch evidence recommends itſelf to the minds of thoſe who read theſe pages, Florio's Montaigne muſt be regarded henceforth with a heightened intereſt; and juſt as we regard the book from having paſſed into the poſſeſſion of ſuch a man as Mr. Hales, muſt its preſervation by him be an additional teſtimony—if ſuch were needed—

needed—in favour of the authenticity of the autograph of Shakeſpere.

Let Hales be "ever-memorable," ſaid Malone, becauſe of his defence of Shakeſpere. Will he not deſerve to be "ever-" memorable," indeed, if it ſhould prove that to his love and reverence we are indebted for the preſervation of the only known article of property that belonged to Shakeſpere?

Thoroughly convinced of the genuineneſs of the autograph, and ſtrongly impreſſed with the belief that after Shakeſpere's death his goods and chattels were ſold, and that this book paſſed into the poſſeſſion of Mr. Hales, of Eton, Florio's Montaigne is regarded by the author as the ſolitary "*In memoriam*" of New Place. New Place is ſwept away; the great houſe has vaniſhed; the Poet's ſword is loſt; the plate and jewels are deſtroyed or ſold, or loſt likewiſe; the broad

broad ſilver-gilt bowl is—melted down perhaps; but one treaſure is ſpared to us, better than plate or jewels, becauſe it is aſſociated with the Poet's play of the *Tempeſt*,—becauſe it bears his autograph, —becauſe, being a book, it is a memento moſt kindred to him who has given to the world, ſuperior to all other products of the human intellect, the Book of books,—and becauſe, having belonged to his library, we know how he muſt have valued it—

> "*Me, poor man! my library*
> *Was dukedom large enough.*"

The attention of the reader has been eſpecially called to the name of "Charles "Hales," as one of the commiſſioners of the inquiſition for inquiry regarding the eſtate of Ambroſe, Earl of Warwick. It will be obſerved that in Shakeſpere's time a Charles Hales is connected with Stratford. Then a John Hales is peculiarly intereſted

interested in upholding the Poet's fame; and on a book bearing his autograph the name "A. Hales" is found inscribed.

A visit to Heralds' College, and a little of the "Old Mortality" spirit of mural research in Canterbury, Warwick, and Somerset, gives us information of considerable interest, and seems to the author to add value to the folio of Montaigne. The fact is, the Hales family was connected with Snitterfield, and one branch of it was seated there both before and after Shakespere's time. This distinguished stock, which yielded so many servants to the Crown in the high offices of the law, belonged, *ex stirpe*, to Canterbury, and may be traced as located at the Dane John, or Dungeon, of that city, at Hales Place, at Tenterden, and elsewhere. By reference to the appended Pedigree, it will be seen how the junior descents of this house became seated at Coventry,

Coventry, at Newland near Coventry, and at Snitterfield. John Hales (A) acquired the celebrated Priory of Coventry, which ſingularly enough had been granted by patent of Henry VIII., dated 28th July, 37th anno., to John Combes, Eſq., and Richard Stansfield, their heirs, &c. From them it paſſed to this John Hales, in the 15th of Elizabeth. He died ſeiſed thereof, leaving it to John, his nephew (B), ſon of his brother Chriſtopher, who, it will be obſerved, had married the daughter of Lucy of Charlecote.

If the reader will glance over this Pedigree, it will be obſerved that the Haleſes, Lucys, and Combes became connected by marriages between their families; and it is of ſome intereſt to find that ſuch a magnificent monaſtic eſtabliſhment as the Priory of Coventry—magnificent even in the wreck that remains of it to the preſent time, converted as it is

to

to be a home for the poor—belonged to the father or grandfather of John à Combe, and after him to the Haleſes of Warwickſhire.

The reader will perhaps accuſe the author of taking him a heavy ride acroſs heraldic country to arrive at a very ſimple fact. But in theſe matters of reſearch there is no royal road to knowledge, and it is only by patient ſearch that we arrive at a knowledge of facts calculated to throw light on ſubjects like the preſent.

The pedigree of Hales, if given in all its branches, would require the inſertion of an immenſe map-like ſheet in this place, and therefore it is neceſſary to exclude ſuch branches as are not connected with the hiſtory of Shakeſpere. As the Haleſes wandered away from Kent to Warwickſhire, to Coventry, to Snitterfield, to Newland, ſo one of the branches took root in Somerſetſhire, at a place called

PEDIGREE OF A BRANCH OF THE HALES FAMILY.

(HALES *of High Church, Somerset.*)

Hales =

Richard Hales of High Church, near Bath, Esq. = d. of — Beauchamp, Esq.

John Hales of High Church, Esq. = Joanna, d. of Thomas Burnham, Esq.

Edward Hales of High Church, Esq. = Ann, d. of — Grenfield, Esq.

Children of Edward Hales: (B) John Hales; William. David. Susan. Maria.

(B) John Hales of High Church, Esq. = Bridget, d. of Robert Gouldesborough of Knahill, in the Co. of Wilts, Esq.

Children of John Hales and Bridget: Marvyn. Edward. ob. s. p. Matthew. Robert. Thomas. (C) ANTHONY. (A) JOHN. THE EVER MEMORABLE JOHN HALES OF ETON. Born April 19, 1584. Obiit May 19, 1656. Anne. Gertrude. Cicelie. Melior.

Marvyn = Alice, d. of Richard Thomas of Bishop's Nottle, in the Co. of Wilts, Esq.

John. Ætat. 10, in 1623.

To Face p. 249.

called High Church. To this branch the "ever-memorable John" belonged. His life is familiar to Eton and Oxford men, and to perſons intereſted in Laud, and the Royaliſt troubles. It is not generally known; and therefore a few words on the ſubject may not be inopportune, as John Hales has always appeared to the author to have beer the firſt ſcholar in England who recogniſed, as it deſerves to be recogniſed, the genius and tranſcendent ſuperiority of Skakeſpere to all the poets of ancient or modern days.

He was, as the Pedigree ſhows (A), the ſixth ſon of John Hales, of High Church (B), and was born in 1584. He matriculated at Corpus Chriſti College, Oxford, April 16, 1597, and took his B.A. July 9, 1603; was elected Fellow of Merton, October 13, 1606; took his M.A. in 1609; and was admitted Fellow of Eton, May 24, 1613. He accompanied

accompanied Sir Dudley Carlton to the Hague as his chaplain, and was admitted to the Synod of Dort, with reference to which he wrote his "Golden Remains." His connection with the Synod gave a strong Arminian turn to his opinions, and, as he himself expressed it, he "bid "John Calvin good-night."

In February, 1619, John Hales returned from the Synod, and took up his residence in England; but his peculiar theological opinions rendered him obnoxious to Laud, who summoned him to a lengthened interview, in 1638, at Lambeth Palace, when, by mutual explanations, Laud and Hales became reconciled, so that a very short time afterwards the Archbishop, at a public dinner, presented Hales to a canonry at Windsor, into which he was installed June 27, 1639, though in 1642 he was ejected from the same. About the time of

Laud's

Laud's death, 1644, he retired from his rooms in Eton College, and took up his refidence in a private chamber in Eton, where he concealed himfelf for a quarter of a year, in order to preferve the College books and keys, of which he was Burfar. He lived upon bread and beer, and in his concealment was fo near the College, that he ufed to fay, "thofe who fearched "for him might have fmelt him if he "had eaten garlick." He refufed to take the Covenant, and was confequently regarded as a malignant, and ejected from his fellowfhip at Eton. There are many conflicting ftories about his poverty, and the dire neceffity in which he was compelled to fell, for £700, a part of his library to Cornelius Bee, a London bookfeller. This ftatement, however, obtains weight from the confirmation of Dr. Pearfon, who wrote the preface to "Golden Remains."

John

John Hales died May 19, 1656, and was buried in Eton College Chapel-yard, where a monument was erected to his memory by P. Curwen, Efq., and in 1765 an edition of his works was publifhed, edited by Lord Hailes.

The following extracts from his will, taken from the Eton College Regifter, are interefting :—

"I, JOHN HALES, of Eton, &c. &c., do dispose "of the small remainder of my poor and broken "estate in manner and form following:—1st. I "give to my sister, CICELY COMBES, £5. . . . . "Moreover all my Greek and Latin books I give "to my most deservedly beloved friend, William "Salter of Richkings, Esq. . . . . All my English "books, together with the remainder of all moneys, "goods, and utensils whatsoever, I give and be-"queathe to Mrs. Hannah Dickenson of Eton, "widow, relict of John Dickenson, lately deceased. "In whose house . . . I have for a long time been "with great care and good respect entertained—"and her I do by these presents constitute and or-"dain my sole executrix. . . . . As for my funeral, "I ordain that at the time of the next Evensong "after my departure my body be laid in the

"Church-yard

" Church-yard of the Town of Eton, . . . in plain
" and simple manner, without any Sermon, or
" ringing of the Bell, or calling of the people
" together, without any unseasonable commessa-
" tion or compotation, . . . for as in my life I have
" done the Church no service, so I will not that in
" my death the Church do me any honour."

It will be obſerved in the above detailed facts, that John Hales had taken his degree at Corpus Chriſti College thirteen years before Shakeſpere died, and that he was a Fellow of Eton three years prior to that event. Alſo, that — doubtleſs owing to the family connection with Snitterfield—Cicely Hales, his ſiſter, had married into the family of Combe; and laſtly, that John Hales's younger brother was named Anthony Hales (C). When we come to put all theſe facts together, there can be little doubt as to the origin of John Hales's peculiarly ſtrong intereſt in Shakeſpere; and the ink-printed name A. HALES, on the edges of the leaves of the

the copy of Montaigne, gives additional value to that already moſt valuable volume; becauſe we gather from that name, and from the ſcholarly comments and notes in the book, that John Hales, after Shakeſpere's death, had poſſeſſion of this work,—had annotated it with his own erudition,—and that from him the book paſſed to the poſſeſſion of his brother Anthony! It appears to the author that this circumſtantial evidence is as convincing as any ſuch evidence can be, ſhort of a poſitive entry on the fly-leaf to that effect. That the book ſhould have remained in families connected with Warwickſhire, is moſt natural; and that it ſhould belong to a clergyman in the ſame neighbourhood in 1780, is preciſely what we ſhould expect. Let it be remembered that Mr. Patteſon exhibited the book to his friends as bearing the Poet's ſignature for no mercenary purpoſe, and with

with no view of making a ſale of it. He valued it as it deſerved, and ſacredly preſerved it. His ſon was induced to part with it to the Britiſh Muſeum, becauſe it was urged on him that ſuch a book ought to be depoſited in the National library.

The reader, and particularly the antiquary, will pardon this lengthened diverſion regarding the "ever-memorable "John" and his family; for, believing, as the author does, that the name A. HALES has enticed him into a reſearch which he would otherwiſe have overlooked, ſo he believes it has furniſhed additional evidence in ſupport of Sir Frederick Madden's paper, and—if ſuch were needed—confirmed the authenticity of the autograph in the only remaining book that belonged to the Poet.

Until faith can be driven by overpowering proofs into the wildeſt infidelity, let

let us cling to the belief that the autograph is genuine, and that this volume did belong to our Shakeſpere. Should that laſt plank, which floats us over the gulf of ſeparation that has gone on widening for more than three hundred years, ever drift away, and leave us utterly cut aſunder from the domeſtic life of the man, we ſhall ſtill have, in two of the Palatial Halls of England, monuments that muſt be for ever aſſociated with the genius and glory of the High Prieſt of literature.

A mile away from the Hall in which Shakeſpere charmed his King and the Court, is the Villa to which one of his chief interpreters, David Garrick, retired, after leaving his profeſſion. It is now faſt approaching a century ſince he too ſhuffled off this mortal coil! Half a century after Shakeſpere's death, all the tangible aſſociations connected with him ſeem to have periſhed, or to have been removed from

from Stratford! Not ſo at Garrick's Villa, when a whole century is well-nigh complete ſince his death. His Villa, his garden, his river-ſide pleaſure-grounds, his temple erected to Shakeſpere, remain as he left them. There is the lawn ſkirting the Thames, overhung with noble trees, which Garrick ſhowed with delight to Dr. Johnſon, and received from the Doctor, as he ſurveyed the beauty of the ſcene, the moraliſing rejoinder, "Ah, David, theſe are the "things that make Death terrible!"* There is the tunnel under the road, ſuggeſted by the Doctor;—"Well, David, "if you cannot get over the road, "try and get under it." There is the drawing-room with the Chineſe-patterned

* This anecdote was told me by the Rev. Edward Phillips, of Surbiton, to whoſe family Garrick's Villa now belongs. The ſtory is aſſociated with the place, and is poſſibly now publiſhed for the firſt time.

terned papering, the palm-tree faſhioned fireplaces, the chairs and ſofas, exactly as he left them. There is his bedroom, with its preſſes, its furniture, its bed, and chintz hangings, ſo long delayed in paſſing the Cuſtoms, that David aſſured his Majeſty's officers Mrs. Garrick was breaking her heart over their delay. Could Garrick return to Hampton and re-viſit his home to-morrow, he would find it, its furniture and appointments, as if he had only left it yeſterday. The reverential ſpirit in which this Villa has been preſerved, and the furniture of Garrick's drawing-room and bedroom reſpected, is above all praiſe. In the lapſe of time, through whatever hands the property may paſs, let us hope that centuries to come will find theſe chambers exactly as they are now, at the cloſe of the firſt century ſince the great tragedian's death. But how painful is the contraſt between

between the confervative action exhibited at Hampton, and the deplorable, nay, wicked, neglect, which prevailed at Stratford!

A volume of fuch intereft and importance as Montaigne's "Effays," publifhed in 1603, is precifely the fort of work which we fhould expect to find on Shakefpere's bookfhelf. Florio's tranflation recommends itfelf *becaufe it is a tranflation*, fince it has been fatisfactorily proved to us that Shakefpere's knowledge was largely, if not entirely, gathered from tranflations of Claffical, French, and Italian authors; and, moreover,—the character of Montaigne's mind being peculiarly calculated to intereft Shakefpere,—had the volume in queftion bearing his autograph not exifted, it might with fome confidence be argued that a tranflation of fuch a famous author, publifhed about 1603, by a near relative of Ben Jonfon's, with whom

whom Shakespere was probably personally familiar, would be precisely the sort of book of which the Poet would possess himself, and in which we should expect to find his autograph. Let a catalogue of all the books published in or about that date be placed before any one familiar with Shakespere's cast of mind, and it may be asserted, without fear of contradiction, that were he about to make a purchase out of the lot, one of the first he would select would be Montaigne.

Here, at the threshold, our curiosity to learn something of the favourite books which the Poet may have had about him is cut short. We know nothing of the sources of his learning beyond such internal evidence as his plays and poems afford. If they carry us over the threshold, they take us no further. They favour us with no glimpse of the sanctum—

tum—of the reading-ſtand, the work-table, the inkhorn, or the book-preſs. What early advantages Shakeſpere poſſeſſed—whether from the ſchool "i' the "church," or other ſources—continue a profound myſtery up to this time; though there yet remain quarters for inquiry where ſome information might be gathered. The earlieſt reliable evidence of Shakeſpere's being in London dates in 1589, when he was twenty-five years of age. It is poſſible he may have been connected with London for a year or two previouſly, but certainly not longer. Until he was twenty-three or four he reſided at Stratford; and this fact ſupports the opinion that it was in Stratford the whole groundwork of his knowledge was obtained, as it was in Stratford, in later life, that the greateſt achievements of his genius were accompliſhed. Imagination alone can aid us to picture him at

New

New Place when he was comparatively wealthy, able to purchase property and tythes in Old Stratford, Welcombe, and Bishopton, and to carry on profitable transactions in corn or wool. In his home he had but one child, Judith, who remained unmarried until the year previous to his death! Poor Hamnet, her twin-brother, died the year before they moved into New Place! Mrs. Shakespere and this daughter were his constant companions. His other daughter and her husband, Dr. Hall, lived hard by, and had made a grandfather of him when he was only forty-four years of age. A grandfather! when many Englishmen, as Johnson expressed it, "having frisked "with the dogs," are only beginning to think about marriage, now-a-days!

The glimpses we catch of him as he passed along the last stage of his life are very few, and scarcely take us into his home.

THE ANCIENT CHALICE AND PATEN OF BISHOPTON,

From which SHAKESPERE *is said to have received the Holy Communion.*

(It will be observed that the lid of the Chalice, when inverted, forms the Paten, upon the top of which is engraved the date, 1571).

Face p. 262.

home. Buſineſs tranſactions connected with his purchaſes at Stratford or in London; the poſſeſſion of corn; a viſit to London in 1614 to oppoſe the encloſure of lands at Stratford,—theſe and a few other facts of a like character are all the information regarding him that has reached us. There is infinitely more ſatisfaction in muſing over a couple of lines in Rowe's Life, becauſe their ſtatement depends upon Betterton's inquiries, made at Stratford a few years after Shakeſpere's death. He ſpent his later days "in eaſe, retirement, "and the converſation of his friends."

The words may be applied to the laſt years both of Shakeſpere and of Milton. In retirement and (poor though Milton was) at eaſe, and enjoying the converſation of their friends, their countrymen muſt love to contemplate England's moſt illuſtrious ſons—the Epic and Dramatic Laureates of the Saxon tongue. Of the domeſtic

domeſtic ſcene at Bunhill Fields we know enough to be enabled to picture it. We even know that Milton enjoyed his evening pipe while joining in the fireſide talk. We know his daily habits; his hours of ſtudy; his writings in London and at Chalfont. It is poſſible that Milton, in that year 1614, when Shakeſpere was in town, may have ſeen him paſs down Bread Street, Cheapſide, to the "Mer-"maid Tavern," — that patriarch of London Clubs—there to enjoy a ſtoup of liquor and a jeſt with rare Ben Jonſon. And yet, while a maſs of the moſt intereſting information exiſts regarding the life of the younger of theſe poets, who were actually contemporaneous, nothing ſurvives to admit us into the home and ſociety of him who Milton calls "our "wonder and aſtoniſhment"—

"Dear ſon of memory, great heir of fame,"

There are two circumſtances connected with

with his laſt days at New Place with which we are acquainted. "In perfect "health and memory, God be praiſed," he had his Will drafted 25th January, 1616. February 10th, his daughter Judith married Thomas Quiney. We are led to conclude that the Will was probably drawn up in January with reference to his daughter's marriage; and that ſubſequent to the wedding, Shakeſpere was ſeized with ſome ſudden illneſs, which led to the execution of the Will on the 25th day of March. Theſe few facts, occurring in the firſt three months of the year 1616, conſtitute the entire knowledge we poſſeſs of the cloſing days of Shakeſpere's life. Forty years after his death, the then vicar of Stratford, Mr. Ward, jotted down ſome of the ſtories current in the place regarding the Poet. Among others, he ſtated, "Shakeſpear, Drayton, and Ben Jhonſon "had

" had a merry meeting, and, itt ſeems, " drank too hard, for Skakeſpear died of " a feavour there contracted."

When we remember that Shakeſpere died in the prime of life, and that he was in perfect health and memory twelve weeks prior to his deceaſe, it ſeems likely enough that fever was the cauſe of death. The wedding of Judith would perfectly account for Ben Jonſon and Drayton being his companions at Stratford at ſuch a time, though no evidence has as yet been produced to prove Jonſon's whereabout at that date. The ſtory of drinking too hard is ſuſceptible of explanation in the ſame way; and it is eaſy to be underſtood how the conviviality of a wedding party at New Place would be converted, on the tongues of goſſips, into "hard " drinking at a merry meeting." Village ſtories and traditions, as it has been already admitted, are worthy of conſideration

ſideration, but not of truſt. They are ſeldom abſolutely true in themſelves, and yet they almoſt always direct the hiſtoric inquirer in the right direction to arrive at truth. Traditions are like photographs —diſtorting the prominent features of the ſubjects they repreſent. Accepting the reverend vicar's ſtory as a Stratford tradition, told him in the rough-and-ready phraſeology of the place, and tranſlating the meaning of "hard drinking" into the joyous feſtivity which would be naturally obſerved at ſuch a period as the wedding of the Poet's daughter, when friends like Ben Jonſon and Drayton were gathered around the board of their old companion, to drink to the health and happineſs of the bride and bridegroom,—we have a domeſtic picture preſented to us of the laſt days of Shakeſpere, as happy in itſelf as it is probable from its conſonance with his character.

Though

Though the picture is the bareſt ſketch, yet its touches are true to nature; and all, ſave one, we know to be true in fact. That one, (the coarſeneſs of its colouring toned down), harmoniſes well with the reſt, and gives completeneſs to the outlines. Let fancy fill in the canvas, and the autumn days of the Poet's life be painted in the golden tints of nature's own autumn time, in which ſunnineſs and ſadneſs ſo myſteriouſly blend. Pleaſant it is to think that the happineſs of New Place was not ſhadowed by any tedious or agoniſing ſickneſs. There was no lingering diſeaſe, no protracted pain. "In perfect health "and memory, God be praiſed," our Shakeſpere lived until his fifty-ſecond year. He enjoyed his Merry Chriſtmas, and the converſation of his friends. Then came the preparations for the wedding. New Place was all alive. Mrs. Shakeſpere's ſecond-beſt bed, like enough, was aired

aired and made up for the arrival from town of Ben Jonſon. Shakeſpere thought the time befitted that he ſhould make his Will, which was accordingly drafted. The great garden was neatly trimmed, no doubt, and the borders of ſnowdrops and crocuſes fringed the beds about the mulberry tree. The wedding-day arrived. Parſon Rogers, the vicar, appeared in his beſt caſſock, bands, and tippet; and robed in clean white linen ſurplice, leaned against the tomb of John à Combe, book in hand, until the wedding party came. Coaches in Stratford were unknown; but

"*Slowly—stately—two by two,*"

the train of relatives and friends proceeded from New Place to the church. The merry marriage-bells rang out their welcome, and William Shakeſpere, leading Judith through troops of friends, preſented

presented her at the altar to the vicar, and gave the woman to the man.

There were no signatures of witnesses to the ceremony necessary, else had we seen, perchance, Shakespere's and Rare Ben's upon the same page of the Register.

The ceremony over, and the vicar unrobed, the whole party left the church. It was the last time Shakespere entered it alive, and the last time he left it! The wedding of his child brought him there that day: about nine weeks afterwards his children attended in the same place at his funeral! But on that marriage morn none dreamt of, or anticipated, the impending loss which not New Place only, or Stratford, but England and her literature, were to suffer. The marriage tables were spread; the cakes and ale were plentiful; and Parson Rogers, garnishing his periods with Latinity, after the fashion of his day, told how one of old time, in a little

little town of Galilee, had bleſſed with His preſence that marriage-feaſt at which the "water ſaw its Lord, and bluſhed!"

> "*Meanwhile the day ſinks faſt, the ſun is ſet,*
> *And in the lighted hall the gueſts are met;*
> *The beautiful looked lovelier in the light*
> *Of love, and admiration, and delight.*"

It was a merry, happy evening in Stratford! No doubt the Haieſes, and the Quineys, the Hathaways, "my Couſin "Green," Thomas Combe, and all the lads and laſſes of the varied Shakeſpere connection, as far as Warwick, had collected at New Place to celebrate the wedding,—to "dance and eat plums;" to be merry with the "round" and "wooing dance," and to trip it lightly to the ſtirring notes of "John, come kiſs "me now!" Subſtituting Ben Jonſon for "Couſin Capulet," the Poet's own words beſt ſerve our purpoſe to imagine the ſcene:—

"*Welcome,*

"Welcome, gentlemen! ladies that have their toes
Unplagued with corns will have a bout with you:—
Ah ah, my mistresses! which of you all
Will now deny to dance? . . . .
I have seen the day
That I . . . . could tell
A whispering tale in a fair lady's ear,
Such as would please!—'tis gone, 'tis gone, 'tis gone.
. . . . Come, musicians, play.
A hall! a hall! give room, and foot it, girls.
More light, ye knaves! and turn the tables up,
And quench the fire, the room is grown too hot.—
Nay, sit, nay, sit, good Cousin Capulet,
For you and I are past our dancing days!"

So, while they went on with the dance, and joy was unconfined, we can imagine these *patres conscripti* of Stratford, gathering together in a knot, and the "natural wit" of Shakespere, goaded into point and brilliancy by Ben and Drayton, bursting forth into corruscations of fancy! Then the reminiscenses of London life, of Blackfriars and the Globe, would come up, and the experiences of these wits would astonish and delight their country friends. Shakespere could tell many an anecdote of kings and courts, of Whitehall and

and Hampton; and, perhaps, among the jovial pledges of the ſupper, Ben Jonſon might let ſlip ſomething about Gunpowder Plot. Such a "merry-meeting"—the celebration of his daughter's wedding-day—we have ſufficient reaſon for ſuppoſing, preſents us to Shakeſpere at New Place, in health and vigour, for the laſt time. A fever ſeized him. A few brief days of ſickneſs intervened. Gradually the ſtrength of the hale man ſuccumbed before the invading enemy. Neceſſity compelled the Will to be ſigned. Gloom poſſeſſed the lately happy, feſtive, houſe. At Chapel Street corner, with whiſpered words and ſolemn head-ſhaking, the friends of the dying man told their worſt fears. Then there was another gathering! In Holy Croſs, moſt like, the Church's prayers were heard for him who lay a-dying. By his bedſide Vicar Rogers would ſtand, calming the woes

woes of the living, and pointing to the hopes of the dying; while gradually—but painleſſly as fever does its work—the laſt enemy ſtole in among the group, and the windows of New Place were darkened, and the doors were ſhut, and the keepers of the houſe trembled, and the mourners went about the ſtreet, becauſe man goeth to his long home! "The "reſt is ſilence!"

As

As regards the identification of Shakeſpere's reſidence, there is a popular error. Many writers, and even ſome of the lateſt, aſſert that the Sir Hugh Clopton who ſucceeded to New Place in 1719, "repaired and beautified it, and built a "modern front to it."

This ſtatement is repeated in numerous works down to the preſent day. It is not a mere error; it is more than an error, for it is totally untrue. The evil reſulting from it is, that deſcribers of New Place, whoſe works are eſpecially read by viſitors to Stratford, have betrayed the public into a very undeſerved amount of regret for the deſtruction of the Rev. Francis Gaſtrell's houſe, in 1759; that being the houſe to which

which a "modern front" is reprefented to have been added; the original ftructure of Sir Hugh Clopton being encafed within it, juft as the monaftic Zion Houfe is enclofed within that ponderous ducal pile on the banks of the Thames, which looks like a "Union" outfide, and is decorated as an Italian Villa infide. Thoufands of perfons have mourned Mr. Gaftrell's deftructivenefs, caring nothing for the "modern front," but grieving over the antique interior, where Shake-fpere was fuppofed to have lived and died.

It is defirable that the public fhould be fet right concerning this miftake, and underftand, that, about the year 1720, one Sir Hugh Clopton utterly demolifhed the fabric which another Sir Hugh Clopton, about the year 1490, had erected. It was not a "modern front," but an entirely new houfe, which was erected about 1720; and it was this ftructure (of the

Dutch

New Place: *as it appeared when rebuilt, circa* 1720.

This is the house in which Garrick was entertained, and which was destroyed by Gastrell.

(AN EXACT COPY FROM THE ORIGINAL DRAWING.)

Face p. 277.

Dutch William or Queen Anne's ſtyle of building) which, devoid of all hiſtorical aſſociation, the ruthleſs Gaſtrell razed to the ground.*

Repreſentations of this houſe are extant. They only need to be examined, and the eye learns inſtantly that a complete rebuilding, and not a "modern "fronting," muſt have occurred in or about 1720.

Upon the ground-floor the hall door occupied the centre, flanked right and left with three windows.

On the firſt-floor a row of ſeven windows were diſplayed, the central one opening into a ſmall balcony. The three centre windows and the doorway, ſlightly projecting, were ſurmounted by a pediment, containing the creſt and motto of the Cloptons, "*Loyavte Mon. Honnevr,*" in the tympanum.

The

* Appendix K.

The middle of the roof was occupied with a ſquare platform, ſurrounded by a wooden baluſtrade, as frequently ſeen in houſes of the period. Ruſticated ſtone-work, in long and ſhort blocks, ornamented the corners of the houſe, and a projecting Claſſic cornice, with dentile decoration, gave a finiſh to the roof. On the oppoſite page this houſe is repreſented. In it Mr. Garrick and his friends were entertained at the time of the Jubilee, in 1769.

It was what auctioneers call a ſubſtantial family manſion, very ſquare, very flat, very red, and in its flat-topped roof, with wooden baluſtrades, cloſely related to the ſtyle of ſtructures delighted in by the King of pious and immortal memory.

About Kenſington, Chiſwick, and Hammerſmith, any number of "ſuitable "reſidences," built at the ſame date, may be ſeen, generally conſpicuous as Colle-giate

giate ſchools, or Claſſical and Commercial academies.

However ponderous, raw, and ſelf-aſſerting the architecture of that period may be, let it be confeſſed that it is infinitely grander, more ſtately, and more *real* than that pretentious ſtyle now prevalent in London, in which "whatever is, "is not," and a muddy ſtucco is ſalved over the carcaſes of houſes to make them look what they are not—ſubſtantial.

The name of the Rev. Francis Gaſtrell was execrated in Stratford. He committed great offences againſt the town. This perſon appears to have been the ſon of Dr. Gaſtrell, Biſhop of Cheſter, and to have held the living of Frodſham, in the dioceſe of Cheſter.

He married Jane, the daughter of Sir Thomas Aſton, Bart., whoſe family was ſeated at Aſton, in Cheſhire. At Stow Houſe, Stow, a ſuburb of Lichfield, about half

half a mile to the eaſt of the Cathedral, lived Elizabeth Aſton, ſiſter to Mrs. Gaſtrell, and, as is uſual with ſpinſters when arrived at a mature age, commonly deſignated "Mrs. Aſton."

Subſequently to the Rev. F. Gaſtrell's death, his widow lived on Stow Hill, in a houſe adjoining her ſiſter's.

Letters addreſſed by Dr. Johnſon to this lady are given in Boſwell's Life, as alſo ſeveral to Mrs. Aſton. With both theſe ladies Johnſon had been intimately acquainted from his earlieſt years; and the intimacy continued until the day of his death. The following paragraphs from one of his letters will give the reader ſufficient evidence of the terms on which Johnſon lived with theſe friends:—

"Bolt Court, Fleet Street,
"*January* 2, 1779.

"Dear Madam,

"Now the New Year is come, of which I wiſh you "and dear Mrs. Gaſtrell many and many returns, it is "fit that I give you ſome account of the paſt year.

"In

" In the beginning of it I had a difficulty of breathing, " and other illneſs, from which, however, I by degrees " recovered, and from which I am now tolerably free. . . " But the other day Mr. Prujean called and left word " that you, dear madam, are grown better; and I know " not when I heard anything that pleaſed me ſo much. " I ſhall now long more and more to ſee Lichfield, and " partake the happineſs of your recovery. Now you " begin to mend, you have great encouragement to take " care of yourſelf.

" Do not omit anything that can conduce to your " health, and when I come I ſhall hope to enjoy with " you and deareſt Mrs. Gaſtrell many pleaſing hours.

" Do not be angry at my long omiſſion to write," &c. &c. &c.

" Madam,
" Your moſt humble ſervant,
" SAM. JOHNSON."

There is an old man, by name Mr. Thomas Barnes, now living in Bird Street, Lichfield, who has entered his ninety-firſt year. He was born at Chorley, near Lichfield, the firſt week in February, 1772. He was brought up a wig-maker, and may be ſaid to have followed his trade up to the preſent time. Mr. Barnes is in the enjoyment of all his faculties, able to garden, and while gardening to recur with the greateſt clearneſs of memory

memory to the events of his early life. He is perhaps the only perſon living who can ſay that he remembers Dr. Johnſon. Mr. Barnes informed the author that he clearly recollects Mrs. Aſton and Mrs. Gaſtrell living at Stow; and that he remembers ſeeing the Doctor walking with theſe ladies in Boar Street, Lichfield, oppoſite the Town Hall. Mr. Barnes was alſo well acquainted with Mr. Peter Garrick, brother of the tragedian, whoſe houſe was ſituate in Lichfield, on the ſite now occupied by the newly-erected Literary Inſtitution and Probate Office.

Mr. Barnes had no perſonal acquaintance with Doctor Johnſon or his female friends, Mrs. Aſton and Mrs. Gaſtrell, for whom, it is beyond queſtion, the Doctor entertained the warmeſt and moſt ſincere friendlineſs of feeling.

In glancing round the walls of Lichfield Cathedral, on the north ſide of the great

great weſt door in the nave, and above the door of the ſouthern tranſept, there ſtill ſtand tablets to the memory of Mrs. Aſton and Mrs. Gaſtrell. "Still," becauſe it would be well, for the ſake of the architecture, if thoſe unſightly and unharmonious lumps of maſonry had been removed, in the late elaborate reſtorations at Lichfield, to ſome leſs conſpicuous poſitions. Lichfield Cathedral, as it now appears, will be contemplated for generations to come as a monument whereby to recall the Epiſcopate of Dr. Lonſdale. The lover of church architecture will ponder over and revel in the regenerated lovelineſs of that exquiſite gem of art; and in admiration of the ſpirit and munificence with which the clergy and gentry of the dioceſe have gathered round their venerated Dioceſan, in carrying out the glorious work which has been accompliſhed, contraſt it painfully with ſome of

its

its fifter edifices, where Cathedral bodies are much richer, and far more able, but apparently much lefs willing, to encounter the facrifices neceffary for much-needed reftorations. To wit—look at Durham, a Golden See! That monarch of all Norman piles is ftill disfigured with filthy white-wafh and yellow-wafh. The condition of its nave is a difgrace to any Cathedral chapter; and, as if to prove that ecclefiaftical barbarians ftill furvive, thofe ftupendous pillars—the glory of the Palatinate—have very lately been outraged by having gliftening lead gas-pipes nailed to their fides, furmounted with fittings and fhades of the commoneft and moft vulgar defcription!

As it will be neceffary to fay a few words refpecting Mrs. Gaftrell with regard to the deftruction of the mulberry-tree, it may be the moft chivalric if we anticipate her blame by founding her praife, praiſe, and adminiſter the antidote before the bane. The following inſcription on her monument in Lichfield Cathedral is a grandioſe ſpecimen of teſtamentary gratitude:—

"J. G. died October 30, 1791, aged 81.

"Sacred to the memory of Jane, daughter of Sir "Thomas Aſton, of Aſton, Baronet, and widow of the "Rev. Francis Gaſtrell, Clerk, who, to the laſt moments "of her life, was conſtantly employed in acts of ſecret "and extenſive charity, and on her death bequeathed "to numerous benevolent inſtitutions a conſiderable "portion of her property. This monument was erected "by her five nephews and three nieces, who partook "equally and amply of her bounty.

"*Let not thy alms, the holy* JESUS *cried,*
Be ſeen of men, or dealt with conſcious pride;
So ſhall the LORD, *whoſe eye pervades the breaſt,*
For thee unfold the manſions of the bleſt.

"*O'er her whoſe life this precept held in view,*
A friend to want, when each falſe friend withdrew;
May theſe chaſte lines, to genuine worth aſſign'd,
Pour the full tribute of a grateful mind.

"*Sweet as at noontide's ſultry beam, the ſhower,*
That ſteals refreſhing o'er the wither'd flower,
Her ſilent aid, by ſoothing pity giv'n,
Sank through the heart, the dew of gracious heaven,

"*Deeds ſuch as theſe, pure ſhade, ſhall ever bloom,*
Shall live through time and glow beyond the tomb.
Through thee, the orphan owes parental care,
Bends the glad knee, and breathes the frequent prayer;
Through

Through thee the debtor, from despondence fled,
Clasps his fond babes, and hails his native shed;
Through thee, the slave, unbound his massive chain,
Shouts with new joy, and lives a man again;
Through thee, the savage on a distant shore
His SAVIOUR *hears, and droops with doubt no more.*

" O thou who lingering here, shalt heave the sigh,
The warm tear trembling on thy pensive eye,
Go, and the couch of hopeless sorrow tend,
The poor man's guardian, and the widow's friend;
Go, and the path which ASTON *lately trod,*
Shall guide thy footsteps to the throne of GOD."

The Rev. Francis Gastrell appears to have had a great desire to acquire property in, and also about, Stratford. It does not seem that he intended to make New Place a permanent residence, but merely a temporary retreat for pleasure and repose. In his garden stood "Shakespere's "Mulberry-tree," which all visitors to Stratford were curious to see and sit under. Mr. Gastrell's temper was sorely tried by the perpetual invasions of these visitors, and in his spleen he sent forth the fiat to cut it down—"with Gothic bar-"barity," as Boswell remarks. Dr. Johnson

ſon told him Mr. Gaſtrell did ſo "to vex "his neighbours." Boſwell adds, "His "lady, I have reaſon to believe, *on the* "*ſame authority*, participated in the guilt "of what the enthuſiaſts of our immortal "bard deem almoſt a ſpecies of ſacrilege." This ſacrilege took place in 1756, only three years after Gaſtrell became poſſeſſor of New Place.

The wood of the mulberry-tree was purchaſed by Thomas Sharp, of Stratford, watch and clock maker, who manufactured it into boxes, goblets, and a variety of articles for ſale. Twelve rings made out of the wood were manufactured for the Jubilee, 1769. A few valuable mementoes ſtill remain, highly prized, and carefully treaſured.

Among theſe, the Shakeſpere chair now in the poſſeſſion of Miſs Burdett Coutts, and purchaſed by her for £300, is the moſt valuable. The medallion on the back

back of this chair was carved by William Hogarth.

There is the mulberry cup, which was uſed by Mr. Garrick, and held in his hand when he ſang his own ſong at Stratford:

"Behold this ſair goblet, 'twas carved from the tree,
Which, O my ſweet Shakeſpere, was planted by thee!
As a relic I kiſs it, and bow at the ſhrine,
What comes from thy hand muſt be ever divine:
All ſhall yield to the mulberry-tree.
Bend to thee,
Bleſt mulberry:
Matchleſs was he,
Who planted thee,
And thou, like him, immortal be!"
*Etc. etc.**

W. O. Hunt, Eſq., Town-clerk of Stratford, poſſeſſes a drawing-room table made

* The following receipt for the ſale of mulberry-tree wood to Garrick is intereſting:—

"*9th July*, 1762.

"Received of David Garrick, Esq., by the hands "of Lieutenant Euſebius Silveſter, Two Guineas in "full for four pieces of Mull-berry tree, which, with "the other pieces of the ſame tree, I lately delivered "to the ſaid Mr. Silveſter for the uſe of the ſaid Mr. "Garrick, I do hereby warrant to be part of the "Mulberry

made of walnut, the top of which is beautifully inlaid with wood from the mulberry-tree. The device is unuſual, being formed by a ſeries of thin rounds, into which a branch of the tree muſt have been ſawn. A block of wood occupies the centre of the table, the rounds encircle it, and ſucceſſive circles continue being deſcribed, until they reach the exterior frame of walnut within which they are comprehended. The heart of the tree, and the varying rings of the wood, being ſeen in every round, a piece of furniture has been manufactured which is artiſtic as a ſpecimen of geometrical

"Mulberry Tree commonly called Shakeſpeare's tree:
"and ſaid to be planted by him; and lately cut down
"in the Rev. Mr. Gaſtrell's, late Sir Hugh Clopton's,
"garden, in Stratford-upon-Avon.

"*Witneſs my hand*—GEO. WILLES.

"*Witneſs hereto*—
Wm. Hunt, *Attorney in Stratford.*
John Payton, *Maſter of the White Lion there.*"

trical cabinet-making, and invaluable in its hiſtorical aſſociations. This table belongs to a gentleman who beſt deſerves to poſſeſs it, both on account of the unflagging enthuſiaſm he has exhibited in everything that has reference to Shakeſpere (eſpecially of late in ſecuring New Place to the public); and alſo on account of the urbanity he has ſhown viſitors to Stratford, who have had the honour of being introduced to him.

In 1759 what was thought a greater, but was in reality a minor offence, was committed. Being compelled to pay the aſſeſſment for the poor at Stratford, as well as at Lichfield, his fixed reſidence, Gaſtrell vowed that New Place ſhould never be aſſeſſed again, and pulled it down.

This has been regarded as an unpardonable crime. It was not ſo in reality, becauſe the houſe had no connection with the Poet, as has been ſhown. There can

be

be little doubt that had Homer, Dante, Taſſo, and Shakeſpere all lived in that ſelfsame houſe it would have mattered nothing to the Rev. Mr. Gaſtrell. He would have deſtroyed it, whatever had been its aſſociations.

Even among clergymen, particularly the perverſe and obſtinate, paſſion often dominates veneration.

The Rev. Francis Gaſtrell's diſpoſition is a ſtudy; but it is one which cannot be now purſued. It may be allowable, however, to hint, that inquiry may juſtify Johnſon's communication to Boſwell. Mrs. Gaſtrell poſſibly did more than "participate in the guilt;" and in the murder done upon the mulberry-tree it may hereafter appear that ſhe was the Lady Macbeth, inſtigating the reverend Thane to deeds of "Gothic barbarity."

A Diary written in Scotland by Mr. Gaſtrell has lately been preſented (among other

other gifts) to the embryo, "Stratford "Musuem." Hereafter the public will have accefs to this hitherto private MS. It tells nothing of Stratford; but being a diary, it reveals fomething of the ftyle of thought of the man. A very commonplace and unpoetic ftyle of thought it is, but harmonious with what we fhould conceive fuch a man would be. It may not be gallant to the fair fex, but neverthelefs fomething near the truth, to conjecture that Mr. Gaftrell has been abufed over much: that, as in all great crimes, fo in the mulberry-tree flaughter, "there was "a woman in it," aiding, abetting, and, as Johnfon fays, "participating in the "guilt." Malone, in writing to Dr. Davenport, of Stratford, May, 1788, quotes a letter received from a lady at Lichfield, who afferts that it was Mrs. Gaftrell, and not her hufband, who cut down the mulberry-tree. In the fame letter

letter, Malone's correſpondent gives him a hiſtory of Mrs. Gaſtrell's lateſt performance at Lichfield. Her houſe on Stow Hill had been let to a lady at the rental of £100. The lady had been very kind to the poor in the neighbourhood. Mrs. Gaſtrell having had ſome diſagreement with her tenant, took meaſures to turn her out, and *determined that the poor ſhould derive no benefit from that houſe again*, which ſhe reſolved ſhould remain empty. Malone's correſpondent, in great wrath, ſays, that Mrs. Gaſtrell is "little better "than a fiend."

In this report there is a coincidence that cannot eſcape obſervation. The ſame feeling which prompted the deſtruction of the houſe at Stratford, in order that it might never again be aſſeſſed for the relief of the poor, likewiſe prompted the cloſing of the houſe at Stow Hill, Lichfield, that the poor might derive no further

further aſſiſtance from thence. It is hardly poſſible to reſiſt the concluſion which the peculiarity of theſe circumſtances ſuggeſts; and deſpite Johnſon's friendly regard for Mrs. Gaſtrell, we muſt remember that it is from his own lips we hear of that lady's participation in her huſband's acts. She was undoubtedly a paſſionate and imperious woman; and if the whole truth were known, it ſeems very probable that the inſtigation to the act, if not the carrying it into execution, both in felling the tree and deſtroying the houſe, is attributable rather to Mrs., than to Mr., Gaſtrell.

It has been diſcovered that there was a Chancery Suit pending between Mr. Gaſtrell and the Corporation, ſtrengthening a ſuſpicion that hot blood was rouſed. The public at this moment knows little of the merits of the Gaſtrell caſe, or the amount of provocation under which

which that irrafcible divine fuffered. If all the charges againft him regarding the deftruction of the mulberry tree were proved, and he were found guilty as the real criminal, neverthelefs he cannot be found guilty, as he commonly has been, of deftroying Shakefpere's houfe,—fimply becaufe Shakefpere's houfe did not exift for him to deftroy.

From thefe facts above ground, we now defcend to difcoveries recently made below ground.

During the fpring of 1862, that portion of the garden of New Place fronting the main ftreet, Chapel Street, on the weft, and bounded by Chapel Lane on the fouth, was excavated to the extent of about fixty feet fquare. The workmen, having cleared away the foil ſoil and *débris* over this large ſpace to the depth of eight or ten feet, came upon a ſeries of foundations. Some very intereſting facts have been diſcovered. The leading and moſt manifeſt are, that two ſets of foundations exiſt. The one muſt be thoſe of the manſion built in the Georgian era, *circa* 1720; the other thoſe of Shakeſpere's own houſe—the "Great Houſe" which Sir Hugh built *circa* 1490, and in which both he and the Poet "lived and died." Upon this ſite there never have been more than the two houſes in queſtion. For the ſake of diſtinction, let theſe houſes be deſignated reſpectively, the "Great Houſe" and the "Clopton Houſe."

It is eaſy to diſtinguiſh the foundations of the one from the other, becauſe the lines of walls in the Clopton Houſe at certain points meet, and interſect the walls of the Great Houſe (eſpecially in the foundations

foundations abutting on Chapel Lane). Where they ſo meet and interſect, the Clopton foundations are *built over and acroſs* thoſe of the Great Houſe.

Again: the materials of the Great Houſe are for the moſt part ſtone, which ſuch foundations—built nearly 400 years ago—commonly were. The materials of the Clopton Houſe are red brick, and in many places the plaſter upon the walls of the offices in the baſement is ſtill perfect; and not only perfect, but ſhows the coloured outline of the ſtaircaſe, leading from the offices up to the firſt-floor, as clean and black as if it had been painted yeſterday.

Various evidences prove the date of this portion of the foundations.

Firſt. The bricks of which the party-walls are built have that bright red colour, and are ſet together with that peculiar cloſeneſs and ſharpneſs of edge, which

which particularly charaćterife the period of William, Anne, and George I.

Secondly. The condition of the plafter and painting fhows that they belong to a houfe which muft have been inhabited at a comparatively recent period.

Thirdly. The evidences of habitation revealed in the Clopton foundations prove that they were portions of Gaftrell's houfe, and verify the ftory of its fudden deftruction. The kitchen fire-place was found quite perfect, and the afh-pit filled with the cinders of the coals that may have cooked Mr. Gaftrell's dinner in Stratford the day before he demolifhed the houfe. A great variety of trifling domeftic evidences of this fort abound, fhowing that thefe "Clopton" foundations are the bafement ftory of a houfe of modern ufe, and that the houfe itfelf muft have been erected during the laft century.

Laft

Laſt of all, the ground above theſe foundations when dug out proved to be a *débris* of plaſter-of-Paris mouldings, cornices, and decorations belonging to the ſtyle of ornament commonly introduced in the houſes of the reigns of Anne and the firſt Georges. When the walls of the houſe were knocked down, this plaſter work was buried in the ruins; but it is now carefully arranged in an adjoining houſe for inſpection.

There cannot be a doubt about the foundations of the Clopton Houſe (1720) being identified.

From them we turn to the much ſmaller but far more intereſting remains of the Great Houſe.

It is evident that the Great Houſe was not reſtored with a "modern front," becauſe there are two diſtinct ground plans; and the Clopton Houſe foundations (as already ſtated) run aſkew to thoſe of of the Great Houſe, interſecting them at very acute angles. It is alſo evident that in laying the walls of the Clopton Houſe a great portion of the foundations of the Great Houſe were cleared away entirely, and that thoſe only were left untouched which there was no neceſſity to move. Conſequently the foundations of the Great Houſe in which Shakeſpere lived are comparatively ſmall in extent.

The following facts are illuſtrative :—

Firſt. In two ſeparate places Tudor mullions have been diſcovered, built into the Clopton foundations, ſhowing that ſome of the material of the Great Houſe was cleared out and uſed again in laying the external foundations of the modern one.

Secondly. In that portion of the Clopton foundations where the kitchens and offices ſtood, the ground exhibits no

traces

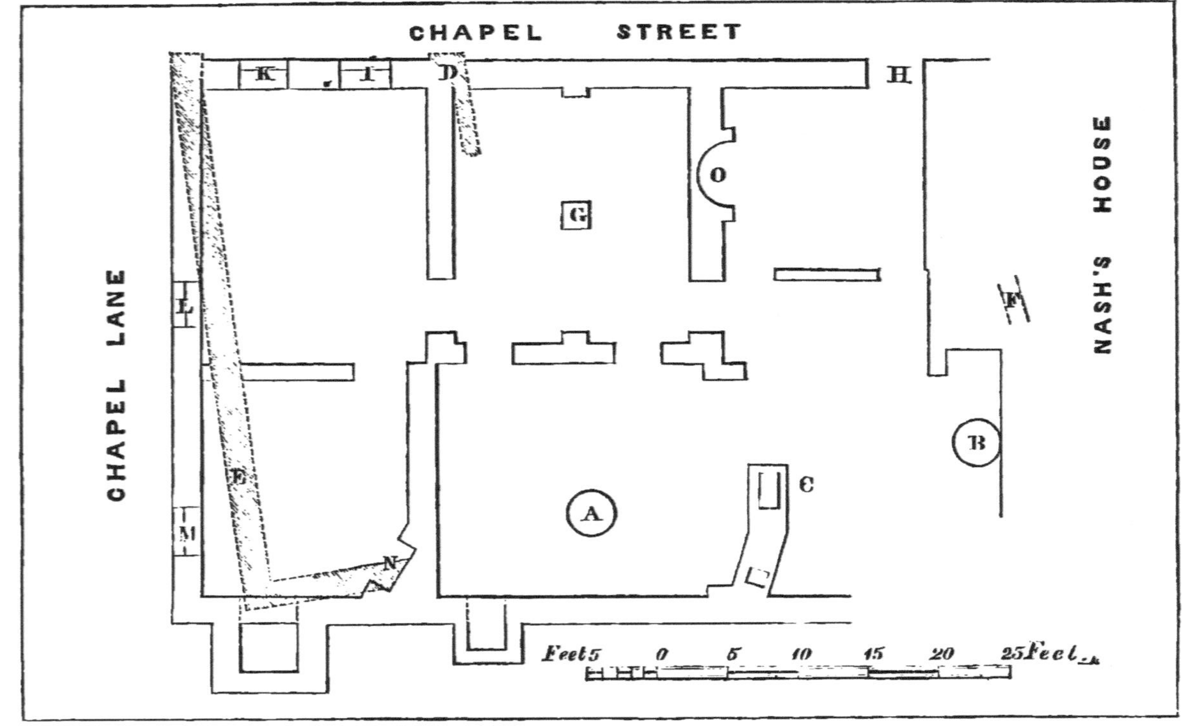
CHAPEL STREET
CHAPEL LANE
NASH'S HOUSE
K
I
D
H
O
G
L
F
B
E
C
A
M
N
Feet 5 0 5 10 15 20 25 Feet

KEY TO THE PLAN

OF THE

FOUNDATIONS: GREAT HOUSE AND CLOPTON HOUSE.

—o—

A. Ancient Well of the Great Houſe.

B. Well, lately diſcovered, which appears to have belonged to Naſh's Houſe.

C. Kitchen Fire-place.

D. Piece of projecting Ancient Wall, belonging to Shakeſpere's, *i.e.* the Great Houſe; conjectured to be the Foundation of the Entrance Porchway.

E. The External Wall of the Ancient Great Houſe, terminating in N, a Fire-place of the Clopton Houſe.

F. The Site of Naſh's Houſe: with Ancient Foundations.

G. The Crown of the Vaulting depoſited in one of the Offices.

H. The Poſition at which the Ancient Mullions have been built into the Clopton Foundations.

I, K, L, M. Cellar Windows in the Clopton Foundations.

N. Fire-place in one of the Offices of ditto.

O. Ditto.

traces of ancient walls, although it is almoſt certain that the Great Houſe entirely covered this ſite, ſince the frontage to Chapel Street, between Chapel Lane on the north, and Naſh's Houſe (the next plot of land on the ſouth, where a reſidence now ſtands, but which never belonged to New Place), is not more than ſixty feet in length.

Two apparent exceptions preſent themſelves, viz., a piece of ancient wall which, extending under the ſtreet, protrudes inwards into the main wall of the Clopton foundations; and a few feet removed from it, in one of the offices, there are the remains of the crown of a vaulting. Both theſe interlopers, looking ſtrangely out of place, are at firſt ſight a complete puzzle. Why they were ſuffered to abide where they now aſſert themſelves, and are undoubtedly in the way, is the natural conjecture.

The

The portion of wall that projects from the foundations (and outward, under the footpath of Chapel Street) is palpably, both from position and construction, part of the Great House, and may probably be one of the foundations of the porch-way or entrance of the Great House, which would necessarily require to be very strong, if above the porch (with its ponderous oak beams, and its elaborately carved arcades) there rose an overhanging chamber, with oriel window commanding the street. This is mere conjecture, which, though it seems probably correct, must be taken for what it appears worth.

The crown of the vaulting obtrusively thrusting itself into one of the Clopton offices would be a marvel and a mystery, supposing it to belong to the Great House; but, with all humility, it may be questioned whether it ever did! May it not, after all, be one (and the only

one)

one) maſs of vaulting, which did not break aſunder when that reverend Samſon pulled down a domeſtic Gaza about the ears of his enemies—the Philiſtines of Stratford? May not this conglomerate have quietly dropped from its vaulted eminence to the humble poſition on the floor which it now occupies, and (inſtantly covered in with lighter materials) have eſcaped being daſhed aſunder? This ſuppoſition, if it be correct, would ſolve a difficulty of which there has, as yet, been no ſatisfactory ſolution offered.

Aſſuming it to be true, the remains of Shakeſpere's Houſe would be the above-mentioned (porch) wall, and the main walls of the Great Houſe adjoining Chapel Lane, which the Clopton walls were built acroſs, and interſected, but which remain in their original ſolid condition. Theſe main walls are preſerved the entire depth of the houſe, commencing

cing from the frontage at the junction of Chapel Street and Chapel Lane, and running eastward along Chapel Lane. Having reached the extreme point to which foundations run in that direction (about forty-five feet in depth), they turn at a right angle northward, and continue about twenty feet, when they encounter a fire-place of the Clopton House, built over and upon them, in which they become lost, and are no farther traceable.

These, then, are the very walls of the very house in which William Shakespere lived and died. They are inconsiderable, it is true, but nevertheless far more extensive than any one could have dared to hope; for when we consider that two houses have occupied this site, and (as is evident) the foundations of the former were in a great measure cleared away in order to lay the foundations of the latter,—moreover, when we recall the

passionate

paſſionate vexation which cauſed the ſudden and total demolition of the latter, it is a matter of no ſmall ſatisfaction to diſcover *at leaſt ſixty feet* of the indiſputable and veritable foundations of the Great Houſe that Sir Hugh Clopton erected nearly four hundred years ago, ſurviving the ravages of time and the work of man's deſtructiveneſs, exhumed and once more brought to light in the middle of the nineteenth century; ſo that all who reverence the name and memory of the greateſt genius of the world, may identify, and, for themſelves, examine the walls of the houſe in which our Shakeſpere lived and died.

In the midſt of theſe foundations there has been ſimultaneouſly revealed an object of peculiar intereſt. It is "Shakeſpere's "Well"—the ancient well of New Place. When the labourers made the diſcovery in digging out the foundations, it was choked

choked with the *débris* of the Gaſtrell ruins. The well was cleared out, and its quoining ſtones were found to be as perfect as ever. On the 5th of Auguſt, 1862, another well, equally as ancient, and, if poſſible, in a better ſtate of preſervation as to its maſonry, was diſcovered in the embankment under Naſh's Houſe, at the extreme northern limit of the New Place plot. Two wells attached to the ſame houſe ſeem uſeleſs; and therefore it may be conjectured, that although this latter well is now within the boundaries of New Place, it may, at ſome diſtant period, have belonged to, and been encloſed in, the adjoining freehold, "Naſh's Houſe," which is now included in the New Place eſtate. On the morning after the clearance, Shakeſpere's well had filled with ſeveral feet of the pureſt and moſt delicious ſpring water. From the bountiful ſupply of this ſpring, every traveller can

now

now ſlake his thirſt, and drink of the ſame well from which the Poet drank.

In the courſe of the excavations a few articles have been dug up, of no particular intereſt or value.

At the bottom of the well, a peculiarly primitive flat-candleſtick, with long, ſtraight handle, and very ſmall ſtand for the candle, was found.

A bone-handled knife, with metal ornaments of an antique character.

A number of tobacco-pipe bowls of the time of Charles II.; the bowls very ſmall, and the clay impreſſed at the elbow with the name of the manufacturer, "Robt. Legg."

Figured tiles belonging to a pavement; glaſs; and various pieces of iron-work, much corroded.

Theſe, and a vaſt amount of ſmall articles of domeſtic uſe, have been found among the *debris*, which are all collected together

together at Naſh's Houſe for the antiquary's examination and diſcuſſion. Among them there may perchance be ſome trifling objects as ancient as the time of Shakeſpere; but it would be almoſt idle to hope that the riddling of the vaſt amount of earth which has been diſplaced will bring to light any objects of real value, or capable of being aſſociated with the Poet's tenancy of New Place.

All

All the boundaries of Shakeſpere's Garden—including the "Great Garden"—have been aſcertained, and proved by the title-deeds (nearly 100 in number) of the ſurrounding properties. The whole of this New Place eſtate is now purchaſed and ſecured to the public, with the exception of one plot occupied by a conventicle-like brick building, entitled "The "Theatre." This ſtructure has neither age, appearance, utility, nor aſſociation to recommend it to the public. The ſpot where it ſtands was never occupied by any former theatre; the building belongs to the preſent century. As a building it is to the laſt degree ugly, and might be miſtaken for a village Bethel or Ebenezer!

Ebenezer! It is an obſtruction and eye-ſore in Shakeſpere's Garden; added to which, to complete its condemnation, it is not a theatre at all! Having been converted into a ſort of lecture-hall or public room, it ſuits the purpoſes either of a Police Court or County Court in the morning, and of Ethiopian Serenaders, Conjurors, and Travelling Wonders at night!

The building belongs to ſhareholders, who are willing to ſell the property for £1,100. In due time it is to be hoped that this hideous fabric will be purchaſed and ſwept away, ſo that New Place may be reſtored to its former condition as a garden, and preſerved as ſuch for ever.

The name of a theatre in Shakeſpere's Garden, catches the ear, and ſuggeſts that it muſt be connected with the traditions of the place. It is apparent that this ſtructure has no claim to the antiquary's conſideration. There is but

one

one building in Stratford that is in any way aſſociated with the paſt—and that is a barn. A barn is ſtill pointed out in which Mrs. Siddons is ſaid to have performed in her youth. The tradition is probably true, becauſe not only was the company of her father, Roger Kemble, accuſtomed to perform in Warwickſhire, but her grandfather, Mr. Ward, was in the habit of acting at Stratford. On the 9th September, 1746, this gentleman gave a benefit performance in the (then) Town Hall, in order to procure funds for repainting the buſt of Shakeſpere on the monument in the church, and reſtoring the original colours. The play enacted was *Othello*, accompanied with a Prologue written for the occaſion by the Rev. Joſeph Greene. Through Ward, a diſtinguiſhed man of the preſent generation was connected with a remote dramatic era: the late Charles Kemble, with

with whoſe perſon and performances thouſands ſtill among us were familiar, was Ward's grandſon; and the grandfather was an actor in the days of Betterton. At one of his benefits in Dublin, the celebrated Peg Woffington made her firſt appearance, according to the ſtatement in Boaden's "Life of Kemble," though his ſtatement "errs in particu-"larity;" for while it fixes the date as April 25th, 1760, the records of the quiet little church at Teddington tell us that on the 3rd of that month, in that ſame year, Peg Woffington had left life's ſtage for ever, and was interred on that day, aged 42. The miſtake made by Boaden aroſe from his confuſing the year of Woffington's death with the year of her firſt appearing for the benefit of Charles Kemble's grandfather. The hall in which Ward produced *Othello*, for the purpoſe of reſtoring the monument at Stratford

Stratford, no longer exiſts ; ſo that the barn which is aſſociated with the name of Mrs. Siddons, ſeems to be the ſole remaining building in the town within which the plays of the Poet were repreſented in the days that are gone and the years that are fled.

At the commencement of this work it was contended that as great a veneration is felt for Shakeſpere by the preſent generation as by any that preceded it. It muſt, at the ſame time, be admitted that the age is eminently practical. With a revived and increaſingly ſpreading taſte for the Beautiful, the men of the Iron age demand that the Beautiful ſhall be combined with the Uſeful. Engliſhmen are ever ready to give their money in honour of a great name; but they ſtipulate that it ſhall not be waſted on uſeleſs

uſeleſs architecture or unprofitable objects. It has been the purpoſe of this work to ſhow what uſe has been made of the money already provided by the public. New Place in its integrity has been ſecured. Shakeſpere's Garden is beyond any riſks from future ſales. The ſite of the Great Houſe has been diſcovered. The few remains of foundations have been brought to light. The garden, as yet in a diſturbed ſtate, will preſently be cleared and reſtored to its former uſe. Once again, and for ever, it will be Shakeſpere's Garden.

In this, a good work has been accompliſhed. Much is done; but much remains to do. To complete the work well begun, public aid will be neceſſary, and for that aid the public muſt be ſought. It might be well if thoſe who were concerned in the various purchaſes of New Place, and have examined all the titles and records connected with it, were to give to the world a detailed hiſtory of them, accompanied by the fulleſt plans and illuſtrations of the property as it exiſted when put into truſt in 1861. Hereafter ſuch a work, which this ſmall volume makes no preſumptuous pretence of undertaking, would be of the higheſt value. There are very few men among us competent to perform it; but among the few, Mr. Halliwell has had rare advantages in his connection with the purchaſes of New Place, which no one elſe has enjoyed. To him the public ſeem to have a right to look for that fair and faithful hiſtory—that compilation of the facts regarding New Place, which have hitherto been obſcure or unknown, but muſt now be beſt known to him.

The object with which theſe pages have been written, will be fully accompliſhed if they ſucceed in attracting public notice to the good work ſo far done, and in ſtimulating

lating the aid which is neceſſary to complete the full redemption of the Poet's property. New Place muſt for ever be aſſociated with the memory of Shakeſpere; and the mere ſight of foundation walls belonging to the houſe in which he lived and died, cannot fail to excite the deepeſt intereſt in the minds of all who are attracted to the ſpot by hearing of the recent diſcoveries. But intereſt having been excited, and curioſity having been gratified, a practical purpoſe will be required, ſooner or later, to ſupport the ſentiment, under the influence of which, Shakeſpere's countrymen have purchaſed his garden. We are often aſſured that "opportunity is everything." If not everything, it is unqueſtionably a great thing; and with regard to the ſubject under conſideration, opportunity has reſolved to do her beſt in lending it a helping hand.

The

The ſwiftly approaching year 1864 will be the Tercentenary Jubilee of the Poet's Birth. Nearly a century ago (in 1769), the celebration of his nativity was held in Stratford under the direction of David Garrick. A ſillier or more uſeleſs exhibition was never witneſſed. Deſpite the excitement which it created at the moment in Stratford, there ſeem to have been ſome of the inhabitants who ſpoke of it in contemptuous language, for the "Garrick Correſpondence" reveals a paſſage of letters between the Rev. Mr. Jago,* of Snitterfield, and George Garrick, the brother of the tragedian, ſhowing that the latter had reſented ſome uncomplimentary animadverſions of Mr. Jago's upon Garrick and the Jubilee. The brother's reſentment was a neceſſary reſult, for never was there a more devoted brother

* Appendix. L.

brother than was George Garrick to David. A charming illuſtration of this is afforded us in the "tender pleaſantry" of Charles Banniſter at the time of Garrick's demiſe. Whenever George was abſent from Drury Lane for any length of time, on returning, his invariable queſtion to the hall-porter was, "Has my brother wanted "me?" It eventuated that the brothers died within a few days of one another. David Garrick expired at his houſe on the Terrace, Adelphi, early on Wedneſday morning, January 20th, 1779, and was buried in Poet's Corner on the 1ſt of February. On the 3rd of February George Garrick expired. When the report reached Drury Lane, Banniſter obſerved, "His brother wanted him!"

But the admiration and affection of George for David could not draw the ſting of the Rev. Mr. Jago's cutting obſervations. Their ſting lay in their truth

truth. Garrick in one of his letters wrote, "When I was bufied about that "foolifh hobby-horfe of mine, the Ju-"bilee!" His language is as correct a defcription of it as could be given, though the wet weather kindly interfered to prevent the greateft abfurdity of the programme — the "pageant proceffion "of Shakefpere's principal characters." Owing to the tremendous downpour of rain, that pageant was never perpetrated at the Jubilee, albeit, there is in the Town Hall of Stratford, a fire-fcreen which gives an amazing pictorial illuftration of the proceffion; and there is alfo a tradition that Mrs. Siddons perfonated Venus in the Jubilee proceffion. The fcreen in queftion—although it reprefents a difplay that never took place,—is well worthy of contemplation. Painted by fome village artift, it is as grotefque and amufing a production as any one with a keen fenfe of the

the ludicrous, would wiſh to contemplate. Diſtant be the day when the Corporation of Stratford remove from their Hall, this humorous repreſentation of an hiſtorical event that never took place !

With reference to Mrs. Siddons appearing as Venus in the proceſſion of the Jubilee, it is true that ſhe did perſonate that part, but not at Stratford. Owing to the proceſſion being waſhed out of the programme, it was dramatiſed the following October (1769), at Drury Lane, by Garrick, who introduced into it the ſongs and the odes that had been given in the Stratford Amphitheatre. We read of it, "Such was the magnificence of the "ſcenery, and the effect given through-"out the piece, that it was ſo far eſta-"bliſhed in public favour as to cauſe its "being repeated during the ſeaſon for "upwards of 100 nights."

It was not even upon this occaſion that

that Mrs. Siddons exhibited as Venus, nor, until 1775,—the ſeaſon before Garrick's final retirement, and that of her firſt appearance at Drury Lane. Garrick revived the *ſpectacle* of the Jubilee Proceſſion during the ſeaſon, and the Lady Ann who had trembled in terror before his glance of reproach in the great ſcene of Gloſter's wooing, was caſt to perſonify Venus. Mrs. Siddons, in her Autograph Recollections, alludes to the Jubilee performance:—“ He (Garrick) would ſome-“ times hand me from my own ſeat in “ the green-room to place me next to his “ own. He alſo ſelected me to perſonate “ Venus at the revival of the Jubilee. “ This gained me the malicious appella-“ tion of ‘ Garrick's Venus,’ and the ladies “ who ſo kindly beſtowed it on me, ruſhed “ before me in the laſt ſcene, ſo that if he “ (Mr. Garrick) had not brought us for-“ ward with him, with his own hands, “ my "my little Cupid, (the subsequent auto-"biographer Thomas Dibdin), and my-"self, whose appointed situations were in "the very front of the stage, might have "as well been in the Island of Paphos. "Mr. Garrick would also flatter me by "sending me into one of the boxes when "he acted any of his great characters."

Such are the facts which connect the name of Mrs. Siddons with the Jubilee Procession, there being no connection at all with the celebration at Stratford, at which, nevertheless, she might have been present; for two years previously (February 12, 1767), Miss Kemble (aged twelve), and her brother, John Philip (aged ten),* had appeared in the parts of the Princess Elizabeth and the Duke of York,

* John Philip Kemble was born at Prescot, in Lancashire, February, 1757. The author was, some years since, curate of Prescot, and a frequent visitor of the humble folks who now inhabit the house in which Kemble first

York, in the theatre at Worceſter, in Havard's tragedy of *Charles the Firſt*, which, though unknown to the modern ſtage, was at one time highly popular, and ſo affecting, that when the part of Charles was performed at Hull by Cummings, the early rival of Kemble, his imperſonation of the miſeries of the King ſo overwhelmed Miſs Terrot, the daughter of a garriſon officer, that her emotions cauſed her inſtantaneous death.

The Stratford Jubilee was celebrated for three days: Wedneſday, Thurſday, and Friday, the 6th, 7th, and 8th of

firſt ſaw light. Like many houſes in the neighbourhood, it is built of the prevailing red ſandſtone, and is whitewaſhed. It has ſolidity enough to laſt for centuries to come. In former years, when Preſcot was the firſt town out of Liverpool on the coaching road, thouſands of travellers would paſs by the door of John Kemble's birthplace. It ſtands in the "Lower Road," going from the market-place of Preſcot to the neighbouring railway ſtation of Rainhill; and the good man of the houſe uſed to take pride in ſhowing the bedroom "i' which th' great actor cum i'th' wuld, welly nigh gang a 'undred yeear."

of September, 1769. The town was thronged with viſitors from London and the ſurrounding counties. There were preſent, among others—

The Duke of Mancheſter.
Duke of Dorſet.

The Earl of Northampton,
Earl of Hertford,
Earl of Plymouth,
Earl of Carliſle,
Earl of Denbigh,
Earl of Shrewſbury,
} And their Counteſſes.

Lord Beauchamp,
Lord Groſvenor,
Lord Windſor,
Lord Catherlough,
Lord and Lady Spencer,
Lord and Lady Archer,
Lord and Lady Craven;

and a large number of Baronets, Members of Parliament, and County gentlemen. Connected with the drama there were—

David Garrick, and his brother George,
Mr. Foote,
Mr. Colman,
Mr. Macklin,
Mr. and Mrs. Yates,
Mr. Roſs (Edinbro),
Mr. Lee (Bath),

and about one hundred and ſeventy actors and

and actresses of minor repute from the London theatres.

Among other notabilities present was James Boswell. Dr. Johnson was staying with the Thrales, at Brighton, and could not be induced to honour the Jubilee with his presence. Boswell says, "I was very sorry that I had not his "company with me at the Jubilee in "honour of Shakespeare, at Stratford-"upon-Avon, the great Poet's native "town. Johnson's connection both with "Shakespeare and Garrick founded a "double claim to his presence, and it "would have been highly gratifying to "Mr. Garrick. Upon this occasion I "particularly lamented that he had not "that warmth of friendship for his "brilliant pupil which we may sup-"pose would have had a benignant "effect on both. When almost every "man of eminence in the literary

" world was happy to partake in this " feſtival of Genius, the abſence of " Johnſon could not but be wondered at " and regretted."

Perhaps the verdict of poſterity may be the reverſe of Boſwell's. The "Great " Cham" was not partial to buffoonery, and it is probable that he kept away from Stratford becauſe he would not encourage his "brilliant pupil" aſtride of his "fooliſh hobby horſe."* Johnſon had no

* A number of letters regarding the Jubilee of 1769, addreſſed by Garrick to Mr. Hunt, of Stratford (grandfather of the preſent Town Clerk), are in exiſtence. In one of them Garrick ſays:—"I heard yeſter-" day, to my ſurpriſe, that the country people did not " ſeem to reliſh our Jubilee, that they looked upon it to " be Popiſh, and that we ſhould raiſe ye d——l, and " would not. I ſuppoſe this may be a joke, but after " all my trouble, pains, labor, and expenſe for their " ſervice and the honour of yr county, I ſhall think it " very hard if I am not to be received kindly by them; " however, I ſhall not be the firſt martyr for my zeal.

" I am, dear Sir,

" Always in a hurry, but yours ſincerely,

" D. GARRICK."

" Pray tell me ſincerely what common people ſay."

no taſte for maſquerading, which Boſwell had. The occaſion was propitious. During the day he appeared in the ſtreets of Stratford with the words "Corſica Boſwell" diſplayed in large letters round his hat; and at the evening entertainment he exhibited himſelf as a Corſican Chief, with "*Viva la Libertà*" inſcribed on the front of his cap! Johnſon's preſence at ſuch fooling, would have been *much to be regretted.*

The only portions of the Jubilee which deſerve record, were the performance, in Stratford Church, of Dr. Arne's Oratorio of *Judith*, under the direction of Arne himſelf, for which he received a payment of £60 from Garrick; and the Oration pronounced by Garrick, in the Amphitheatre. The Odes, which were partly ſpoken by him, and partly ſung, contain nothing to recommend them to our peruſal; but one paſſage from the

"Oration

"Oration in honour of Shakeſpere, "written and ſpoken by Mr. Garrick," may fitly be reproduced. Alluding to the "uſes" and opportunities of life, at the cloſe of his oration, Garrick ſaid,—

"In theſe fields, where we are pleaſed "with the notion of doing him honour, "he is mouldering into duſt.

'*Deaf the prais'd ear, and mute the tuneful tongue.*'

"How awful is the thought! Let me "pauſe. If I ſpeak, it muſt be in my "own character and in yours. We are "men; and we know that the hour "approaches with ſilent but irreſiſtible "rapidity, when *we* alſo ſhall be duſt. "We are now in health and at eaſe; but "the hour approaches when we ſhall be "ſenſible only to ſickneſs and to pain,— "when we ſhall perceive the world gra- "dually to fade from our ſight, and cloſe "our eyes in perpetual darkneſs."

Ten

Ten years ſubſequently the world had faded from Garrick's ſight. Time's courſe is ſo rapid, that another centenary Jubilee is cloſe at hand. What men of eminence in the literary world, what nobles or princes of the land, will collect at Stratford—and in what manner the Jubilee is to be conducted—muſt ſhortly be conſidered. It may, however, be ſuggeſted to thoſe intereſted in the reſtoration of New Place, and to thoſe who will arrange the programme of the Jubilee, that they ſhould remember Garrick's ſolemn peroration on the "uſes" of life, and, eſpecially in this practical age, determine upon ſoliciting public ſympathy and ſupport in April, 1864, for practical purpoſes, and not for a frivolous pageant to the memory of a great man. The beſt honour which can be paid to his memory will be the promotion of objects uſeful to the body of men in connection with whom

whom Shakeſpere made his name and fame.

That the Tercentenary of his birth ſhould be celebrated at his birthplace is a propriety which every one will recognise; but what *muſt* be there, may alſo be elſewhere. There is no reaſon why the people of the Metropolis ſhould not commemorate the occaſion, as well as the ſelect few whoſe time and means will allow them to congregate at Stratford. Such a double celebration ſeems almoſt a certainty. But, whatever be the form of feſtival held, whether in London or in Stratford, the age we live in, warns all ſenſible men againſt the repetition of any ſuch mumming as took place under Garrick's programme of 1769. Foote, who was preſent, has given us his definition of that occaſion:—" A Jubilee is a public " invitation, circulated by puffing, to go " poſt without horſes, to a borough

" without

“ without reprefentatives, governed by “ a mayor and aldermen who are no “ magiftrates, to celebrate a great poet, “ whofe own works have made him im- “ mortal, by an ode without poetry, “ mufic without melody, dinners with- “ out victuals, and lodgings without “ beds; a mafquerade, where half the “ people are bare-faced; a horfe-race up “ to the knees in water; fireworks extin- “ guifhed as foon as they were lighted; “ and a gingerbread amphitheatre, which, “ like a houfe of cards, tumbled to pieces “ as foon as it was finifhed.” Foote's cauftic humour, if not true in its defcription of the Jubilee, is perfectly true in outline; the grotefque colouring of the picture is its only untruth.

It is devoutly to be wifhed, that the follies of 1769, may be a warning to the people of 1864. To begin and end with a fhow, and to accomplifh no permanent good,

good, is not confonant with the tafte of the prefent day. Whether at Stratford or in London, or at both places, the Tercentenary celebrations muft feek the public fympathy on behalf of fome public good. If there were but the one celebration at Stratford, it might be well to devote all the funds collected, to the completion of the propofed purchafes, the laying-out of New Place Gardens, and the erection of fome monumental ftructure, commemorative of the purchafe and of the 300th celebration of the Poet's Birth, but, while beautiful as a piece of architecture, at the fame time a ftructure that fhould be practically ufeful for literary purpofes, and a benefit to Stratford and the nation. In the Metropolis, the refults of a Jubilee celebration, might probably be devoted to fome other object. It appears natural, that the object fhould be Metropolitan; and if fuggeftions were wanted, numberlefs numberleſs ſchemes, without doubt, would quickly be propoſed. But it ſhould never be forgotten that the Jubilee is in honour of Shakeſpere, and that thoſe have the beſt claim to enjoy the benefits of the public largeſs, who, in this day and generation, follow the calling of the man, to whoſe honoured memory, the commemoration is dedicated.

True it is, there are many who profeſs a conſcientious diſapproval of the drama, and who, neither directly nor indirectly, would encourage the "poor player." It may be a ſubject of regret—but, nevertheleſs, it is a fact which cannot be denied—that ſome perſons affect to condemn the works of Shakeſpere himſelf. With this undoubted fact in mind, it will be deſirable, having due reſpect to tender conſciences and hopeleſs prejudices, to preſent ſome object for public ſympathy at the Jubilee, which may, if poſſible, diſarm all cavil and objection.

If

If the depreciators of Shakefpere, and the difapprovers of the profeffion to which he belonged, be taken on their own ground—and, for the fake of argument it be momentarily granted that the Puritanical view of the drama is its righteous and proper eftimate; in the fame proportion that its influence is af-ferted to be evil and deftructive, muft the fympathies and folicitude of fuch perfons, if fincere in their belief, be aroufed on behalf of one helplefs clafs connected with Shakefpere's profeffion. Whatever the player may be, the player's child muft be an object of concern to all who are interefted in the education of the young;—but he muft be doubly fo to thofe, whofe duty it is, in the fincerity of their principles, to attempt the refcue of that child, from influences which they believe deftructive of its foul's welfare!

It

It is to be hoped that the ſubject of education would preſent a common ground, whereon diverſities of opinions might meet to accompliſh, a truly Chriſtian and beneficial object.

In the abundant philanthropy of the preſent age, ſchools and inſtitutions have ſprung up on every ſide, wherein the greater the degradation of the young, the greater the ſympathy of the profeſſed religious world! The fallen, the friendleſs, the erring, and the outcaſt, have been the recipients of Chriſtian compaſſion and ſolicitude. Every right-feeling perſon muſt pray that God's bleſſing may protect and proſper our Ragged Schools, our Reformatories, our Penitentiaries, and that they may, in their proſperity, reflect bleſſings on the heads of all earneſt men and women, who, in their ſupport, have practically evinced the firſt of Chriſtian virtues. But there are ſpheres

ſpheres in life, removed alike from abſolute want, and aſſociation with crime; where ſympathy is not leſs needed, and where reſpectable poverty — that owes no man anything—ſhrinks from ſeeking aid, and values ſelf-dependence with as honourable a love, as the wealthieſt and nobleſt of the land!

Among Shakeſpere's profeſſional deſcendants, there are many ſuch, who, owing to the ſmallneſs of their ſalaries, are hindered from procuring for their progeny that ſound teaching which every Engliſh child ſhould enjoy; and who, conſtrained by need, are compelled to introduce their offſpring in their early years to ſubordinate ſituations in the theatres, at a time when the child's moral and phyſical conſtitution require, the one bringing up in the way it ſhould go, the other, the vigour derived from regular habits, early riſing, early reſt, and unbroken repoſe.

repoſe. It is unneceſſary to point out that the oppoſite of all this, is the inevitable reſult of engaging a child in the arduous buſineſs of a theatre. The intellect is left untrained, the ſtrength of the body is ſapped and undermined, and it is to be feared that in a calling peculiarly open to temptation, moral deterioration may frequently accompany phyſical exhauſtion.

In that Royal College which has been honoured with the patronage of, and has been watched over with intereſt by, the higheſt perſonages in the realm, the deſign of the promoters is underſtood to be, not only the proviſion of homes for decayed actors and actreſſes, but alſo the completion of a Dramatic College in the fuller ſenſe of the phraſe, wherein childhood and old age may be aſſociated—wherein Spring and Winter may flouriſh together, and both put forth their ſeaſon-

able

able flowers. Some of the nobleſt of Old England's charities exhibit this touching union; and never has the ſatiriſt of this age more tenderly moved the hearts of his readers, than in that paſſage of the Newcomes, where the aged brother of the Charter Houſe, liſtens to the chapel-bell calling the ſchoolboys to their prayers, and replies to his own ſolemn ſummons, "*Adſum!*" The Charter Houſe is one of many ſimilar foundations ſcattered about the land. It was a happy thought on the part of thoſe who were moſt earneſt in inſtituting the Dramatic College, to deſire that, within the boundaries of the ſame inſtitution, a ſchool for the player's child ſhould be erected hard by the homes of thoſe who had fallen into the ſere and yellow leaf. The homes are completed, but this good work has not yet been begun!

Is there not, in ſuch an undertaking, a beneficial

beneficial and charitable object, to which the profits of a Metropolitan Tercentenary celebration of Shakespere's nativity might be dedicated? The education of the children of actors can be objected to by none, and is a righteous and goodly aim, that may properly be approved by all!

It would be a great work accomplished —a work of genuine and practical honour to the memory of the Poet, if on a festival, which can only be celebrated by every third generation, a sufficient fund were raised for building and endowing with a few "Shakespere Scholarships," a Dramatic College School, wherein the children of the hard-worked and humbly-salaried artists could be provided with sound and liberal education, fitting them, when adults, to take their choice of other callings in life than those of their parents, if so disposed; but, under any circum-

stances

ſtances, preſerving them in their childhood, from the turmoil, fatigue, premature conſtitutional decline, and inevitable precocity, of baby actors, and Theſpian phenomena.

By the erection of ſuch a ſchool, Shakeſpere's Jubilee, in 1864, would be made a genuine and abiding Jubilee in the families of hundreds of our countrymen, who are painſtaking, ſtriving, and reſpectable men, — who would bleſs, with grateful hearts, the friends that ſympathiſe with them in their narrow circumſtances,—friends that abhor the aſſumption of patronage, and cordially embrace a rare opportunity of ſhowing concern and care for the player's children, on the feſtival which commemorates that red-letter day in England's calendar, when, three hundred years ago, ſweet Shakeſpere was himſelf a child!

APPENDIX.

****

A—page 16.

The Family of Bott.

THOUGH confiderable information has been difcovered in the preparation of this work regarding the Botts, as given at pp. 75 to 85, neverthelefs, I have not thought it worth while to purfue my inquiries far into their hiftory, as I fhould had there been anything of intereft as regards Shakefpere likely to be arrived at by the refearch.

It will be obferved that I have fpoken in ftrong language regarding W. Bott; and, at p. 86, have called him a "grafping lawyer." From the evidence which has come into my poffeffion in refearches regarding the fales of New Place, I find that Bott muft have been a thoroughly unprincipled, pettifogging attorney, doing all the dirty work of Stratford and its neighbourhood. His character oozes out through the medium of the following proceedings taken in the Star Chamber (*temp.* Elizabeth); and however meagre the details may be, ftill new light is difcernible regarding fome members of his family and his pofition with reference to W. Underhill.

By the Bill of Complaint we are informed that John Harper, of Henley-on-Arderne, co. Warwick, who was poffeffed of certain lands and tenements in Henley, Ownall, Wotton, and Whitley, in the county aforefaid, was in danger of being taken in execution under a diftrefs at the fuit of Sir Edward Afton, Knight. Under which circumftances, being himfelf a plain and fimpleſimple-minded man, he was induced to ſeek the aſſiſtance of W. Bott, of Stratford, a man of about fifty years of age, and reputed of ſome experience and ability, to adviſe him properly.

Bott had two ſons and three daughters, and finding his client poſſeſſed of ſome ſubſtance, although under age, made up a match between him and his daughter Iſabel; and further, on the 10th of April, 1563, deviſed a deed of feoffment, whereby Harper ſhould aſſure to him and others, in fee ſimple, all his lands to certain uſes, unknown to the petitioner, but as far as he conceives, to the uſe of petitioner and wife, and their heirs, &c., with remainder to one of Bott's ſons, promiſing to extricate him from his difficulties, alleging it was for the better advancement of his wife; and that the ſaid deed was only a conveyance of his goods, and "*that becauſe the goods remained in the houſe, he* "*muſt make livery of them by the ring of the door.*" The unſuſpecting youth fell into the ſnare, being eaſily led to do whatever his father-in-law inſtructed him, who, not content with this, if we may believe the allegations of the petitioner, forged, eraſed, and altered other deeds concerning the ſaid conveyance; indeed, in the preamble of the bill, which we muſt bear in mind was framed probably ſome ſix or ſeven years after (Mrs. Harper being dead in the interim, without children), he denounces him as "*a man* "*clearly void of all honeſty, fidelity, or fear of God, and* "*openly detected of divers great and notorious crimes, as,* "*namely, felony, adultery, whoredom, falſehood, and* "*forging, a procurer of the diſinheriſon of divers gentle-* "*men your Majesty's ſubjects, a common barretour, and* "*ſtirrer of ſedition amongſt your Majeſty's poor ſub-* "*jects.*"

This nefarious proceeding, executed without the conſent or privity of petitioner, places him in the poſition that he cannot leaſe his lands, &c., without Bott's conſent, and that, in point of fact, he is only tenant thereto for life. Having thus wreſted petitioner's tioner's poſſeſſions, he withholds too the evidences and muniments of the ſame—the contents, and even the number of which are utterly unknown to petitioner. He prays, therefore, a writ of ſubpena for W. Bott perſonally to appear and anſwer theſe charges. Thus far the complainant's ſtatement.

Bott denies the facts alleged as ſlanders emanating from complainant and his adherents, and declares that if the premiſes were true, it were determinable at common law, and not in the court of Star Chamber, ſtating that about ſix years ago, complainant being a minor, did marry his daughter Iſabel, at which time he promiſed on arriving at twenty-one he would make her a jointure; but inſtead thereof, becoming improvident, he mortgaged his lands, and fell into difficulties. Thereupon, coming to his father-in-law in tears, he beſought his aſſiſtance, which he readily promiſed on theſe conditions, viz., that he ſhould aſſure his eſtate, or rather the portion left unſquandered, to himſelf and wife, or the longeſt liver of them, then to their iſſue, failing which, to the various ſons and daughters of the ſaid Bott in ſucceſſion, for which defendant undertook to ſatisfy Sir Edward Aſton and divers other creditors. The catalogue of crimes hurled at his reputation he meets by a countercharge, and declares it to be by the "*falſe and malicious procurement of one William Under-*" *hill and Rowland Whelar, which that the ſaid defen-*" *dant is ready to aver and prove that the ſaid Underhill*" *is a ſtirrer of ſedition, and of a very evil conſcience,*" *and ſo meet to join with the ſaid Whelar, a very common*" *barretour and a vagabond.*" Further, he denies the truth of the ſtatement about his own procurement of the marriage, for the complainant was married three or four years before the affair of Sir Edward Aſton. All the other charges he denies *in toto ſeriatim.*

The replication of Harper denies the ſtatement about the jointure, and that whatever mortgage he made, which would be but trifling, was at Bott's inſtigation. The debts, too, as paid by defendant, were of no no magnitude; ſome eight pounds would cover the whole, including that of Sir Edward Aſton, in diſcharge of which defendant yet detaineth £9, which petitioner recovered againſt Sir Edward, and detains moreover a ſum of 40 marks which he promiſed to give with his daughter as her dowry, &c.

So far from W. Underhill being meet to be matched with any vagabond, he is, on the contrary, "*a gentle-*" *man of a worſhipful calling in his country, and very* " *well known to all honeſt men to be of good eſtimation,* " *and of very good name, report, and credit, a maintainer* " *of juſtice, and a repreſſer of evil doers.*" That Sir Edward Aſton's ſuit againſt petitioner was commenced long before his marriage, is alſo untruly alleged.

The rejoinder by Bott denies generally the truth of the ſtatements in the foregoing replication, and ſays further that he never did promiſe complainant any bigger ſum than £20, which he did pay before they went to the church to be married, and avers that complainant is maintained and ſupported in his ſlanders by the ſaid W. Underhill and his companion, Rowland Whelar, as named in the anſwer.

By taking the year 1563 as the date of the marriage, or thereabouts, and adding ſix years, the time noted by Bott in his anſwer, the probable date of theſe proceedings would be about 1569.

It will be ſeen at p. 77, that there was a near relationſhip at one period between the Botts and the Cloptons. In the Domeſtic Correſpondence, Eliz., vol. cxxxvii., art. 68, anno. 1580, among the Gentlemen and Freeholders in the Countie of Warwick appears,

"Hundred of Hemlingford,
"George Bott."

In another ſimilar work appears,

"Solyhull,
"George Boote."

(Intended for Bott, as there was a family ſo named at Solyhull at that date.)

From

From various traces of the name, cropping-up in this way, I have satisfied myself that an extensive family of the Botts was scattered about Warwickshire in Shakespere's time; and if it were worth while, a very slight inquiry in the parish registers in the neighbourhood of Stratford would probably supply abundant evidence concerning them. There was a moment when I entertained the suspicion that the Botts had been mixed up with some foul play perpetrated in the Clopton family, in the time of William and Anne Clopton.

On perusing the following documents, any reader would naturally suppose, as I at first did, that a William Clopton, and Anne his wife, living about the years 1580 to 1589, would be the William and Anne marked "C" upon the Pedigree, more especially as the circumstance of this William Clopton dying without an heir, gives countenance to the allegations in the following Bill of Complaint. I had not then compiled the Clopton Pedigree, and consequently was not aware that William Clopton (C) lived until 1592, and that Kentwell, in Suffolk, was no part of the property of that branch of the Clopton family seated at Clopton, Warwickshire. This proves the necessity for an intimate acquaintance with family pedigrees when we deal with public records, otherwise a confounding of persons may easily arise, such as in this instance would be most natural, where we find documents relating to persons of particular names at a fixed date, and then discover that persons of the same names—*man and wife*—and at the same date, lived in another county.

Bill of Complaint of Anne Clopton, &c.*

"Showing that her late husband, William Clopton,
"Esq.

* Proceedings in Chancery, *temp.* Eliz., C. c. 13, No. 3. Date inscribed on the top, 12 May, 1589. Counts of three documents only, the answer of the defendants not appearing to be extant.

"Esq., of Kentwell, in county of Suffolk, leased sundry "manors and lands to William Clopton of Groughton, "and another, to pay £40 per annum for the same, "&c. &c. Thomas Clopton (a brother of the half "blood to the said William, complainant's late husband) "used subtle means to obtain the lands from the right "heirs, persuading the said William Clopton who was "enfeebled by long sickness, to disinherit his next heirs, "and to convey his whole estate to the said Thomas "Clopton, inducing him to make his will by the which "he left only one legacy of very small amount to one "of his servants, and nothing to his wife or his sisters, "or sisters' children, &c. &c. Prays a writ of subpœna, "&c. &c., as Thomas Clopton, William Clopton of "Groughton, and John Bowsell, the other defendant, "have procured the property to be conveyed to them-"selves, and have made themselves masters of all."

Replication of Anne Clopton to the Answer of William Clopton and John Bowsell:

"States that John Bowsell, defendant, was servant "to William Clopton, complainant's late husband, and "that during his long continued illness it was insinuated "by defendants to William Clopton, that Anne his "wife, and one Thomas Smith, a nephew of William "Clopton, employed poison, whereupon she desired that "she might go away from him for some little time, "until he were recovered and better persuaded con-"cerning such slander; to which her husband replied "that Thomas Clopton was a bad, lewd fellow, and "used such speeches of her as were not decent to "rehearse. Finally, she went to the house of one "Lady Pelham, of Sussex, and there abode until "Edward Lovell, now servant to Thomas Clopton, "administered a potion to William Clopton, which "was a purgative or such like, from the effects of "which he died, whereas had it happened during her "residence with him, she would have been charged as "accessory to his death."

The

The Rejoinder of Thomas Clopton, Esq., and John Bowsell, to the above Replication of Anne Clopton:

"Denies the allegations attributing her leaving to the "indiscreet behaviour of complainant, and unnatural "dealing towards her late husband, whom she neither "loved nor obeyed; condemns the statement about "Lovell as slander; deposes to the perfect state of "the faculties of William Clopton, and his powers of "memory and appetite, &c."

B—page 16.

It would appear from the mention in this place "between 1563 and 1570," that there is some uncertainty about the date of sale by W. Bott to W. Underhill, whereas the exact date, Michaelmas Term, 1567, is given with a copy of the Fine at p. 85. The truth is, that when paragraph 3rd, p. 16, was stereotyped, I had not discovered the Fine given at p. 85; and rather than cancel the page, I preferred to make the correction in this place.

C—page 19.

The general reader had better be warned, particularly if he should be a reader of Malone, against falling into the error into which that author, in the original edition of his Shakespere's Works, would betray him.

The statement there made, both as to the Nash pedigree, and as to the manner in which New Place passed from owner to owner, is completely erroneous. The fact is well known to every Shakesperian scholar but it may be as well to set it forth distinctly. Malone says—

"Sir

"Sir John Clopton, Knt. (the father of Edward "Clopton, Efq., and Sir Hugh Clopton), who died at "Stratford-upon-Avon in April, 1719, purchafed the "eftate of New Place, etc., fome time after the year "1685, from Sir Reginald Forfter, Bart., who married "Mary, the daughter of Edward Nafh, Efq., coufin-"german to Thomas Nafh, Efq., who married our "poet's grand-daughter, Eliz. Hall. Edward Nafh "bought it after the death of her fecond hufband, "Sir John Barnard, Knt. By her will, fhe directed "her truftee, Henry Smith, to fell the New Place, "etc. (after the death of her hufband), and to make "the firft offer of it to her coufin, Edward Nafh, "who purchafed it accordingly. His fon, Thomas "Nafh (whom, for the fake of diftinction, I fhall call the "younger), having died without iffue in Auguft, 1652, "Edward Nafh, by his will, made on the 16th March, "1678-9, devifed the principal part of his property to "his daughter Mary, and her hufband, Reginald "Forfter, Efq., afterwards Sir Reginald Forfter; but "in confequence of the teftator's only referring to a "deed of fettlement executed three days before, with-"out reciting the fubftance of it, no particular mention "of New Place is made in his will. After Sir John "Clopton had bought it from Sir Reginald Forfter, he "gave it by deed to his younger fon, Sir Hugh, who "pulled down our poet's houfe and built one more "elegant on the fame fpot."

Malone's errors in the above paffage are extraordinary, becaufe they are not only errors as to pedigree, but errors as to fales and purchafes, which the fmalleft amount of inveftigation would have proved to him to have been incorrect. It is eafy to fet him right upon the pedigree, but impoffible to conceive how he could be fo mifled as to make the feries of egregious blunders which will appear in the above extract when it is compared with the correct ftatement, in par. 7, p. 19.

I give the pedigree which was accepted by Stevens and Malone firft, and then the correct one. By the firft

"gave Mr. Ireland his firſt information on which "he created his viſionary falſehood (the Shakeſpere "forgeries)."

Ditto, 1809, September, p. 885.—"It is conjectured "that many of his (Jordan's) tales reſpecting Shake-"ſpere were from his own inventive genius."

E—page 57.

The Clopton Arms.

The porch of the Chapel of the Holy Croſs has been allowed to fall into ſuch a ſtate of decay, that only one of the four ſhields which once adorned it can now be read. It is the one bearing the arms of London.

The ſhields, as they originally appeared, are given by Dugdale, and could eaſily be reſtored. A beautiful coat of the Cloptons will be found inſide the chapel, adorning the porch at the entrance. It is unfortunately buried under the clumſy and offenſive gallery which has been erected over the line of the ſcreen which originally divided the chapel from a ſmall ante-chapel. Holy Croſs is one of the moſt painful ſpecimens of plaſterers', painters', and carpenters' church reſtoration. Its pews and fittings are moſt ſubſtantial, moſt ſervice-able, and moſt deteſtable.

It is well known to every one acquainted with the building, that its walls are adorned with a ſeries of freſcoes of the moſt intereſting deſcription. Theſe have been carefully hidden under coats of yellow waſh. Everything that the Corporation of Stratford could do to diſguiſe this venerable pile, has been done. The ancient oak ſcreen has been hidden behind the gallery; the exquiſite ſtonework of the porchway has been mutilated; and all that the moſt barbaric Proteſtant taſte could accompliſh to convert the building into the appearance of a comfortable conventicle, has been thoroughly

thoroughly carried out. There are only three features, internally, of this building, that carry us back in imagination to Sir Hugh Clopton's time. 1ſt. His ſhield and quarterings, which have happily eſcaped deſtruction on one ſide of the doorway. 2nd. The tracery of the windows. 3rd. A beautiful piece of mediæval iron-work—the handle of the prieſts' door, paſſing from the chancel to the garden formerly occupied by the prieſts' houſes, attached to the preſent grammar ſchool.

The ſooner the Corporation of Stratford ſet about a reſtoration of this chapel — clean the walls and reproduce the freſcoes; remove the frightful and uſeleſs gallery blocking up the lovely tower arch; reſtore the ſcreen to its proper place, and fit up the building with open benches and ſtalls—the more it will be to their credit.

Inſtead of introducing the following facts in the Clopton Pedigree, I have reſerved them to be inſerted here. It will have been ſeen that on the death of Mrs. Partheriche, the Clopton Houſe Eſtate paſſed under her will to Charles Boothby Scrimſher, Eſq. (I), who took the name of Clopton. The Pedigree ſhows that he was the ſon of Anne Clopton, who married Thomas Boothby, Eſq., and the heir-at-law of Mrs. Partheriche at her deceaſe. According to the proviſions of that lady's will, in default of iſſue the eſtate was to paſs to Edward Ingram, Esq. (K, Pedigree), the ſon of Barbara Clopton and Aſhton Ingram; and, in caſe of default, to his brother John or his heirs, all of whom were tenants for life. In caſe of no iſſue in any of theſe families, the eſtate was to paſs to one Anthony Clopton, of Ireland, who had perſuaded Mrs. Partheriche that he was deſcended from the Clopton family. C. B. Scrimſher Clopton died 1815, without iſſue; Edward Ingram died 1818, without iſſue; John Ingram died, aged 90, November 20, 1824, without iſſue. The ſaid Anthony Clopton died in like manner without iſſue. The eſtate then came to a Mrs. Noel (L),

(L), a ſiſter of the above C. B. Scrimſher Clopton. She, being next heir to the eſtate, during its poſſeſſion by the above-named John Ingram Clopton (for, by the will, every poſſeſſor was bound to aſſume the name of Clopton) ſold the reverſion to Charles Meynell, Eſq., for £10,000 in money, and an annuity of £300 per annum; the £10,000 being to pay the debts of her brother Charles Boothby, who, having been greatly embarraſſed, committed ſuicide.

Charles Meynell, Eſq., the purchaſer of the reverſion, died in 1815, leaving two ſons and a widow, Elizabeth, who married Samuel Stoddart, Eſq.; and they conjointly, by a decree of the Court of Chancery, ſold Clopton Houſe and eſtate for £50 an acre, the purchaſe-money (279 acres) amounting to £13,975; the buildings on the eſtate being further valued at £781. The timber ſold for £548; and the Clopton pews, in Stratford church, with two ſmaller ones, for £100; the Clopton meadow, for £1,500; and the furniture and FAMILY PICTURES IN THE HOUSE, for £55!!! The whole were purchaſed for £16,959 15*s.* 6*d.*, by George Loyd, Eſq., of Welcombe, Stratford, in October, 1830. Mr. Loyd died in July, 1831, leaving the Clopton and Welcombe eſtate to his brother, John Gamaliel Loyd, Eſq., for his life, and afterwards to his nephew, Charles Warde, Eſq., the preſent poſſeſſor. There were ſome legal difficulties, owing to the non-completion of the purchaſe prior to Mr. Loyd's death, which were ſet right by an order in Chancery, but they are of no intereſt to the public. The above facts furniſh thoſe who may be intereſted in the ſubject with a correct account of the hands through which the Clopton eſtate has paſſed ſince the extinction of the direct deſcent, as traced upon the Pedigree, down to the preſent moment.

F—page 87.

Underhill.

The hiſtory of the ſettlement of the Underhill family at Eatington, near Stratford, is curious and amuſing. The facts now related are gathered from the elaborate notice of Eatington and of the Shirley family contained in the MSS. of the late Rev. Mr. Warde.

The Pedigree I have given ſhows that the Underhills came originally from Wolverhampton. They ſettled at Eatington in the firſt year of the reign of Henry VIII., owing to John Underhill marrying for his ſecond wife one Agnes Porter, of Eatington. This John obtained a leaſe for 80 years of the manor of Eatington, from Sir Ralph Shirley, Knight. This was an amorous knight, who married in ſucceſſion four wives,—the laſt in the year 1514. This lady, a daughter of Sir Robert Sheffield, bore him a ſon, Francis, who was left fatherleſs in the firſt year of his life—January, 1517. Being very much his own maſter, before he was of age this fooliſh youth married a widow, the relict of Sir John Congreve, of Stretton, county Stafford, and likewiſe the daughter of his guardian, Sir John Giffard. The widow Congreve brought with her to her young huſband's home two daughters by her late ſpouſe, Elizabeth and Urſula Congreve.

By turning to the Underhill Pedigree, it will be ſeen that the two ſons of Edward Underhill, of Eatington, eventually married theſe two young ladies, and the reader will not be ſurpriſed to hear what followed.

By a leaſe, dated April 28, 1541, the above-named Francis Shirley was induced to grant the whole of his ancient Warwickſhire property, except the right of preſentation to the church of Nether Eatington, to Edward Underhill and his eldeſt ſon, Thomas, for a term of 100 years. This leaſe was the cauſe of much unpleaſantneſs and of a long ſeries of lawſuits, which were

were not finally determined until the year 1652. The Underhills were accufed of having obtained this valuable leafe of the Shirleys' lands by the procurement of the mother of the young ladies, Dorothy Congreve, who had married Francis Shirley. The following extracts, made from depofitions taken at Shipfton-upon-Stour, illuftrate the times, and the characters of Francis Shirley and his wife:—

"Ralph Brokefby, of Sholbye, in the county of "Leicefter, Efq., being examined, depofed—

"That Francis Shirley did not meddle in the "management of his eftate, only in his horfes, hounds, "and deer in his park at Staunton, wherein he took "great delight; but referred the refidue to be ordered, "and for the moft part to be difpofed of, by the faid "Dorothy his wife, and her friends, who ruled the "fame, and efpecially his hofpitality and houfekeeping, "with great frugality and worfhip, to her fingular com-"mendation, as well for prefervation of his woods, "keeping his houfe in good repair, and all other "things whatfoever. From fuch converfation and deal-"ings as he had with and for the faid Francis Shirley, "and his fon, John Shirley, he judged that Eatington "be now (1613) worth £200 per annum more than "the 40 marks paid for it (by the Underhills). More-"over, he depofeth, that Thomas Underhill, and Eliza-"beth his wife, did make an attempt to have had "from Francis Shirley the Fee farm of the manor of "Eatington for £200 in money, wherein they had "prevailed if they had not been providently prevented "by John Shirley, and further he gave his advice to "John Shirley fo to do."

Defpite the litigation, the fenior branch of the Underhills retained poffeffion of Eatington until the expiration of the leafe, in 1641, when the heir removed to Upthrop, in the parifh of Alderminfter, county of Worcefter.

During the reign of Elizabeth, the profperity of the Underhills was at its height; and it was in Shakefpere's time

time that they acquired lands in and about Stratford, and in numerous pariſhes about Eatington.

Our intereſt, in this work, is directed to the junior branch of the family, and therefore the ſenior line has not been given in the Pedigree. The founder of this junior line was William (A), (the younger ſon of the above-named Edward), who married one of the ſiſters Congreve—Urſula.

He was the father of William Underhill (B), who purchaſed New Place from Bott, and ſold it ſubſequently to Shakeſpere. Concerning theſe perſons, I have gathered ſome intereſting information, which will ſhow their connection with the county, and particularly with Stratford-upon-Avon.

(S.P.O. Domeſtic Correſp. Elizabeth, vol. cxxxvii. art. 68, 69).

Art. 68.—"*A Booke of the Names of the Gentlemen and Freeholders in the Countie of Warwick.* 1580."

"Hundred de Kington:

* * * *

Tho. Undrill, gent.

* * * *

"Hundred de Barlichway:

* * * *

Wm. Clopton, Eſqr.

* * * *

Wm. Underhill, gent.

* * * *

John Coomes, gent.

* * * *

John Shakeſpeare.

* * * *

Thomas Shakſpeare.

* * * *

John Shakſper.

* * * *

Art. 69.—

Art. 69.—Another Book, intituled, "*A Booke of the Names and Dwelling-places of the Gentlemen and Freeholders in the Countie of Warwick.* 1580."

(Under Idlicote, no Underhills are placed; the names of Richd. Hall and Wm. Merſhall occurring only.)

"Allington Inferior:

* * * *

Tho. Underhill, gent.

* * * *

"Stretford-upon-Avon:

* * * *

Wm. Claptun, Eſquier.

* * * *

John Shaxper.

* * * *

Wm. Underhill, gent.

* * * *

"Rowington:

* * * *

Tho. Shaxpere.

* * * *

The following documents, an abſtract of the will of William Underhill (A), and the will in full of his ſon (B)—Shakeſpere's Underhill—ſeem to me to complete all the information regarding this family which it is neceſſary to publiſh.

G—page 88.

G—page 88.

Abstract of Will of William Underhill.

(*Vide Pedigree*, A).

William Underhill makes his will on the 1st day of December, anno. 12 Eliz. (1569), and describes himself therein as of "Newbold Revell, in Com: Warr. "Gent."* In the first place he expresses his desire to be buried by his dearly beloved wife, in the parish of Nether Eatington. He then proceeds to express his intentions as to the disposition of his property, as follows:—To his heir, &c., the third part of all his manors, lands, and tenements; the rest (the manor of Idlicote being held *in capite*) to his executors, with all "leases, goodes, cattell, plate, and household stuffe," to fulfil the intents and meaning of his will, and to bring up his children.

He prohibits most emphatically to his heirs the alienation of his lands, except for their lives, their wives' lives, or leases for xxj years. Prohibits his son, W. Underhill, from marrying before the age of twenty-four, without the consent of his brother Shirley, brother Broketby, brother Thomas Underhill, and brother Congreve, or their heirs, &c., &c.

In the event of his son dying, or going about to alienate or sell his lands, he provides that they shall pass

* I find that the manor of Idlicote was alienated by Louis Greville to William Underhill (A), in the 10th of Eliz., and that in the following year the same Louis Greville alienated to the same William Underhill the manor of Loxley. It will be observed that on the Pedigree I have described this William (A), as of Idlicote and Loxley, while in his will he describes himself as of "Newbold Revell." The above facts will explain the reason. He was commonly known, when he made his will (1569), as Underhill of Newbold Revell, the Idlicote and Loxley property having been acquired only during the two years previous.

paſs to teſtator's brother, John. The properties in the will enumerated are the manor of Idlicote, lands and tenements in Idlicote, Coxley, and Hollington, lands in Kington-Baſſet, Barton, Meryden, Alſpathe, and Eſenell, in the county of Warwick aforeſaid. The teſtator mentions a brother Humphrey. Alſo a brother Thomas, and the ſaid Thomas's ſon, Francis (his godſon), as follows :—

" And alſo I do give to my brother Thomas, untell his " ſon Frauncis Underhill my godſon be of the age of " xxiiij yeres and then only to the ſaid Frauncis and to " the heires males of the very body of the ſaid Frauncis " lawfully begotten as is aforeſaid and with like condi- " cion and untill ſuch time as is aforeſaid all my landes " and tenementes with their appurtenances in Haſelor " *Stretforde-upon-Aven* and Drayton in the county of " Warwick and in the pariſh of Wolverhampton in " the county of Stafford " &c.

Two more ſons of his brother Thomas are alſo mentioned, viz., George and Humphrey. Alſo Humphrey, ſon of his brother John. Teſtator mentions by name his three daughters, Dorothy, Margaret, and Anne, to each of whom there is a bequeſt of £500.

To his ſon William, he leaves his ſignet of gold. To each of his daughters "*one* ſilver ſpone;" to Dorothie her mother's wedding-ring and one bracelet of gold; to his ſecond daughter, " my late moſt loving wife " Newport's* wedding-ringe;" to my youngeſt daughter, "a little chain of gold, and one other of my firſt " wife's ringes."

Legacies are bequeathed to his brother John's children,

* This was his second wife, who had pre-deceased him little more than a year, her will (which was made by license of her husband) having been proved on the 28th of January, 1569. She was the widow of Richard Newport, of Hemingham, by whom she had a son, John, and four daughters, Constance, Elizabeth, Ursula, and Mary.

dren, to his fifter Dalby's children, to his fifter Wykeham's children, and to his fifter Mynofa.

Allufion is made to an Elizabeth Underhill, his god-daughter, his fifter Wynifred's daughters, and his fifter Tamer's daughters. He provides, in the event of any difficulty arifing about the interpretation of his will, that it fhall be referred to the judgment and arbitration of his friend, Sir James Dier, Lord Chief Juftice of the Common Pleas.

He ftrenuoufly urges more than once (reiterating the fame defire at the conclufion) the non-alienation of his lands, and particularly requefts that his daughters do not throw themfelves away in marriage; and fhould they marry contrary to his determination and appointment, or "offend and myfufe "themfelfes in carnall or adulterous lyvyng and the "fame be duely proved" that then the portions and bequefts allotted them fhall be null and void.

This will was proved at London on the 10th day of April, A.D. 1570, the teftator having departed this life, according to the *inquifition poft mortem*, on the laft day of March preceding.

H—page 90.

The Will of William Underhill. (*Vide Pedigree*, B.)

"In the Name of God Amen WILLIAM UNDER-"HILL of Idlicott in the countie of Warwicke "Efquier beinge of perfect minde and memorie did as "well in the fixth daie of Julie anno domini 1597 as "at divers other tymes or at leaft once in the tyme of "his ficknes whereof he died make and declare his "laft will and teftament nuncupative in manner and "forme followeing or the like in effect viz. Firft he "revoked all former wills and teftamentes by him "made

"made or declared and willed that his daughter Do-
"rothie ſhold have for her parte five hundred poundes
"and all her jewells and that his younger daughter
"named Valentine ſhold alſo have other five hundred
"poundes Likewiſe he willed that his eldeſt ſonne
"Foulke Underhill ſhold have all his landes and that
"in regarde thereof if he lived he ſhould be charge-
"able to perform all ſuch promiſes and grauntes as
"ſhall at anie tyme hereafter appeare to be made by
"him the ſaide William Underhill in his life time for
"which he had received monie And further he
"willed that if the ſaide Foulke Underhill ſhould
"happen to die, then his next heire that ſhall inherite
"ſhold be chargeable to performe the ſame his pro-
"miſes and grauntes. Alſo he willed that everie of his
"other ſonnes ſhould have two hundred poundes a peece.
"Likewiſe he the ſame William Underhill declared
"that he had oweinge unto him two thouſande poundes
"for the which he had ſpecialties. And that one
"Maſter Baſſet owed unto him threeſcore and tenne
"poundes for which he had nothing to ſhewe. Laſtlie
"he conſtituted and appointed Maſter George Sherley
"Eſquier and Maſter Thomas Sherley his brother
"executors of the ſame his laſt will and teſtament and
"humblie deſired that it wold pleaſe them to take
"uppon them the execution thereof. And this his ſaide
"laſt will and teſtament he ſoe made and by worde
"declared in the preſence of divers credible witneſſes.

"Proved at London, on the 9th day of Auguſt
"AD 1597, by the oath of Alexander Serle
"notary public, the proctor of George Sherley
"Eſq. and Thomas Sherley, the executors
"above named."

It will be obſerved that in the above will of W. Underhill (B), he leaves two members of the Shirley family his executors; from which we may gather that the diſpute between the Shirleys and ſenior branch of the

the Underhills of Eatington did not affect the junior branch at Idlicote.

For those who are fond of church-hunting, and reading heraldic achievements, Eatington offers peculiar attractions. It is the burial-place of the distinguished families of Shirley and Ferrers, and is rich in monumental remains. There are memorials likewise to several of the Underhills. Edward Underhill, whose sons married the twin Congreves, is thus remembered—

"Here lyeth buried under this stone Edward
"Underhill, sometime gentleman of this Town,
"with Margaret, sometime his Wife: which Edward
"disseased this world the fifth day of November,
"A.D. M.D.XLVI.

"*On whose sollys Jhesu have mercy. Amen.*"

Thomas, the eldest son of the above, and Elizabeth Congreve, his wife, are also held in memory, with a very lengthy inscription, of which the following is but a small part. Their monumental virtues are immense:

"Here lyeth buried the bodyes of Thomas Under-
"hill, of this Towne, Esquier, and Elizabeth his wife,
"who lived married together in perfect amitie about
"65 years, and had issue between them xx children:
"viz. xiii sons, and vii daughters. . . . . She dyed
"24 Junii, An. D. 1603; and he the 6th day of Octo-
"ber next after. . . . .

"*God they feared: God they served: God they loved:*
"*and to God they dyed.*"

As far as this book is concerned, the most interesting of all the monuments is that of the William Underhill (A) from whose son Shakespere purchased New Place. The inscription runs as follows:—

"Here lyeth William Underhill of the Inner
"Temple of London, gentleman: of Edward Underhill,
"Esquier, second son; and Ursula his dearly beloved
"wife

" wife, youngeſt daughter of John Congreve of Stret-
" ton, in Com. Staff. Eſquier, whoſe life was a ſpectacle
" unto all honeſt, virtuous, and obedient wifes: ſhe dyed
" the XIIIth day of May, An: Dom: M.D.L.X.I.

" *Upon whoſe ſouls Chriſt have mercy. Amen.*"

(No date is given of the death of this William Underhill (A); but the period is fixed by the proving of his will in April, 1570, as above.)

I—page 131.

De Quincey.

De Quincey's article on Shakeſpere in the old edition of the " Encyclopædia Britannica," is probably known to a comparatively ſmall number of perſons. Probably had he been alive at this time, and having ſuch an article to write, he would not have produced the one in queſtion; probably, alſo, in his complete works, now iſſuing from the preſs, and ſo beautifully got up, we ſhall never find the article in queſtion. But the well-worn phraſe is painfully applicable, "*literæ ſcriptæ manent.*" Whatever ſuch a man as De Quincey might write, is ſure to leave its mark; and therefore, when a giant hits a giant's blow, we muſt look for the neceſſary contuſion. De Quincey uſed his ſtrength to bruiſe the reputation of Shakeſpere; and it is a very ſorry apology, when you have disfigured a man, to beg his pardon, and ſay you did not intend to hit ſo hard.

The reſult of De Quincey's article has been preciſely what any one might expect. Men who have never read that article, perhaps never heard of it, have received through other channels of information the impreſſion made by De Quincey. In this way, minds receive prejudices which no regret on the part of the writer of an article

article can prevent. I can quite believe that if De Quincey could, years ago, have torn out from the pages of the Encyclopædia his article on Shakeſpere, he would have done ſo. But that can never be done; and though it be ſuppreſſed in his works, or otherwiſe huddled away, it cannot be obliterated from the pages of the work in which it remains, unaſſailable. For this reaſon I have dwelt upon it, and referred to it, hoping that the attention of thoſe who read theſe pages may thereby be drawn to the ſubject, and that a proper antidote may be adminiſtered to the baneful influence which ſuch an article as De Quincey's has had, and would ſtill have if treated with ſilence. It is far more healthy and more juſt to drag it into the open day, point to its injurious paragraphs, and ſay openly—Theſe words ought never to have been written; they are unjuſtifiable; they are the mere conjectures of a man who muſt have regretted writing them, and who never would have written them had he acquainted himſelf thoroughly with the cuſtoms of the times in which Shakeſpere lived.

I give one extract from De Quincey to ſhow how he wrote, and to explain the tone aſſumed by me in the body of this work.

He is commenting on the marriage bond (pp. 29, 30, 31):—

"What are we to think of this document? Trepi-
"dation and anxiety are written upon its face. . . . .
"As the daughter of a ſubſtantial yeoman, who would
"expect ſome fortune in his daughter's ſuitor, ſhe (Anne
"Hathaway) had, to ſpeak coarſely, a little outlived
"her market. Time, ſhe had none to loſe. William
"Shakeſpere pleaſed her eye, and the gentleneſs of
"his nature made him an apt ſubject for female bland-
"iſhments—poſſibly for female arts. Without imputing
"to this Anne Hathaway anything ſo hateful as a
"ſettled plot for enſnaring him, it was eaſy enough
"for a mature woman, armed with ſuch inevitable
"advantages of experience and of ſelf-poſſeſſion, to
"draw

" draw onward a bluſhing novice, and, without directly " creating opportunities, to place him in the way of " turning to account ſuch as naturally offered.

" Young boys are generally flattered by the conde- " ſcending notice of grown-up women," &c. . . . . . " Once, indeed, entangled in ſuch a purſuit, any perſon " of manly feelings would be ſenſible that he had no " retreat; *that* would be to inſult a woman grievouſly— " to wound her ſexual pride—and to inſure her laſting " ſcorn and hatred. Theſe were conſequences which " the gentle-minded Shakeſpere could not face. He " purſued his good fortunes, half perhaps in heedleſſ- " neſs, half in deſperation, until he was rouſed by the " clamorous diſpleaſure of her family upon firſt diſco- " vering the ſituation of their kinſwoman. For ſuch " a ſituation there could be but one atonement, and " that was hurried forward by both parties, whilſt, out " of delicacy towards the bride, the wedding was not " celebrated in Stratford, where the regiſter contains " no notice of ſuch an event." . . . . . . (and much more to the ſame effect).

The reader will now underſtand the emphaſis uſed in various portions of this book; and will, perhaps, wonder with me that Shakeſpere's was not too honoured a name to be dealt with ſo flippantly by a famed author in a great national work.

Let it be ſaid of the above, that it is—every ſyllable —an unſupported and degrading conjecture; that the motives and the acts are the baſe inventions of De Quincey's own imagination; and that the man who uſes his pen to hurt the fair fame of the dead in ſuch a faſhion, were he twenty times the author and writer that De Quincey was, deſerves the ſevereſt condemnation.

J—page 148.

J – page 148.

CLOPTON PEDIGREE.

COMBE, or COMBES.

To work out the Combe Pedigree, and to bring it down correctly to the union between the heiress Martha Combe and Edward Clopton, has cost me an amount of labour, which none but those acquainted with the difficulties of such work will give me credit for.

By the courtesy and kindness of Herald's College, I was enabled to take a copy of the pedigree contained in "Vincent's Warwickshire" (1619). This book was presented by Sheldon to the College in 1684, and is always regarded as a most trustworthy guide. Having possessed myself of this, I next consulted all the Visitations and MSS. at the British Museum which would give any light on the subject, and next I ransacked the registers of Stratford Church. I have at last compiled that Pedigree which will be found on one part of the "Clopton" sheet.

In the main features of this Pedigree I have thought it my duty to accept the authority of Vincent, but I confess I do so with great hesitation, being unable (except upon a conjecture which I have embodied in the Pedigree) to reconcile the conflicting evidence of Vincent's MS. and the unbending entries which I find in the Stratford Register.

To those who are curious in such matters this subject cannot fail to be interesting, and therefore I will go into it fully.

After having gone over the Stratford Register with great care, and assisted by Mr. Butcher, the Parish Clerk, who has revised all my quotations, I find the following to be the whole of the entries with regard to the Combes family about the dates with which we are interested.

Marriages.

Marriages.

1561. Auguſt 27.—Johannes Combes, generoſus, et Roſa Cloptonne.

Burials.

1573. April 4.—Jone, filia Johannis Combes.

1575. April 8.—Francis, ſonne to Mr. John Combs.

1576. June 11.—Francis, ſonne to Mr. John Combes.

1577. January 29. — John, ſonne to Mr. John Coombes.

1579. Oct. 14.—Miſtreſs Roſe, wife to Mr. John Combes.

1584. Feb. 2.—Will, ſonne to Mr. John Combes.

1584. May 24.—Miſtreſs Elizabeth, wife to Mr. John Combes.

1614. July 12.—*Mr. John Combes, gentleman.*

We naturally aſk, who was this Mr. John Combes? On turning to the inſcription upon the altar tomb of John à Combe, in the chancel of Stratford Church, we find it terminating in this faſhion. After enumerating the bequeſts of the deceaſed, it concludes,—"Ye wich "increaſe he apoynted to be diſtributed towards the "reliefe of ye almes-people theire. More he gave to "the poore of Stratford Twenty LI."

What does that 51 mean? Can it be intended to denote the age of John à Combe at the time of his death? Probably not; but if not, what poſſible meaning can it have?

The reader will ſoon ſee the intereſt of this inquiry. There is no evidence, that I am aware of, to tell us at what

what age John à Combe died; and there are, unfortunately, ſo many Combes in the Pedigree named "John," that we are in great danger of confuſing one with another. John à Combe, Shakeſpere's friend, is commonly reputed to have been an old man at the time of his death; but he is alſo reported to have been an old bachelor. In a MS. given by Mr. Hunter in his New Illuſtrations, we read of "an old gentleman, "a batchelor, Mr. Combe, upon whoſe name the "poet," &c., &c.

Aſſuming that John à Combe was an old bachelor, who was the John with all the children?

The Pedigree ſhows us that there was another John Combe, living at Warwick, but he had married one Johanna Murcote, and therefore he could not be the huſband of Roſe Clopton, married in 1561, and dead in 1579, nor yet of "Miſtreſs Elizabeth," who died in 1584.

We are driven, therefore, to the neceſſity of trying to ſhow that one of the *above-named ladies was the wife of John à Combe's father.* This is what Vincent ſets forth in his Pedigree, and it is ſupported by a note of Malone's. He ſays, "Mr. Combe married Mrs. Roſe "Clopton, the youngeſt daughter of William Clopton "of Clopton, Eſq. [*it was old John who married Roſe "Clopton*], Auguſt 27, 1561; and therefore was, pro"bably, when he died, eighty years old."

As Vincent was a Warwickſhire man, and had full opportunity of acquainting himſelf perſonally with the hiſtories of the families he catalogued in his Viſitation, we ſeem bound to conclude that John à Combe's father (John of Stratford) was the huſband of Roſe Clopton. The regiſter above quoted ſhows that ſhe lived in wedlock from 1561 to 1579.

During that period, four children of Mr. John Combe's were interred in Stratford Church, viz., Jone, Francis, Francis, John. They evidently were Roſe Clopton's offspring, and died in infancy; *but of them there is no mention made in Vincent's Pedigree.* I have introduced

introduced theſe names with dotted lines, according to heraldic cuſtom, to ſignify that the deſcent is doubtful, though there cannot be any doubt upon the point, becauſe the evidence of the Stratford regiſter is overpowering; and therefore in the above omiſſions, Vincent's Pedigree at Herald's College muſt be ſo far incorrect.

But Vincent inſtructs us that "old John" took Roſe Clopton for his *ſecond wife*, and that his celebrated ſon, John à Combe, was the third offspring of the firſt marriage with Jocoſa, the daughter of Edward Blount, of Kidderminſter. It will be ſeen, on reference, that there were four children by that marriage. Aſſuming that Jocoſa Blount died the year prior to her huſband's ſecond marriage, and that her children were born one year after the other, ſhe could not have been married later than 1555 (moſt probably the date would be two or three years earlier); and aſſuming that "old "John" was twenty years of age when he married, it would give his date of birth about 1535. It is moſt likely that he was born ſomewhat earlier, but as marriages were contracted in very young years in thoſe days, we could hardly conjecture his birth as prior to 1532. At the death of his ſecond wife, therefore, he would be about 47 years of age, and not at all too old to marry for the third time. That he did ſo ſeems almoſt certain, becauſe we are encountered with the entry, in 1584, "Miſtreſs Elizabeth, wife to Mr. John "Combes." It is quite poſſible that this lady might have been the wife of John à Combe, for at that date he was probably five and twenty years of age. But as John à Combe is univerſally reported to have been an old bachelor, this cannot be correct. We have no alternative, therefore, but to conclude that "old John" did marry for the third time, after the death of Roſe Clopton, and that "Miſtreſs Elizabeth" was the mother of the child "Will," who was buried February 2, 1584. It was only three months afterwards that the mother followed the child to the grave, and therefore it appears probable

probable that the child's birth and death coſt the mother her life alſo. With the entry of "Miſtreſs "Elizabeth's" funeral, all knowledge of "old John," as far as I am acquainted, ends. I am at a loſs to underſtand why Malone gueſſes "old John" as probably "eighty years old when he died," ſimply becauſe he married his ſecond wife, Roſe, in 1561, at which date he was poſſibly about thirty years of age—probably ſomewhat younger. Diſproportionate alliances as to years were not faſhionable in thoſe days; and we can with certainty conclude that "old John" muſt have been a youthful bridegroom when he married Roſe, becauſe, in 1561, ſhe muſt have been quite a girl, ſince her eldeſt brother, William Clopton (C), was only born in 1537, and was therefore but twenty-four years of age when his ſiſter, the third younger than himſelf, was married. Roſe could not have been more than eighteen or nineteen when ſhe married John Combe; and it is not likely that a girl of eighteen, *in thoſe days*, would marry a man many years older than herſelf.

It is quite poſſible that "old John" may have lived until he was eighty years of age. If ſo, he only died four or five years before his ſon, John à Combe. The regiſter of Stratford is totally ſilent on the ſubject, and I can find no trace there of his death or burial. He may poſſibly have been interred at Aſtley, from whence his family came.

It will be ſeen that on the Pedigree I have, with the dotted lines of doubt, ſupplied "old John's" third marriage, and the burial both of his wife and his child, concerning whom Vincent is altogether ſilent. I conclude his Pedigree *muſt be defective,* becauſe the Stratford regiſters will admit of no queſtions or doubts; their entries are abſolute and concluſive evidence.

I confeſs I have had, and ſtill have, ſome doubts as to the correctneſs of Vincent in repreſenting John à Combe as the third child of Jocoſa Blount—"Old "John's" firſt wife; though I dare not venture to call in queſtion his pedigree, becauſe it clears up one great

great difficulty which has never before been explained, and in this reſpect is evidently correct. Thoſe who have ſtudied John à Combes' Will cannot fail to have been ſtruck with the manner in which he conſiſtently ſpeaks of his "brother John and his children," though he alſo ſpeaks of his "*Couſin Thomas Combe*," and ſubſequently calls him "my ſaid nephew, Thomas "Combe."

"Item. I will and bequeath and deviſe to my Cousin "Thomas Combe, &c.," . . . . "that he the ſaid "Thomas Combe, his heirs and aſſigns, ſhall yearly and "every year for every year for ever pay to a learned "preacher twenty ſhillings to make a ſermon twice a "year at Stretford Church, &c., &c.," . . . . "and if "my ſaid Nephew Thomas Combe . . . . ſhall or "do not pay the ſaid twenty ſhillings yearly to a "preacher," &c.

There can be no queſtion as to the perſon here deſcribed, nor to the miſtake in the drafting of the Will, calling him in the one inſtance Couſin, and in the other Nephew.

Having diſcovered one ſuch miſtake, I was led to ſuſpect that the term "brother" might be alſo open to ſome ſuch explanation, becauſe, though it was conſtantly the cuſtom, after the death of one child, to chriſten another by the ſame Chriſtian name (as we ſee in the caſe of the infants "Francis," the ſons of "Old John"), nevertheleſs, we ſhould hardly expect to find two brothers living and both bearing the ſame title. Vincent's pedigree explains the matter at once. We there ſee that theſe Johns, though both ſons of "Old John," were, nevertheleſs, only *half-brothers*—the one being the child of Jocoſa Blount, the other of Roſe Clopton. Hence at their chriſtenings each received the name "John;" and when John à Combe was making his Will, it was very natural for him to ſpeak of "my brother John."

Having thus fairly acknowledged Vincent's ſtrength and authority, I will frankly allow that I have only weakneſs to oppoſe to him in ſupport of my doubts and

and hesitations. I have undoubtedly proved one of two things. Either Vincent's Pedigree is incorrect in not having supplied us with the names of Rose Clopton's children in full, and with "Old John's" third marriage, and the name both of his wife and child; or he has altogether dropped out of notice some John Combe, of Stratford, and a member of this family, whose wife and family are proved by the register to have existed.

The difficulty might easily be solved if we entertained the idea of John à Combes having once married—his children having died—and that he was left a widower, instead of being a bachelor. This would make things smooth at once; but unfortunately every sort of evidence and tradition agrees with the pedigree in making John à Combe always and ever a bachelor.

We must conclude, therefore, that Vincent altogether overlooked "Old John's" third marriage. May he not, possibly, have confounded the one John with the other, and have made John à Combe by mistake the son of Jocosa Blount, rather than of Rose Clopton?

There is a strong impression on my mind that I have seen it stated that John à Combe was the son of Rose Clopton. If the figures LI upon his tomb are intended to indicate his age, *he must have been*; for reckoning from 1562, the year after Rose Clopton was married, to the year in which John à Combe died, he would have been 51 at the date of his death, July, 1614; added to which, it must be remarked that Vincent's Pedigree does make a "John Combe" to have been Rose Clopton's eldest child, only it represents him as the "brother John," and makes John à Combe the son of the first wife.

As regards the property or the descent coming down to Martha Combe, wife of Edward Clopton, it matters not whether Vincent is right or wrong. The point is of some interest to those who are endeavouring to put together the facts and associations of Shakespere's day, and to trace out the precise relations of those persons among

among whom he moved in ſocial friendſhip and intimacy. As I ſaid before, I know my poſition is weak, and Vincent's very ſtrong. I ſubmit, therefore, to his authority, with the ſtrongeſt inclination to diſpute it. When John à Combe died, in 1614, *he could not, under any circumſtances, have been an old man.* I cannot calculate him, though the ſon of Jocoſa Blount, to have been more than ſixty at his death. Should it, however, at any time appear that the figures on his tomb denote his real age, it would be a ſingular coincidence to find that both Shakeſpere and his attached friend died in their fifty-ſecond year; and thoſe figures would alſo eſtabliſh the fact that John à Combe came of the Clopton race, *and muſt have been the ſon of Roſe Clopton.*

K—page 277.

In caſe the reader ſhould have a curioſity to ſee a houſe exactly like New Place in the laſt century, I may mention that the new line of railway between Waterloo Station and London Bridge has lately diſcloſed one. In paſſing along Union Street, in the Borough, in the narrow part, where the ſeries of arches runs cloſe to the back of the houſes on the left (going towards London Bridge), there is a ſmall ſtreet, called Gravel Lane. In that ſtreet I lately came upon the houſe referred to, and as it is preciſely ſimilar, even in ſmall details, to the prints of New Place (1720), it may be an object of intereſt to ſome of my readers.

As it ſtands cloſe into the angle where the Chatham and Dover Railway, going to Blackfriars Bridge, croſſes the extenſion line from Waterloo to London Bridge, and the Act of Parliament gives powers to purchaſe this property, it may be well to draw attention to this intereſting old houſe, before the iron Viſigoths ſweep it away. It belongs to George Vaughan, Eſq., of Weſtbourne Terrace, and has been in poſſeſſion of his family

family for a confiderable period. Mr. Vaughan's tenants, J. H. and G. T. James, hatters, have a worthy affection for the old—old place, which ftands an ancient landmark in the midft of modern buildings.

Over the doorway, upon a lozenge, is the following infcription:—

I.
D. H.
1703.

The old leaden tank bears date, J. C. E. 1669.

The broad ftaircafe and the panelled rooms are carefully preferved, with the exception of the oak out of one of the rooms, which Mr. Vaughan has lately, and very properly, removed to preferve it, in cafe he fhould be compelled to part with his cherifhed houfe. Gravel Lane leads down to the Thames, and to the fite of the Globe Theatre. The following facts, therefore, become interefting. Mr. James remembers, when he was a boy, fome forty years ago, that rows of elm trees fkirted the lane; and he can recall the fact of an aged carman in the employ of Meffrs. Vaughan, telling him about the year 1820, that when he was a youth, in taking the carts down to the Thames, he was obliged to pufh the bufhes and brambles out of the way to enable the cart to pafs.

Thefe facts are ftriking, becaufe they prove that the land behind the Globe Theatre retained the fame rural character to the end of the laft century which it muft have familiarly prefented to the eyes of William Shakefpere.

There was, until a few months ago, a large garden at the back of Gravel Lane Houfe. It is now being built upon by the piers of the Chatham and Dover railway arches. In it, from time to time, many relics have been dug up. Of courfe there are many houfes around London of the fame character and date as this houfe, but none in the direction where it ftill exifts. I have not, however, feen anywhere a houfe

fo

ſo exactly correſponding to the elevation of New Place (1720). It is the veriſimilitude; and, therefore, if the Londoner wiſhes to ſee what New Place was like at that date, he has only (before it is too late) to take a walk over Southwark Bridge, and penetrate the now denſely-populated and uninviting heart of the Borough, called Gravel Lane.

L—page 317.

The Rev. R. Jago is buried in the ſide aiſle of the nave of Snitterfield Church, of which he was Vicar. As a poet, he was well and deſervedly known about Stratford, and many of his productions obtained a much wider popularity. He lives in the pages of "Elegant "Extracts." One of the beſt parodies in the Engliſh language, upon Hamlet's ſoliloquy, "To be or not to "be," will be found in that work. It was written by Mr. Jago, and deſcribes the miſeries of a would-be poet longing after bays. It commences, "To print, "or not to print," and while adhering moſt cloſely to the language of Shakeſpere, admirably depicts the fears and hopes of the depreſſed rhymeſter, working up to this climax—

"Thus critics do make cowards of us all."

Mr. Jago died in 1781, Æt. 69.

HATHAWAY, M.

(See Shakespere Pedigree.)

It appeared to me perfectly unneceſſary to encumber the Shakeſpere Pedigree with the deſcents of the Hathaways down to their extinction—in the Shottery branch —during the preſent century. To any one curious on the ſubject, the Stratford regiſters will always ſupply an abundant fund of information.

I have contented myſelf, therefore, by merely introducing in Shakeſpere's Pedigree thoſe names which were abſolutely neceſſary to ſhow the connection with him by marriage; and in this place I have collected together ſuch material as ſeems to me valuable, in order to preſerve a correct record of the lateſt deſcents of the Shottery family, and of the way in which the property paſſed from them to its preſent owner. As no one has previouſly undertaken to do what I have thus done, I believe that the following information will not only be valuable on the inſtant, but in ſome few years hence will become very valuable to the antiquary, who will thank me for reſcuing from oblivion many details which in another generation would have been loſt for ever. I am under obligation to Mr. William Thompſon, of Stratford, the preſent owner of Ann Hathaway's Cottage, and alſo to his ſolicitors, for the prompt manner in which they laid the title-deeds open to my inſpection, and for the manner in which they ſhowed themſelves anxious to give me any information they poſſeſſed. Though Mr. Thompſon is yet a very young man, it was exceedingly agreeable to me to find that the Shottery property had come into the poſſeſſion of a gentleman who thoroughly appreciates its hiſtoric aſſociations, and aſſures me of his intention to preſerve the fabric from ſpoliation or decay. My thanks are alſo due to Mrs. Baker, of the Cottage, who, I truſt, will have no reaſon to regret the length of time that we puzzled together in her kitchen over the old family Bible, until we got the Pedigree correct, as far as her knowledge went. It muſt, indeed, be a ſource of unending regret to this good woman, when ſhe recalls from day to day her father's ſale of the houſe, which belonged for centuries to the long line of her anceſtors. It was a bitter neceſſity; and every viſitor to Ann Hathaway's Cottage muſt feel with her, and for her.

By the help of Mrs. Baker, Mr. Thompſon, his lawyer, and the pariſh clerk, I have been enabled to

put

put together the accompanying Pedigree. By reading it through, and then perusing the abstracts I have made of deeds in Mr. Thompson's possession, the reader will be put in possession of the history of the Hathaway family during the last hundred years.

Abstracts of Title Deeds, &c., regarding Ann Hathaway's Cottage, Shottery.

1.

Will of John Hathaway of Shottery (Pedigree, A).

"Bequeathes to Ursula Good, now Ursula Kamill, "5*s*., payable 12 months after the decease of my "mother, Sarah Hathaway.

"Also to my sister, Jane Hathaway, now Jane "Webb (B), the sum of Twenty Pounds.

"Also all Freehold Lands, *i.e.* in fee simple, to my "loving mother, Sarah Hathaway, during her life; and "after her decease, I devise the said

"To my three sisters, *Sarah* Hathaway (C), Elizabeth "Hathaway (D), and Susannah Hathaway (E), and "their heirs.

"And I hereby nominate my mother, Sarah Hatha-"way (L), executrix, &c.

"I have hereunto set my seal this 7th day of August, "in the 17th year of the reign of our Sovereign Lord, "George II.

"Proved April 2, 1746."

2.

Will of Sarah Hathaway (C), dated May 3, 1779.

"I give, devise, and bequeath unto my brother-in-"law, William Taylor (F), and Susannah (E), his wife, "during their joint lives, and the life of the longest "liver of them, all that my third part or share of and "in a messuage or tenement, lands, hereditaments, and "premises which I may die seized or possessed of or "entitled unto, situate at Shottery aforesaid, in the "possession of the said William Taylor, or elsewhere—

"and

HATHAWAY.
Hathaway.
(M) Robert Hathaway of Shottery
(L) Sarah
(H) Elizabeth Hathaway
Standley of Chipping Campden, co. of Gloucester.
(G) Richard Standley
Mary.
(A) John Hathaway.
(B) Jane
Webb.
(C) Sarah.
By her will, proved at Worcester,
she bequeaths the premises at Shottery to her nephew, John Hathaway Taylor.
(D) Elizabeth.
(E) Susan Hathaway of Shottery
(F) William Taylor.
(I) John Hathaway Taylor.
(J) Mary Hamp
Buried at Stratford,
(K) William Taylor
Lived at Shottery, at the Cottage, until his death. Buried at Stratford.
Kitty Dobbin
After her death the Cottage was divided into three parts
John
Buried at Stratford,
Betsy
John Jevons
at Aston Cantlow.
Sarah
Thomas
Mary Taylor.
George Baker,
at Shottery.
William Hathaway Baker

"and from and after the ſeveral deceaſes of the ſaid "William Taylor and Suſannah his wife, then I give, "deviſe, and bequeath all and ſingular the premiſes "aforeſaid unto my nephew, John Hathaway Taylor (H).

"Proved October 13, 1785, at Worceſter."

3.

Conveyance, July 22, 1795—

"Between Richard Standley (G), of Chipping Camp- "den, County of Glouceſter, Flax-dreſſer, eldeſt ſon and "heir-at-law of Elizabeth Standley (H), his late mother, "deceaſed, who was one of the ſiſters, and a devizee "named in the laſt will and teſtament of Robert "Hathaway (M), heretofore of Shottery, pariſh of Old "Stratford, County of Warwick, Yeoman, deceaſed, "and Mary, the wife of the ſaid Richard Standley, of "the firſt part; John Hathaway Taylor (I), of Shottery "aforeſaid, yeoman, of the ſecond part; Thomas Hunt, "of Stratford-upon-Avon, County of Warwick, gentle- "man, of the third part; in conſideration of £55 to "ſaid Richard Standley, paid by ſaid John Hathaway "Taylor, the ſaid Richard Standley did convey unto "ſaid John Hathaway Taylor, all that one undivided "third part or ſhare, the whole into three equal parts "to be divided, of and in all thoſe two ſeveral cottages "or tenements, and two orchards, &c. &c., ſituated in "Shottery, aforeſaid.

"Conveyed in fee to John Hathaway Taylor."

4.

Fine, Michaelmas Term, 36 George III.—

"Between Thomas Hunt, gentleman, plaintive, "Richard Standley, and Mary his wife, to bar dower."

5.

Will of John Hathaway Taylor (I), dated July 18, 1816.

"John Hathaway Taylor, of Shottery, Lime-burner, "bequeathes unto my wife, Mary Taylor (J), and her "aſſigns,

"aſſigns, for and during the term of her natural life, "all thoſe my ſeveral meſſuages or tenements, &c., "ſituate lying and being in Shottery, pariſh of Old "Stratford aforeſaid, and now in my own and Samuel "Bridges' occupation as tenant thereof to me; and "from and after the deceaſe of my ſaid wife, I give "and deviſe the ſaid meſſuages, &c., unto my ſon, "William Taylor (L), his heirs and aſſigns for ever.

"Proved, 9th September, 1820."

6.

Mortgage, January 5, 1836.

"William Taylor (K) to Thomas Taſker; mortgage "of Houſes and Premiſes at Shottery, for ſecuring "£100 and intereſt.

W. S.

7.

Conveyance, October 30, 1838—

"By William Taylor (K) and the Mortgagee to Mr. "Thomas Barnes, in fee of two meſſuages, orchards "and gardens and premiſes, at Shottery, pariſh of Old "Stratford, County of Warwick. William Taylor re-"ceived £245, conſideration money, and Thomas "Taſker, the mortgagee, £100 from Mr. Thomas "Barnes, of Luddington."

8.

Mr. Thomas Barnes, by will, dated January 5, 1855—

"Deviſed all thoſe three cottages or tenements—"formerly Hathaways—and ſituated in Shottery afore-"ſaid, unto William Thompſon, his heirs and aſſigns "for ever."

Baptiſm,

Baptiſm, 1747.—December 18, John Hathaway, ſon of William Taylor.

1809.—John Taylor and Elizabeth Barnett, married, January 3, at Stratford.

1828.—September 5, John Taylor, buried, aged 49.

1835.—January 10, Mary Taylor, aged 82.

I append a few entries from the Marriage Regiſter of Stratford which are not familiar; though attention has been previouſly drawn to that of Jan. 17, 1579, when one William Wilſonne married one "*Anne* "*Hathaway of Shotterye.*"

The extracts from churchwardens' accounts I have not ſeen before in print. Theſe accounts are full of the names and ſignatures of perſons with whom we are familiar as living in Shakeſpere's time.

Marriage Regiſter, Stratford.

1567. January 13.—Lawrentius Walker et Phillippa Hathaway.

1570. October 22.—George Hathaway et Anne Catan, of Loxley.

1572. May 18.—Henry Smith, of Banbury, to Ales Hathaway, of Shottery.

1575. Thomas Hathaway et Margaret Smith.

1579. *January 17.—William Wilſonne et Anne Hathaway, of Shotterye.*

June 22.—David Jones et Ffrances Hathaway.

1634.—Regiſter ſigned by John Hathaway, churchwarden.

Churchwarden's Accounts.

1633. July 18.

Signed, Tho. Naſhe.

"A Levy of Taxation" . . . . . of £40 throughout the whole pariſh.

The

The account of William Walford, ... April, 1618, churchwarden for the year paſt. Borough of Stratford:

"Henley St. Ward.
"Received of Rich. Hathaway . . iij$^{s.}$ iiij$^{d.}$"

Sept. die. Junii, Anno 1619.
Accounts ſigned, Richard Hathway.

The fifteenth of April, 1628.
Mr. John Hall, Churchwarden for the Borough.

7th day of April, 1629.
Surveyors for the highways.
George Barker, } for the County.
John Hathaway, }

24th day of February, 1627.
Will. Combe.
Ge. Combe.
Richard Hathaway.

8th day of October, 1626, } R. Hathaway, Bayliffe.
27th March, 1627. }

3rd day of April, 1621.
Batholomew Hathaway,
George Quiney, Curat.

Ditto, April, 28, 1620.

Oct. 17, 1641. Tho. Clopton.

The name of Barnard appears frequently.

FINIS.

J. S. Virtue, Printer, City Road, London.

NEW WORKS AND NEW EDITIONS

PUBLISHED BY

VIRTUE BROTHERS & CO.,

1, AMEN CORNER, PATERNOSTER ROW.

HISTORY OF ENGLAND,

DURING THE REIGN OF GEORGE THE THIRD.

By JOHN GEORGE PHILLIMORE. [*In preparation.*

In 1 vol. post 8vo.,

SHAKESPERE'S HOME AT NEW PLACE,

STRATFORD-UPON-AVON.

A History of New Place, from its Original Erection by Sir Hugh Clopton, 1490, to its Destruction in 1759, together with an account of the "Great Garden;" accompanied with Illustrations, Copies of Fines, Indentures, &c., Pedigrees of the Shakespere and Clopton Families, a Ground Plan of the Estates at New Place, and Plan of Excavations lately made.

By J. C. M. BELLEW.

In 1 vol. fcap. 8vo. antique, price 3s. 6d.,

PATTIE DURANT;

A TALE OF 1662.

By "CYCLA," Author of "Aunt Dorothy's Will," "Passing Clouds," &c.

In 1 vol. 8vo., cloth, price 6s.,

THE DEAD LOCK:

A STORY IN ELEVEN CHAPTERS. Also, TALES OF ADVENTURE.

By C. MANBY SMITH, Author of "The Working Man's Way in the World."

In 1 vol. 12mo. limp cloth, with Illustrations, price 1s.,

EXPERIMENTAL ESSAYS.

I.—ON THE MOTIONS OF CAMPHOR ON THE SURFACE OF WATER.
II.—ON THE MOTION OF CAMPHOR TOWARDS THE LIGHT.
III.—HISTORY OF THE MODERN THEORY OF DEW.

By CHARLES TOMLINSON, Lecturer on Physical Science, King's College School, London.

In 1 vol. 12mo. limp cloth, with illustrations, price 2s.,

THE OUTLINES OF MODERN FARMING.

By R. SCOTT BURN.

WORKS BY THE AUTHOR OF "MARY POWELL."

WORKS BY THE AUTHOR OF "MARY POWELL" (*continued*).

In post 8vo., price 7s. 6d., cloth gilt,

FAMILY PICTURES.

TWILIGHT IN AN UNINHABITED HOUSE.
OF A FINE OLD ENGLISH MERCHANT.
FATHER AND SON.
A GENTLEMAN OF THE OLD SCHOOL.
A GHOST STORY.
CHARLES LAMB.
SIR FRANCIS BARING.
ON LEAVING AN OLD FAMILY HOUSE.
LONE HEATHS AND HIGHWAYMEN.
ON THE SACRED AFFECTIONS.
A SCRAP OF AUTOBIOGRAPHY.
THE EMPEROR ALEXANDER.
THE EVELYNS OF WOTTON.
FABIAN'S DILEMMA.
CLAREMONT AND THE PRINCESS CHARLOTTE.
THE FATHER OF A FAMILY.

In post 8vo., price 7s. 6d., cloth gilt, with Frontispiece,

THE YEAR NINE.

A Tale of the Tyrol.

"A highly interesting volume, in which the noble stand made by an army of peasants for independence is told with great power and pathos."—*Morning Herald.*

"Sweet 'Mary Powell' exchanges her lute for a cymbal, clanging with her white fingers upon the sounding brass. The subject is well chosen, and the theme inspiriting. 'Hofer' is the hero of her lute."—*Art-Journal.*

New Edition, price 7s. 6d., cloth gilt, with Coloured Frontispiece after WARREN,

CLAUDE THE COLPORTEUR.

"The hero of the narrative is, in plain English, a Bible hawker among Roman Catholics chiefly; and his difficulties, ill-treatment, conversations, and beneficial influence, form the staple of the book—his character is well drawn."—*English Churchman.*

"The volume is one of no ordinary merit; for it throws intense interest around common occurrences and common characters, and presents not only a vivid series of pictures, but a well-sustained tale."—*Church and State Gazette.*

Post 8vo., cloth, price 7s. 6d., with Frontispiece,

SOME ACCOUNT OF MRS. CLARINDA SINGLEHART.

"It may be said of all her works, that of their kind they are very good; and this cannot fail to give pleasure to every reader capable of appreciating literary merit, and it will commend itself for family reading, on account of the genial tone of the morality which runs throughout."—*Atlas.*

Third Edition, post 8vo., price 7s. 6d., antique,

YE MAIDEN & MARRIED LIFE OF MARY POWELL.

Afterwards MISTRESS MILTON.

"This is a charming little book; and whether we regard its subject, cleverness, or delicacy of sentiment and expression,—to say nothing of its type and orthography,—it is likely to be a most acceptable present to young or old, be their peculiar taste for religion, morals, poetry, history, or romance."—*Christian Observer.*

VIRTUE BROTHERS & CO., 1, AMEN CORNER.

CHEAP AND POPULAR TALES BY F. E. SMEDLEY.

Price 2s. 6d. boards; 3s. 6d. cloth,

FRANK FAIRLEGH;

OR, SCENES FROM THE LIFE OF A PRIVATE PUPIL.

"If our readers wish to read a very entertaining and laughter-provoking story, we cannot do better than suggest a perusal of 'Frank Fairlegh.'"—*Somerset Gazette.*

Price 3s. boards; 4s. cloth,

LEWIS ARUNDEL;

OR, THE RAILROAD OF LIFE.

"The task of the reviewer becomes a pleasant one when such works as the one before us is forced upon his perusal."—*Weekly Times.*

New Edition, post 8vo. cloth gilt, price 3s. 6d., boards 2s. 6d.

HARRY COVERDALE'S COURTSHIP,

AND ALL THAT CAME OF IT.

By F. E. SMEDLEY, author of "Frank Fairlegh," &c.

Price 1s. 6d. boards; 2s. 6d. cloth,

THE FORTUNES OF THE COLVILLE FAMILY;

OR, A CLOUD AND ITS SILVER LINING.

This day, in fcap., price 2s. boards; 2s. 6d. cloth,

SEVEN TALES BY SEVEN AUTHORS.

Edited by F. E. SMEDLEY, Esq., Author of "Frank Fairlegh," &c.

New Edition, with Illustrations on Steel, post 8vo. cloth, price 8s.,

THE OLD FOREST RANGER;

OR, WILD SPORTS OF INDIA ON THE NEILGHERRY HILLS, THE JUNGLES, AND THE PLAINS.

By MAJOR WALTER CAMPBELL, of Skipness.

VIRTUE BROTHERS & CO., 1, AMEN CORNER.

32mo. cloth, gilt edges, 1s.,

BASKET OF FLOWERS;

OR, PIETY AND TRUTH TRIUMPHANT.

A Tale for the Young.

16mo. gilt edges, 2s. 6d.,

THE BOY AND THE BIRDS.

By Emily Taylor. With Sixteen fine Woodcuts, from Landseer's Designs.

"A delightful book for children. The birds tell of their habits to a little inquiring boy, who goes peeping into their nests and watching their doings, and a very pleasant way they have of talking, sure to engage the young reader's attention. The designs are pretty, and nicely cut on wood."—*Spectator*.

In foolscap 8vo. cloth, 2s. 6d.,

COLA MONTI;

OR, THE STORY OF A GENIUS.

A Tale for Boys. By the Author of "John Halifax Gentleman," &c. With Four Illustrations by Franklin.

"No one possessing common sensibility can read this book without a thoughtful brow and a glistening eye."—*Chambers's Edinburgh Journal*.

"A lively narrative of school-boy adventures."

"A simple and pleasing story of school-boy life."—*John Bull*.

In fcap. 8vo., 7s. 6d., elegantly bound and gilt,

DOCTOR'S LITTLE DAUGHTER.

THE STORY OF A CHILD'S LIFE AMIDST THE WOODS AND HILLS.

By Eliza Meteyard. With numerous Illustrations by Harvey.

Second Edition, in square 16mo., handsomely bound in cloth, price 2s. 6d. with gilt edges,

HOW TO WIN LOVE;

OR, RHODA'S LESSON.

A Story Book for the Young. By the Author of "Life for a Life," &c. With Illustrations on Steel.

"A very captivating story."—*Morning Post*.

"Just what a story for children ought to be."

VIRTUE BROTHERS & CO., 1, AMEN CORNER.

16mo. cloth, price 2s.,

OPEN AND SEE;

OR, FIRST READING LESSONS.

By the Author of "Aids to Development," &c. &c. With Twenty-four Engravings on Wood.

Fcap. 8vo., price 3s. 6d. cloth gilt,

RECOLLECTIONS OF MRS. ANDERSON'S SCHOOL.

A Book for Girls. By JANE WINNARD HOOPER. Illustrated by FRANKLIN.

"A pretty unpretentious volume, neatly embellished, and gay in its livery of green and gold. Outside and in 'tis precisely the *beau ideal* of a present or a prize-book for a young lady. More fresh and more delightful reading than this book it has rarely been our fortune to meet."—*Morning Advertiser.*

18mo. cloth, price 2s.,

ROBINSON CRUSOE.

With Illustrations.

A New and Revised Edition, with Eighty-eight cuts, 18mo. cloth lettered, price 2s.,

RURAL SCENES;

OR, A PEEP INTO THE COUNTRY.

In 18mo. cloth, price 2s.,

SANDFORD AND MERTON.

With Cuts.

New Edition, cloth, 1s.; gilt edges, 1s. 6d.,

WATTS'S (Dr.) DIVINE AND MORAL SONGS FOR CHILDREN.

With Anecdotes and Reflections, by the Rev. INGRAM COBBIN, M.A. With Frontispiece and Fifty-seven Woodcuts.

WORKS BY THE REV. J. CUMMING, D.D., F.R.S.E.

In Three Vols., price 18s., cloth,

APOCALYPTIC SKETCHES;

OR, LECTURES ON THE BOOK OF REVELATION.

New Edition, thoroughly revised, corrected, and arranged.

I. THINGS THAT WERE.
II. THINGS THAT ARE.
III. THINGS THAT WILL BE.

This Work has undergone a most elaborate revision and correction by the Author. New matter of great value has been introduced, allusions to circumstances now obsolete have been expunged, and fresh and interesting evidence of the fulfilment of the prophecies of the book have been added. These volumes form a LIBRARY EDITION of a work of unprecedented popularity, replete with interest, and strikingly illustrative of a much neglected portion of the Word of God.

In fcap., price 3s. 6d., cloth,

RUTH:

A CHAPTER IN PROVIDENCE.

Second and Cheaper Edition, in fcap., price 5s., cloth,

CONSOLATIONS;

OR, LEAVES FROM THE TREE OF LIFE.

Cheap Edition, Tenth Thousand, in One Volume, containing 688 pages, price 6s., cloth lettered,

THE CELEBRATED PROTESTANT DISCUSSION,

Between the Rev. JOHN CUMMING, D.D., and DANIEL FRENCH, Esq., Barrister-at-Law, held at Hammersmith, in 1839.

Price 1s. 6d. each.
THE FINGER OF GOD.
CHRIST OUR PASSOVER.
THE COMFORTER.
Or 2s. 6d. in cloth gilt.

Price 1s. each.
INFANT SALVATION.
MESSAGE FROM GOD.
BAPTISMAL FONT.
Or 2s. with gilt edges.

VIRTUE BROTHERS & CO., 1, AMEN CORNER.

WORKS BY THE REV. JOHN CUMMING, D.D., F.R.S.E. (*continued*).

In 4to., cloth, gilt edges, 21s.,

DAILY FAMILY DEVOTION;

OR, GUIDE TO FAMILY WORSHIP.

With Twenty-four Engravings.

SCRIPTURE READINGS;

OR, POPULAR AND PRACTICAL EXPOSITIONS OF THE NEW TESTAMENT.

Vol. XII.—THE EPISTLES OF ST. JAMES, &c., price 6s. in cloth.

Into the Comments and Expositions will be introduced illustrative extracts from a variety of valuable sources, giving clear illustrations of disputed passages; so that when the series on the New Testament is finished, every family may find in the library a storehouse of useful, interesting, Protestant, and evangelical instruction.

ALREADY COMPLETE:

Vols. I. to IV.—THE FOUR GOSPELS, price 20s.
Vol. V.—THE ACTS OF THE APOSTLES, price 7s.
Vol. VI.—EPISTLE TO THE ROMANS, price 4s. 6d.
Vol. VII.—THE CORINTHIANS, price 5s.
Vol. VIII.—GALATIANS, EPHESIANS, AND PHILIPPIANS, price 6s.
Vol. IX.—COLOSSIANS AND THESSALONIANS, price 4s. 6d.
Vol. X.—TIMOTHY, &c., price 4s.
Vol. XI.—THE HEBREWS, price 5s.
THE REVELATIONS, price 7s. 6d.

READINGS ON THE PROPHETS.

In monthly numbers, price 4d.,

SABBATH MORNING READINGS ON THE BOOK OF DANIEL.

By the Rev. JOHN CUMMING, D.D., F.R.S.E.

"The Author has not published any exposition of the last prophecy of Daniel, but having studied and lectured on it in the light of existing complications and events, he is satisfied that it will prove interesting and instructive."

Price 3s. complete, in cloth.

LATELY PUBLISHED:

THE BOOKS OF SAMUEL, price 5s.

THE BOOKS OF KINGS, price 4s. 6d.

VIRTUE BROTHERS & CO., 1, AMEN CORNER.

Fourth and Cheaper Edition, revised, fcap. 8vo. cloth, price 3s. 6d.,

THE DAILY LIFE;

OR, PRECEPTS AND PRESCRIPTIONS FOR CHRISTIAN LIVING.

"Popular, clear, captivating, and animated."—*British Banner.*

"Dr. Cumming is famous for the number and variety of his illustrations, chiefly drawn from natural and familiar objects. The volume before us strikes us as being remarkably felicitous."—*Clerical Journal.*

"It is written in the same terse and vigorous style and earnestness of tone as those of its predecessors, and the strong common sense with which its teaching is enforced, will attract while it improves the student."—*Church and State Gazette.*

Sixth Edition, in fcap. 8vo., price 3s. cloth, gilt edges,

OUR FATHER.

Manual of Family Prayers for General and Special Occasions, with Short Prayers for Spare Minutes, and Passages for Reflection.

CHEAP EDITIONS.

CHURCH BEFORE THE FLOOD.

Fcap. 8vo., price 3s. 6d.

PROPHETIC STUDIES;

Or, Lectures on the Book of Daniel. Fcap., price 3s. 6d.

TENT AND ALTAR.

Fcap., price 3s. 6d.

APOCALYPTIC SKETCHES.

Original Edition, with Index, &c. Three Vols., price 3s. 6d. each.

FORESHADOWS;

Or, Lectures on our Lord's Miracles and Parables. Two Vols., price 3s. 6d. each.

VIRTUE BROTHERS & CO., 1, AMEN CORNER.

WORKS RECENTLY PUBLISHED.

Nineteenth Edition, 800 pp., 8vo. cl., strongly bound, 21s.; or in calf, 26s.,

TABLES OF SIMPLE INTEREST

FOR EVERY DAY IN THE YEAR,

At 5, 4½, 4, 3½, 3, and 2½ per cent. per annum, from £1 to £100, &c.

By JAMES LAURIE.

"In the great requisites of simplicity of arrangement and comprehensiveness, we have none better adapted for general use."—*M'Culloch's Commercial Dictionary.*

"Mr. Laurie was well known as one of the most correct and industrious authorities on commercial calculations, and the practical value of his various tables have long been recognised."—*Times.*

Third Edition, 8vo. cloth, 7s.,

HIGH RATE TABLES,

At 5, 6, 7, 8, 9, and 9½ per cent. per annum, from 1 day to 100 days.

By JAMES LAURIE.

In post 8vo., price 12s.,

THE CELT, ROMAN, AND SAXON.

A History of the Early Inhabitants of Britain, down to the Conversion of the Anglo-Saxons to Christianity. Illustrated by the Ancient Remains brought to light by recent research. By THOMAS WRIGHT, Esq., M.A., F.S.A. With numerous Engravings. New edition, enlarged.

One Vol., fcap. 4to., price 21s., appropriately bound,

DOMESTIC MANNERS AND SENTIMENTS IN ENGLAND DURING THE MIDDLE AGES.

By T. WRIGHT, Esq., M.A.

With numerous Illustrations by F. W. FAIRHOLT, Esq.

New Edition, fcap. cloth, 3s.; gilt edges, 3s. 6d.,

MANUAL OF HERALDRY,

Being a concise Description of the several Terms used, and containing a Dictionary of every Designation in the Science. Illustrated by 400 Engravings on Wood.

VIRTUE BROTHERS & CO., 1, AMEN CORNER.

New Editions.

RIPPON'S (Dr.) SELECTION OF HYMNS

FROM THE BEST AUTHORS,

Including a great number of Originals, intended as an Appendix to Dr. Watts's Psalms and Hymns.

Nonpareil 32*mo.*	*s.*	*d.*	*Long Primer* 24*mo.*	*s.*	*d.*	*Large Type.*	*s.*	*d.*
Roan	1	6	Roan	2	6	Sheep	5	0
——, gilt edges . .	2	0	——, gilt edges . .	3	0	Roan, gilt edges . .	6	0
Morocco	5	0	Morocco	6	0	Morocco	9	0

BOUND WITH WATTS'S HYMNS,

1 vol. 32mo., roan, 3s.; gilt edges, 3s. 6d.; morocco, 6s. 6d.

BIBLE CHANTS, ADAPTED FOR PUBLIC WORSHIP.

New Edition, fcap. 8vo. cloth gilt, 1s.,

THE CHANT-BOOK:

A SELECTION OF THE PSALMS AND OTHER PORTIONS OF HOLY SCRIPTURE, ARRANGED AND MARKED FOR CHANTING.

By WILLIAM SHELMERDINE, Conductor of the Sacred Harmonic Society, and Organist of the Mechanics' Hall, &c., &c., Nottingham.

With a Preface by the Rev. J. A. BAYNES.

In crown 8vo., price 2s. 6d.,

ONE HUNDRED AND EIGHTY CHANTS,

ANCIENT AND MODERN.

Arranged for four Voices, with an Accompaniment for the Organ or Pianoforte.

To accompany the above.

Price 4s. post 8vo. cloth, gilt edges,

SCRIPTURE SITES AND SCENES,

FROM ACTUAL SURVEY, IN EGYPT, ARABIA, AND PALESTINE.

Illustrated by Seventeen Steel Engravings, Three Maps, and Thirty-Seven Woodcuts. By W. H. BARTLETT.

VIRTUE BROTHERS & CO., 1, AMEN CORNER.

Works Recently Published (*continued*).

In fcap. 8vo., price 5s., cloth gilt,

THE PRINCE OF THE HOUSE OF DAVID;

Or, THREE YEARS IN THE HOLY CITY.

Edited by the Rev. Professor J. H. Ingraham, Rector of St. John's Church, Mobile. Illustrated with Engravings.

"Our perusal of it has been only to impress us with the ability of the author in the use of the materials, and in the structure of a pleasing and most affecting tale." —*Clerical Journal.*

"This is the best production of its class that has come to our hands for a long time, and it is but candid and just to say that it adds very much to the stores of knowledge already existing about the East."—*British Standard.*

"We hardly know what to say about this book; it is written in beautiful style, and it conveys much valuable information as to the customs and manners of the inhabitants of the Holy Land."—*Wesleyan Times.*

"The whole is written in a semi-poetical style, which will prove attractive to religious readers."—*Leader.*

"The volume contains much information as to Jewish manners and customs." —*Baptist Magazine.*

"Professor Ingraham has worked out his plan with diligence and reverence."—*Literary Gazette.*

In post 8vo., price 7s. 6d., cloth gilt,

FATHER AND DAUGHTER.

A Portraiture from the Life. By Fredrika Bremer.

"Another of those beautiful stories of home-life in Sweden for which Miss Bremer is so justly famed."—*Patriot.*

"A work by Miss Bremer can never fail to delight a great number of readers. It is like a walk through the fields on a frosty day—so free and buoyant is the air—so fresh and sparkling the aspect of nature and human nature in these northern regions."—*John Bull.*

"'Father and Daughter' might have made a name for a less distinguished writer. . . . . Of course the book will be read by everybody. Many will applaud." —*Leader.*

"The book introduces us to people and things which are new to the novel-reading public, and which possess in themselves no ordinary degree of interest."—*Atlas.*

In fcap., with Frontispiece, price 5s., cloth,

THE MILL IN THE VALLEY.

A Tale of German Rural Life. By the Author of "An English Girl's Account of a Moravian Settlement in the Black Forest."

"A pretty tale, from the pen of a young but ready writer. . . . . A religious story —simple, sketchy, and quietly romantic." —*Athenæum.*

"This pretty volume is grave, thoughtful, and frequently pathetic;—a poem in prose, abounding in striking incident, rapid transitions, and pleasing surprise. It is likely to be admired by young persons, and extensively read."—*Christian Witness.*

VIRTUE BROTHERS & CO., 1, AMEN CORNER.

EDUCATIONAL WORKS.

Improved Edition, 18mo., cloth lettered, price 1s. 6d.,

ACKWORTH VOCABULARY;

Or, ENGLISH SPELLING-BOOK; with the meaning attached to each Word. Compiled for the use of Ackworth School.

New Edition, 18mo., cloth lettered, price 2s.,

BARBAULD'S LEÇONS POUR DES ENFANS,

Depuis l'âge de Deux Ans jusqu'à Cinq. Avec une Interprétation Anglaise.

18mo., sewed, price 1s.,

BARBAULD'S HYMNS EN PROSE.

Traduits de l'Anglais. Par M. CLEMENCE.

12mo. cloth, price 1s. 6d.,

BELLENGER'S ONE HUNDRED CHOICE FABLES,

Imitated from LA FONTAINE. Intended for Persons about to learn the French language. With a DICTIONARY. New Edition, revised and corrected by C. J. DELILLE, Professor at Christ's Hospital.

Crown 8vo., cloth, price 4s.,

MANUAL OF THE ANALOGY AND PHYSIOLOGY OF THE HUMAN MIND.

By the Rev. J. CARLILE, D.D. New Edition, enlarged.

Seventh Edition, 12mo. cloth, price 1s. 6d.,

CHRISTIE'S CONSTRUCTIVE ETYMOLOGICAL SPELLING-BOOK.

Exhibiting the Etymology and Meanings of 8,000 Words, with Lessons on Etymology, and Notes.

Crown 8vo., cloth, with Frontispiece, price 5s.,

THE EARTH AND ITS INHABITANTS.

By MARGARET E. DARTON.

"This is a valuable volume, containing a very clear, correct account of the leading facts connected with the surface of the earth, and its inhabitants. . . . . . As far as it goes, it is comprehensive, well written, and interesting, worthy of the daughter of Maria Hack, whose books will always be dear to the young and the old."—*Gentleman's Magazine.*

"We have rarely met with a volume containing so much valuable information for educational purposes as is brought together in this volume. It is prepared, too, in a manner which will immediately attract the interest of the young, in whose minds it will indelibly fix the numerous facts, with which every page abounds."—*Bell's Messenger.*

VIRTUE BROTHERS & CO., 1, AMEN CORNER.

Improved Edition, 12mo. cloth, price 2s.,

GILES'S ENGLISH PARSING;

Comprising the Rules of Syntax, exemplified by appropriate Lessons under each Rule.

New Edition, 18mo., cloth, price 1s. 6d.,

HOPKINS' EXERCISES IN ORTHOGRAPHY,

On an Improved Plan.

New Edition, price 1s. 6d., in cloth,

PICTORIAL SPELLING-BOOK;

Or, Lessons on Facts and Objects. With 130 Graphic Illustrations.

16mo. cloth, price 2s. 6d.,

CHILD'S FIRST STEP TO ENGLISH HISTORY.

By ANN RODWELL. With many Cuts. New Edition, revised by JULIA CORNER.

New Edition, 12mo. cloth, price 1s. 6d.,

DERIVATIVE SPELLING-BOOK,

In which the origin of each word is given from the Greek, Latin, Saxon, German, Teutonic, Dutch, French, Spanish, and other Languages, with the Parts of Speech, and the Pronunciation accented. By J. ROWBOTHAM, F.R.S.A.

New and Enlarged Edition, fcap. 8vo., price 5s. cloth, red edges,

STUDIES IN ENGLISH POETRY,

With short Biographical Sketches, and Notes Explanatory and Critical, intended as a Text-book for the higher Classes in Schools, and as an Introduction to the Study of English Literature. By JOSEPH PAYNE.

"The plan and the execution are equally good; altogether it is an excellent reading book of poetry."—*Watchman.*

"The work is deserving of commendation, as comprehending much that is excellent—the very flowers and gems of English poetry—and nothing exceptionable."

New and Improved Edition, 12mo. cloth, price 2s. 6d.,

A CATECHISM OF FAMILIAR THINGS,

Their History, and the Events which led to their discovery: with a short Explanation of some of the principal Natural Phenomena. For the use of Schools and Families. By E. A. WILLEMENT.

VIRTUE BROTHERS & CO., 1, AMEN CORNER.

In demy 8vo., price 15s., cloth lettered,

THE RUDIMENTS OF BOTANY.

Illustrated with nearly 600 Engravings. By CHRISTOPHER DRESSER, Ph.D., Lecturer on Botany in the Department of Science and Art, South Kensington Museum.

By the same Author, in demy 8vo., price 10s. 6d., cloth lettered,

UNITY IN VARIETY,

As Deduced from the Vegetable Kingdom. Being an attempt at developing that oneness which is discoverable in the habits, mode of growth, and principles of construction of all plants. Illustrated by 300 Engravings.

Second Edition, in 1 vol. 8vo., cloth gilt, price 5s., with many Woodcuts, and Forty Engraved Plates.

SCHOOL PERSPECTIVE;

Being a Progressive Course of Instruction in Linear Perspective, specially designed for the use of Schools. By J. R. DICKSEE, Principal Drawing Master to the City of London School.

McHENRY'S SPANISH COURSE.

New Edition, revised, 12mo. bound, price 6s.,

NEW AND IMPROVED GRAMMAR,

Designed for every Class of Learners, and especially for Self-instruction. Containing the Elements of the SPANISH Language, and the Rules of Etymology and Syntax Exemplified; with NOTES and APPENDIX, consisting of Dialogues, Select Poetry, Commercial Correspondence, &c.

Fifth Edition, price 3s., bound,

EXERCISES ON THE ETYMOLOGY, SYNTAX, AND IDIOMS, &c., OF THE SPANISH LANGUAGE.

KEY TO THE EXERCISES. Price 4s., bound.

Price 5s. 6d. in 12mo. and 8vo.,

SYNONYMES OF THE SPANISH LANGUAGE EXPLAINED.

VIRTUE BROTHERS & CO., 1, AMEN CORNER.

OXFORD AND CAMBRIDGE ANALYSES AND SUMMARIES

OF

OLD AND NEW TESTAMENT HISTORY AND GEOGRAPHY.

Sixth edition, revised and improved, post 8vo., cloth, red edges, price 5s. 6d.,

ANALYSIS AND SUMMARY OF OLD TESTAMENT HISTORY AND THE LAWS OF MOSES;

With a Connexion between the Old and New Testaments; an Introductory Outline of the Geography, Political History, &c. By J. T. WHEELER, F.R.G.S., &c.

Fourth Edition, revised, post 8vo., cloth, red edges, price 5s. 6d.,

ANALYSIS AND SUMMARY OF NEW TESTAMENT HISTORY.

The whole illustrated by copious Historical, Geographical, and Antiquarian Notes, Chronological Tables, &c.

COMPANION ATLAS TO THE SERIES.

Small folio, illustrated by large coloured Maps, and a View and Plan of Jerusalem, extra cloth, price 7s. 6d.,

AN ANALYSIS AND SUMMARY OF THE HISTORICAL GEOGRAPHY

OF THE OLD AND NEW TESTAMENTS;

Comprising a Geographical Account of every Nation mentioned in the Old and New Testaments.

WHEELER'S ABRIDGMENTS.

In Two Volumes, 18mo. cloth, price 2s. each,

A POPULAR ABRIDGMENT OF OLD AND NEW TESTAMENT HISTORY,

For Schools, Families, and General Reading. Explained by Historical and Geographical Illustrations, and numerous Map Diagrams.

A COMPLETE COURSE OF INSTRUCTION IN THE FRENCH LANGUAGE.

Obviating entirely all necessity for leaving England to learn French.

NEW FRENCH SCHOOL, BY M. LE PAGE,

PROFESSOR OF FRENCH IN LONDON.

"The sale of many thousands, and the almost universal adoption of these clever little books by M. LE PAGE, sufficiently prove the public approbation of his plan of teaching French, which is in accordance with the natural operation of a child learning its native language."

Twenty-eighth Edition, with Additions and numerous Woodcuts, in 12mo., neatly bound in cloth, price 3s. 6d.,

LE PAGE'S FRENCH SCHOOL—PART I.

LE PAGE'S L'ECHO DE PARIS.

Being a Selection of Familiar Phrases which a Person would hear daily if living in France. With a vocabulary of the Words and Idioms.

Twelfth Edition, with Additions, 12mo., neatly bound in cloth, price 2s. 6d.,

LE PAGE'S FRENCH SCHOOL—PART II.

LE PAGE'S GIFT OF FLUENCY IN FRENCH CONVERSATION.

A Set of Exercises for the learner of the French Language, calculated to enable him, by means of practice, to express himself fluently on the ordinary topics of life. With Notes.

Seventh Edition, 12mo., neatly bound in cloth, price 2s. 6d.,

LE PAGE'S FRENCH SCHOOL — PART III.

LE PAGE'S LAST STEP TO FRENCH;

Or, the Principles of French Grammar displayed in a series of short lessons, each of which is followed by questions and exercises: with the versification.

VIRTUE BROTHERS & CO., 1, AMEN CORNER.

*** *Mons.* LE PAGE *has also published, for the use of Junior Classes,*

Royal 18mo. neatly bound, price reduced to 2s. 6d.,

LE PAGE'S FRENCH MASTER FOR BEGINNERS;

Or, Easy Lessons in French. New and Improved Edition, with additions.

New and Improved Edition, price 1s. 6d.,

LE PAGE'S PETIT CAUSEUR;

Or, First Chatterings in French, being

A KEY TO THE GIFT OF FRENCH CONVERSATION.

The Key gives the correct translation of the French, thereby showing which is the proper expression for every topic of life.

LE PAGE'S NICETIES of PARISIAN PRONUNCIATION.

ETRENNES AUX DAMES ANGLAISES;

Being a Key to French Pronunciation in all its niceties. Price 6d.

Just published, price 1s.,

LE PAGE'S KEY TO "L'ECHO DE PARIS."

LE PAGE'S JUVENILE TREASURY OF FRENCH CONVERSATION;

With the English before the French. Price 3s.

VIRTUE BROTHERS & CO., 1, AMEN CORNER.

Seventh Edition, in a neat pocket volume, pp. 420, price 4s.,

LE PAGE'S FRENCH PROMPTER;

A HANDBOOK FOR TRAVELLERS ON THE CONTINENT AND STUDENTS IN FRENCH.

A Complete Manual of Conversation, arranged in alphabetical order, so as to obviate all difficulty of reference. Each English word is followed by the phrases and idiomatic French in constant use, forming a perfect English and French dictionary.

Third Edition, in 12mo., neatly bound in cloth, price 3s. 6d.,

LE PAGE'S READY GUIDE TO FRENCH COMPOSITION.

FRENCH GRAMMAR BY EXAMPLES.

Giving Models as Leading-Strings throughout Accidence and Syntax, and presenting a comparative view of the English and French idioms in their principal differences.

New and Approved School Books.

WITH FULL ALLOWANCE TO SCHOOLS AND PRIVATE TEACHERS.

Fifth Edition, improved and corrected,
In 1 vol. 12mo., neatly bound, price 2s. 6d.,

TATE'S ELEMENTS OF COMMERCIAL ARITHMETIC.

Containing a minute Investigation of the Principles of the Science, and their General Application to Commercial Calculations, in accordance with the present Monetary System of the world. By W. TATE.

Recently published, neatly bound, price 3s. 6d.,

KEY TO THE ELEMENTS OF COMMERCIAL ARITHMETIC.

Continuing the exposition of the principles of the science and of the more intricate portions of their application; exhibiting variations in the modes of performing arithmetical operations; and conveying still further information respecting those commercial regulations, by which the pupil must hereafter be guided in his commercial calculations. By W. TATE.

VIRTUE BROTHERS & CO., 1, AMEN CORNER.

WORKS ON MECHANICS AND THE ARTS.

In 2 vols. super-royal 8vo., price £2 5s., cloth gilt,

TOMLINSON'S CYCLOPÆDIA OF USEFUL ARTS, Mechanical and Chemical, Manufactures, Mining, and Engineering; with 40 Engravings on Steel, and 2,477 Woodcuts.

In 3 vols. royal 4to., price £4 14s. 6d.,

TREDGOLD ON THE STEAM ENGINE; Its Principles, Practice, and Construction. Illustrated by upwards of 200 Engravings, and 160 Woodcuts and Diagrams.

In 1 vol. post 8vo., price 10s. 6d., cloth,

A DICTIONARY OF TERMS IN ART: Edited and illustrated by F. W. Fairholt, F.S.A., Author of "Costume in England," &c. Illustrated by 500 Engravings.

In demy 4to., price 12s., cloth lettered,

PRACTICAL HINTS ON PORTRAIT PAINTING; Illustrated by Examples from the Works of Vandyke and other Artists. By John Burnet, F.R.S. With 12 Engravings on Steel. Re-edited, and with an Appendix, by Henry Murray, F.S.A.

In demy 4to., price 12s., cloth lettered,

REMBRANDT AND HIS WORKS: comprising a Short Account of his Life: with a Critical Examination into his Principles and Practices of Design, Light, Shade, and Colour. Illustrated by Examples from the Etchings of Rembrandt. With 14 Engravings on Steel. By John Burnet, F.R.S., Author of "Practical Hints on Painting." Re-edited by H. Murray, F.S.A.

In demy 4to., price 12s., cloth lettered,

LANDSCAPE PAINTING IN OIL COLOURS, Explained in Letters on the Theory and Practice of the Art, and illustrated by Examples from the several Schools. By John Burnet, F.R.S. Re-edited, with an Appendix, by Henry Murray, F.S.A. Illustrated with 11 Steel Engravings.

In demy 4to., price 12s., cloth lettered,

TURNER AND HIS WORKS: illustrated with Examples from his Pictures, and Critical Remarks on his Principles of Painting. With 10 Engravings on Steel. By John Burnet, F.R.S., Author of "Practical Hints on Painting," "Rembrandt and his Works," &c. The Memoir by Peter Cunningham, F.S.A., Author of "A Handbook to London," &c. Re-edited by Henry Murray, F.S.A.

VIRTUE BROTHERS & CO., 1, AMEN CORNER.

THE ART-JOURNAL:

A RECORD OF THE FINE ARTS AND THE ARTS INDUSTRIAL.

PRICE 2s. 6d. MONTHLY.

A NEW VOLUME of the ART-JOURNAL was commenced with the 1st of January, 1863, in which arrangements have been made for largely augmenting its interest and value. It will be seen that the services of several eminent and popular writers on Art and Science have been obtained; and that while

THREE STEEL ENGRAVINGS WILL BE GIVEN MONTHLY,

The Illustrations by Engravings on Wood will be continued, principally of the more attractive and instructive objects contained in the International Exhibition, the ILLUSTRATED CATALOGUE of which will thus be so comprehensive as to include nearly all its prominent works, and accord honour to every leading manufacturer of Europe.

BRITISH AND FOREIGN SCULPTURE.

These Engravings will be resumed in the present year, and comprise beautiful copies of some of the leading Works of Living Artists.

SEVEN CHURCHES OF ASIA MINOR.

A Series of Seven Line Engravings will be given, representing the present state of EPHESUS, SMYRNA, PERGAMOS, THYATIRA, SARDIS, PHILADELPHIA, and LAODICEA, from Paintings by THOMAS ALLOM, the artist-architect, by whom they were visited with that view. They will be engraved by COUSEN, BRANDARD, WILLMORE, and ALLEN.

THE "TURNER GALLERY"

Will supply engravings of the leading pictures bequeathed to the nation by the great artist.

SELECTED PICTURES.

These have been chosen chiefly from the private collections of British Art-patrons, who have liberally placed them at the disposal of the Editor. They consist exclusively of the productions of British Artists, and will include at least one example of every painter who has achieved fame in Great Britain. The Engravings are executed by the best engravers of England, Germany, and France.

The Letter-press will, as heretofore, consist of several Illustrated articles, such as may derive additional value from association with Engravings; of Essays on the higher and more important purposes of Art, endeavouring to render the subject in all its ramifications popular; while attention will be given to every topic that can forward the interests of Art and Art-manufacture, so as to render the ART-JOURNAL indispensable in the Atelier and the Workshop, as a source of instruction, as well as welcome in the Drawing-room, by its elegance of character and the graceful and beautiful nature of its varied contents.

VIRTUE BROTHERS & CO., 1, AMEN CORNER.

www.ingramcontent.com/pod-product-compliance
Lightning Source LLC
Chambersburg PA
CBHW021233300426
44111CB00007B/525

* 9 7 8 3 3 3 7 3 0 9 8 9 3 *